"*Creation and Hope* is like a tapestry that calls for artistic appreciation as it pulls together threads that are often discrepant. Theological and scientific, Trinitarian and Christocentric, anthropological and ecological, phenomenological and biblical, woven together with vibrancy and color creating a pattern that eliminates fragmentation, disintegration, and disconnectedness. And the strand that brings it all together is a substantive hope, not one that ignores reality with superficial optimism but one that invites rigorous action."

—**Rod Wilson**, Former President, Regent College, Vancouver; Canada, Senior Advisor, A Rocha, Canada

"This collection of essays brings to an international readership, threatened by climate change, the voices of those whose hope-filled eco-theology is profoundly informed by their context of Aotearoa, New Zealand. Readers will encounter the braided rivers of the Canterbury plains, the A Rocha project to restore biodiversity to Mount Karioi, and the animal in Derrida's Bible. These and other such engagements are brought into creative dialogue with biblical text and theological tradition. A rich new contribution."

—**Elaine Wainwright**, Professor Emerita, University of Auckland

"It is a privilege to have such a wide variety of perspectives and experience gathered under one cover with this collection of fascinating papers. When theological and ecological reflection come together it is always fruitful, but it is immeasurably more valuable when they are grounded in a particular place as they were in Aotearoa by those who have contributed, and by the work of Nicola Hoggard Creegan in particular. . . However unreflective activism carries its own dangers, and so I trust that *Creation and Hope* will find the readership it deserves."

—**Peter Harris**, President, A Rocha International

"This volume offers informed and fresh insights that contribute to a more nuanced understanding of ourselves as 'deeply embedded creatures'. By exploring the symbolic inheritance and lived experience of the Christian faith in relation to the natural world, it offers a vision of human flourishing in concert with other beings in the natural world—and ecological hope."

—**Vicky Balabanski**, College of Humanities, Arts and Social Sciences, Flinders University

Creation and Hope

Creation and Hope

Reflections on Ecological Anticipation and Action from Aotearoa New Zealand

EDITED BY

Nicola Hoggard Creegan

AND

Andrew Shepherd

PICKWICK *Publications* • Eugene, Oregon

CREATION AND HOPE
Reflections on Ecological Anticipation and Action from Aotearoa New Zealand

Pickwick Publications
An Imprint of Wipf and Stock Publishers
199 W. 8th Ave., Suite 3
Eugene, OR 97401

www.wipfandstock.com

PAPERBACK ISBN: 978-1-5326-0973-2
HARDCOVER ISBN: 978-1-5326-0975-6
EBOOK ISBN: 978-1-5326-0974-9

Cataloguing-in-Publication data:

Names: Hoggard Creegan, Nicola, editor. | Shepherd, Andrew, editor.

Title: Creation and hope : reflections on ecological anticipation and action from Aotearoa New Zealand / Edited by Nicola Hoggard Creegan and Andrew Shepherd.

Description: Eugene, OR: Pickwick Publications, 2018 | Includes bibliographical references.

Identifiers: ISBN 978-1-5326-0973-2 (paperback) | ISBN 978-1-5326-0975-6 (hardcover) | ISBN 978-1-5326-0974-9 (ebook)

Subjects: LCSH: Conservation of natural resources—Religious aspects—Christianity | Environmental degradation—religious aspects—Christianity | Ecotheology | Religion and science

Classification: BT695.5 C54 2018 (print) | BT695.5 (ebook)

04/04/18

Contents

Acknowledgments | vii

Abbreviations | viii

Introduction

1. Introduction | 3
—Andrew Shepherd

2. Evolutionary Anthropology, Entanglement, and Creaturely Hope: A Theology for Conservation Ethics | 9
—Celia Deane-Drummond

Phenomenology

3. The Phenomenology of Hope | 29
—Nicola Hoggard Creegan

4. Spirit, Seabirds, and Sacramentality: Ponderings on Petrels and Pneumatology | 44
—Andrew Shepherd

5. Listening in the Landscape of Aotearoa New Zealand | 62
—Sue Burns

Text

6. The Animal in Derrida's Bible | 77
—Yael Klangwisan

7. Waterlings from Water: Exploring a Cosmological, Eschatological Reading of "Living Water" in John 4:4–42 amidst the Braided Rivers of Canterbury, Aotearoa New Zealand | 90
—Kathleen P. Rushton

8. God So Loved the Cosmos | 109
—Stephen Pattemore

9. "What Are Human Beings That You Are Mindful of them" (Heb 2:5): An Anthropological/Ecological Reading of Hebrews 2:5–9 | 123
—Philip Church

Theology

10. Jesus, the Sabbath, and the Hope of Creation | 141
—Selwyn Yeoman

11. Creative, Apophatic Hopes: Temporality, Resonance Machines, and Entangled Misty Futures | 162
—Scott Kirkland

12. On Finishing Well: The Deification of Nature | 175
—Myk Habets

Conclusion

13. In Praise of Creatures: Pope Francis's Message of Hope for a Fragile Earth | 195
—Celia Deane-Drummond

14. Conclusion | 211
—Nicola Hoggard Creegan

Author Biographies | 215

Acknowledgments

THIS BOOK DERIVES MOSTLY from papers delivered at the *Ecology and Hope* conference held in Auckland in January 2016. We would like to thank all the authors in the collection, but especially Professor Celia Deane-Drummond, who came to Aotearoa New Zealand with her family in January 2016 to be our keynote speaker. Her insightful scholarly contributions and thoughtful presence were inestimable and much appreciated by all.

Our thanks are also due to Carey Baptist College, and Myk Habets and Carol Fearon, for providing a venue for the aforementioned event and assisting with conference logistics. We are also appreciative of the Nga Whaea Atawhai o Aotearoa/Sisters of Mercy New Zealand and Caritas who co-sponsored the conference—providing funding and a lively and supportive presence on the day itself. We acknowledge the contribution too of Tear Fund NZ, and the Auckland Diocesan Climate Change Action Group who provided shorter practical papers at the conference.

A Rocha Aotearoa New Zealand (ARANZ) backed and funded the conference and this book is the result of a partnership between the editors—ARANZ National Co-Director (Andrew) and Board Member (Nicola). Both of us have been involved in A Rocha since its origins in Aotearoa New Zealand a decade ago. We would like to thank the larger A Rocha organisation and family for their support and encouragement in this enterprise, especially National Co-Director Kristel Van Houte, and board Chairman, Murray Sheard. Fellow Board member, Philip Church, contributed a chapter, helped with financial management, and provided a final proofreading eye.

And finally, but most significantly, we owe special thanks to our families for their support during the writing and editing of this volume. As well as providing copy editing and proofreading assistance, our respective spouses, Ingrid Shepherd and Charlie Creegan, provide incredible support to our research and writing, and also provide warm hospitality to a range of guests who pass through our respective homes in Makarora and Auckland.

Easter 2017
Markaroa and Auckland

Abbreviations

AB	Anchor Bible
ANE	Ancient Near East
BAGD	Bauer, W., W. F. Arndt, F. W. Gingrich and F. W. Danker (eds). *Greek-English Lexicon of the New Testament and Other Early Christian Literature*. 2nd ed. Chicago: University of Chicago Press, 1979.
BCOTWP	Baker Commentary on the OT Wisdom and Psalms
EDNT	Balz, H., and G. Schneider, eds. *Exegetical Dictionary of the New Testament*. Eerdmans: Grand Rapids, 1990–1993.
HALOT	Koehler, Ludwig, and Walter Baumgartner. *The Hebrew and Aramaic Lexicon of the Old Testament*. Leiden: Brill, 1994–2000.
LSJ	Liddell, Henry George, Robert Scott, Henry Stuart Jones. *A Greek-English Lexicon*. 9th ed. with revised supplement. Oxford: Clarendon, 1996.
LXX	Septuagint
NICNT	New International Commentary on the New Testament
NIGTC	New International Greek Text Commentary
NIVAC	New International Version Application Commentary
NRSV	New Revised Standard Version
NTS	New Testament Studies
PNTC	Pillar New Testament Commentary
RT	Relevance Theory

SBL	Society of Biblical Literature
TDNT	Kittel, G., and G. Friedrich, eds. *Theological Dictionary of the New Testament*. Translated by G. W. Bromiley. 10 vols. Grand Rapids: Eerdmans, 1964–1976.
UBS	United Bible Societies
VT	Vetus Testamentum
WBC	Word Biblical Commentary
WUNT	Wissenschaftliche Untersuchungen zum Neuen Testament

Introduction

1

Introduction

Andrew Shepherd,
A Rocha Aotearoa New Zealand

We live in an ecological age. Ecology and physics have made us aware of our interconnectedness and dependency upon the web of life. And, as human activity propels us toward a sixth great mass-extinction, there is increasing awareness of the fragility of life on this planet. In such a context, what is the nature of Christian hope with regard to creation? St. Paul declares that all of creation "will be set free from its bondage to decay and will obtain the freedom of the glory of the children of God" (Rom 8:21). How are we to imagine this "freedom" when death and decay are essential to biological life as we currently experience it, when species extinction is part of the evolutionary story, and when the scientific predictions for life in both the immediate and the far future are bleak at best?

Jürgen Moltmann writes: "Christianity is eschatology, is hope, forward looking and forward moving, and therefore also revolutionizing and transforming the present. The eschatological is not one element *of* Christianity, but it is the medium of Christian faith."[1] How does this forward gaze of Christianity relate to a conservation ethic of preserving and restoring degraded ecosystems? Are there specific theologies and eschatologies that fund an ethic of ecological care? How, in the light of grim ecological indicators and statistics does hope motivate, sustain, and shape the nature of Christian life in an ecological age? It is such questions that this book seeks to reflect upon.

Many of the assembled chapters that follow had their origins in a day-long conference, "Ecology & Hope," held at Carey Baptist College in

1. Moltmann, *Theology of Hope*, 16.

Auckland, New Zealand in January 2016. The conference, hosted by A Rocha Aotearoa New Zealand with the generous support of Catholic organizations Nga Whaea Atawhai o Aotearoa/Sisters of Mercy New Zealand and Caritas, was an ecumenical affair. Buoyed by the release of Pope Francis's *Laudato si'* and the perhaps unexpected, but welcome agreement reached by delegates at the UN Climate Change Conference (COP21) in Paris in December 2015, conference attendees were privileged to hear keynote lectures from Professor Celia Deane-Drummond. Originally from the UK, and now based at the University of Notre Dame in the States, Deane-Drummond has been one of the pioneers researching the interface of theology and the natural sciences—particularly in the areas of ecology, evolution, animal behavior, and anthropology. This collection opens with a chapter from Professor Deane-Drummond in which she explores how the classical neo-Darwinian biological account of the world has tended to depict nature as blind to the future and mechanical in its workings. Pointing to the way in which scientific beliefs assume certain values and teleological vision, Deane-Drummond reflects upon the emerging "extended evolutionary synthesis," which recognizes "a myriad of entangled agents in the processes of human becoming." Deane-Drummond suggests that the extended evolutionary synthesis offers a more nuanced understanding of human anthropology that complicates the value questions that lie at the heart of biodiversity conservation.

The chapters that follow offer phenomenological, textual, and theological responses to the themes of creation and hope, while also explicitly and obliquely continuing dialogue with Deane-Drummond's contribution. Nicola Hoggard Creegan picks up on Deane-Drummond's emphasis on the narrative of science, noting that recent theorists are placing greater emphasis upon the cooperative relations that are present in ecosystems. Read from the "underside," Hoggard Creegan believes that in the insights of phenomenology and evolutionary theory "can be found a different kind of story, one that shows us the discarded selves of our inward natures." Taking account of our "long history," recognizing the depth in nature, and rediscovering that as *homo sapiens* we are "deeply embedded creatures," Hoggard Creegan believes, gives us a hope that "is less brittle and more robust." Hoggard Creegan begins to trace a nuanced form of natural theology—arguing that "the only stories that offer real hope are ones that come to terms with our radical embeddedness in and dependence on matter—and with the Incarnation's radical ongoing embeddedness as well."

The sustaining embeddedness of God in the world of matter is the theme too of my contribution in which I offer a phenomenological and pneumatological reflection upon the community bio-diversity project that A Rocha leads in Aotearoa—the Karioi Project. What does it mean to take seriously the concept of sacrament and of a transcendent God, who, while radically Other, is present within creation? If we were to understand God's Spirit in avian terms—as elsewhere in Scripture and the Christian theological tradition—then how might this fund a vision of hope and shape our practical conservation activities, both in Aotearoa and globally?

The contextual nature continues in the final phenomenological chapter in which Sue Burns reflects upon how language shapes our relationship to both land and people. In Aotearoa New Zealand, to what extent is it appropriate to speak of Christian mission using the term "pioneers"? How does such language alienate Pākehā from our relationship with land and prevent the deepening of our relationships with Māori (*tangata whenua*—first people of the land)? Sue's chapter is particularly interesting in light of the increasing engagement of churches, Christian agencies, and organizations in the field of ecological action and care. In my role, as National Co-Director of A Rocha Aotearoa NZ (in 2017 celebrating our tenth year), people often refer to A Rocha's existence as a Christian conservation organization as, "pioneering." But how appropriate is such a label? To what extent does such language prevent us from seeing the presence and activity of God's Spirit within Aotearoa New Zealand prior to the arrival of Europeans, or to push the clock back further, prior to the arrival of *homo sapiens*?

The next section of the book deals with text. The power of symbolic language to shape our relationship with the rest of the created world is one that *homo sapiens* use both for ill and good. Yael Klangwisan provocatively explores how the Western theological/philosophical tradition has distanced us from truly *seeing* other creatures and therefore from recognizing our own *animality*. In a dialogue between Derrida and ANE creation accounts, Klangwisan suggests that it is through being stripped "naked under the gaze" of other creatures, that we begins to gain a new perspective on who we are as humanity and our place and responsibilities in the created order.

The contextual reflections offered by myself and Sue Burns comes to the fore again in the exegetical work of Kathleen Rushton. Where Genesis 2:7 states: *adam* from *adamah*, Rushton suggests we are also "waterlings from water." We are a species dependent, like the rest of biological life on our planet, on the presence of H2O. Utilizing an eschatological and cosmological lens, Rushton explores the richness of water imagery within the Gospel of John, arguing that evident within this biblical eschatological cosmology is a "worldly wisdom" to shape our ethics and ecological actions. Continuing with the text of John's Gospel, Stephen Pattemore challenges the anthropocentric soteriology held by much of the evangelical stream of the church. Dealing directly with the central and public "salvation" text of John

3:16, Pattemore utilizes Relevance Theory to argue that the original hearers of John's Gospel would have understood this passage in cosmic terms.

Earlier contributors recognize our embeddedness in the world and our entanglement due to a shared evolutionary story with other species. Yet, while recent discoveries in the field of evolutionary biology and anthropology and in animal behavior have blurred the hard line drawn between *homo sapiens* and other species, nevertheless, there is no denying that *homo sapiens* are, in some ways, distinctive from other species. While the larger size of our frontal cortex gives us the capacity for tool use and symbolic language it also, as noted by Iain McGilchrist,[2] gives us the ability to step back from the world and create a mental picture—that is, to interpret and order past events, and also conceive a vision of the future. Arguably, it is this ability to narrate a history and a hope that makes us *homo sapiens* (wise). Philip Church offers an anthropological and ecological reading of Hebrews 2:5–9, which takes into account this immense power that *homo sapiens* have to interpret and thus shape the world around them. With the Lynn White thesis ever-present in the background, Church suggests that human "dominion" need not be read as "domination." The passage from Hebrews, he argues, offers a vision of humanity exercising faithful dominion ("diligent exercise of rule") for the benefit of all creation.

The final section of the book moves to theological descriptions on the nature of lives shaped by hope. Selwyn Yeoman contends that the practices of Sabbath and Jubilee present in the life of Israel, the ministry of Jesus, and the patristic writers, are deeply ecological and eschatological. As such, these motifs need to be rediscovered in our current age of ecological crisis. Scott Kirkland engages closely with the work of fourteenth-century German mystical theologian Meister Eckhart to offer a theological critique of the ontology that underlies late-modern global capitalism. Kirkland contends that faced with the "indeterminacy of our futures," we are summoned to rethink our desire. Recognizing our "relation with other creatures is entirely mutually constitutive," Kirkland posits that humans are summoned to "the rhapsodic site of gift-exchange," engaging in the work of constructing an *oikos* that can be home for all. Myk Habets's chapter picks up on this imagery of gift-giving, utilizing the eucharistic eco-theology present in the Orthodox tradition to offer a vision of humanity as "priests of creation" engaged in the activity of offering all of creation back to its creator.

One of the riches of Christianity within Aotearoa New Zealand is the strong sense of ecumenicity. Contributors to this volume come from a range of denominations: Anglican, Catholic, Open Brethren, Baptist, Presbyterian,

2. McGilchrist, *The Master and His Emissary*.

and they draw upon a range of traditions: evangelical, sacramental, Orthodox, Catholic, phenomenologist and post-structuralist philosophers, and Māoritanga. Accordingly, it is appropriate that the final chapter is a reflection offered by Celia Deane-Drummond on Pope Francis's *Laudato si'*—itself a work that draws upon a range of theological traditions (Franciscan, Thomistic, Liberation Theology) and that, as Deane-Drummond notes, is an encyclical written for wide readership—beyond the Catholic and Christian world.

Two of the key elements within *Laudato si'* are that of *hope* and *joy*. Elsewhere, in a well-quoted passage, Moltmann writes:

> In the present situation of our world, facile consolation is as fatal as melancholy hopelessness. No one can assure us that the worst will not happen. According to all the laws of experience: it will. We can only trust that even the end of the world hides a new beginning if we trust the God who calls into being the things that are not, and out of death creates new life . . . . In view of the deadly dangers threatening the world, Christian remembrance makes ever present the death of Christ in its apocalyptic dimensions, in order to draw forth from his resurrection from the dead, hope for "the life of the world to come," and from his rebirth to eternal life hope for the rebirth of the cosmos . . . Life out of this hope then means already acting here and today in accordance with that world of justice and righteousness and peace, contrary to appearances, and contrary to all historical chances of success.[3]

In an age of seeming despair, facing an uncertain ecological future, the Christian belief in the power of the resurrection provides the grounding for actions of hope. And yet, in face of the enormity of the reality of climate-change, declining bio-diversity and ecological degradation, one can become overwhelmed, and even seemingly hope-filled actions can become onerous activism that quenches life. Accordingly, it is both necessary and refreshing that at the very conclusion of the encyclical Francis writes: "Let us sing as we go. May our struggles and our concern for this planet never take away the joy of our hope."[4]

The relationship between joy and hope that Francis points to is, I believe, essential as we move into potentially dark and troubling decades ahead. Moltmann, writing in 1971 during a period of political turbulence and activism (Vietnam War and anti-war protests), noted:

3. Moltmann *The Coming of God*, 235.

4. Pope Francis, *Laudato si'*, §244.

> Our social and political tasks, if we take them seriously, loom larger than life. Yet infinite responsibility destroys a human being because he is only man and not god. I have an idea that laughter is able to mediate between the infinite magnitude of our tasks and the limitations of our strength. Many people, who really get down to work, are saying—and rightly so: "Unless we do a lot of joking, we have to cry and cannot get anything done."[5]

It is our prayer that readers of this book will be inspired to live lives of joyous actions that witness to the hope that the Triune God, the creator of all, is in the process of bringing all of creation toward its future glory.

Bibliography

McGilchrist, Iain. *The Master and His Emissary: The Divided Brain and the Making of the Western World.* New Haven, CT: Yale University Press, 2009.

Moltmann, Jürgen. *The Coming of God.* Translated by Margaret Kohl. London: SCM, 1996.

———. *Theology and Joy.* Translated by Richard Ulrich. London: SCM, 1973.

———. *Theology of Hope: On the Ground and the Implications of a Christian Eschatology.* Translated by James W. Leitch. Minneapolis: Fortress, 1993.

Pope Francis. *Encyclical Letter Laudato si' of the Holy Father Francis on Care for our Common Home.* Rome: Libreria Editrice Vaticana, 2015.

5. Moltmann, *Theology and Joy*, 46.

2

Evolutionary Anthropology, Entanglement, and Creaturely Hope

A Theology for Conservation Ethics[1]

Celia Deane-Drummond,
Department of Theology,
University of Notre Dame.

Introduction

EVOLUTIONARY APPROACHES TO ANTHROPOLOGY are beginning to take much greater account of the community basis of human becoming, widening out in order to include other species with whom humans interact. The notion of inter-specific *entanglement* in a shared niche finds common ground with the field of ecology more generally. But the challenging issue for practical ethics is how far and in what sense acknowledgment of such niche construction offers any kind of reasonable guide for conservation practices and for adjudicating between Nature Preservationists and Social Conservationists. Humans are capable of a distinctive visionary hope that puts them in particular position of trust in relation to other creatures. I will argue in this paper that the way that hope is worked out in practice must not

1. This contribution was made possible in part by support (in the form of an International Travel Award) from the Institute for Scholarship in the Liberal Arts, College of Arts and Letters, University of Notre Dame. I am also grateful to Nicola Hoggard Creegan and A Rocha Aotearoa New Zealand for the invitation to deliver a lecture as part of the Ecology and Hope Conference hosted by Carey Baptist College, Auckland on January 8th, 2016, on which this chapter is based. I am also grateful to Craig Iffland for background research and editorial support.

betray the specific *theological* vocation for reasoned ("just") and compassionate care entrusted to human beings.

Ecological ethics has always included some reference to the sciences, though the extent and measure of that interaction will vary depending on the particular emphasis. The ethics of conservation, on the other hand, understood in a traditional sense as preservation, generally always presupposes that biological diversity is worth preserving. I suggest there are four broad difficulties in engendering positive (hope-filled) approaches to conservation. First, a temporary truce in the 1990s between preservationists, who argued for the protection of "wild areas" regardless of the cost to humans, and those who campaigned for human development goals for impoverished indigenous communities in fragile areas, has reopened in heated debate about the value of and the basis for conservation. Second, there are political and social issues at stake in climate change that mitigate against the idea that the planet will be a livable one for humans, never mind other species, in years to come. The relentless decline in biodiversity speaks of untold loss of species, many of which have not even been identified before they disappear. The Paris meeting of the Conference of Parties in December 2015 reached an Accord, with the aim of 1.5 degree limits, but such agreements seem fragile, especially in their implementation. Third, scientific consensus on the existing or threatened violations of planetary boundaries necessary for the stability of the earth as a whole system means that emboldened attempts to halt habitat disappearance, including biodiversity loss, seem doomed, at least in the long run.[2] Even within the planetary boundaries schema, criticism has come from those working with impoverished communities that human needs have not been properly accounted for, as argued by Oxfam director, Kate Raworth.[3] We need to find a way to live within the "doughnut" area of a habitable space for humanity. Ironically, perhaps, just as humanity is discovering other potential habitable planets in the universe, it is making this fragile planet *un*inhabitable, at least in the long term. Fourth, inasmuch as the agencies involved in conservation are Christian ones, there are divided theological standpoints related to all of the above, including distinct visions about how and in what sense theology might have something to say with respect to ecological ethics.

Where can hope be found? While hope engendered by religious belief in general and Christian expectation in particular is important, I intend to show in this chapter that paying attention to the deep history of human

2. Rockström et al., "A Safe Operating Space," 472–75; and Rockström et al., "Planetary Boundaries," 32. See also Steffen et al., "Planetary Boundaries: Guiding Human Development."

3. Raworth, "A Safe and Just Space."

cooperation and interaction with other animals is significant in (a) ameliorating the internal divide in the conservation literature between people or wildlife, (b) accommodating the planetary boundaries debate, and (c) providing an alternative to the fractious divisions between different theological approaches. In other words, in order to counter a scientific narrative that seems all too depressing and in order to inspire the widest possible commitment, we need not just religious counter-factual cosmologies, but another powerful scientific story that is *then* subsequently given a theological interpretation. After that, perhaps we can turn to religious narratives to help understand the more specific contribution that theology can make.

Nature Preservationists vs. Social Conservationists

Before I embark on that account, I intend to mention what is no doubt familiar to many conservationists, namely the divide between management of wildlife, wilderness and other natural assets for the sake of human benefit, as against protecting "natural" areas of wildlife from *any* interference, at least as far as it is ever possible to achieve such a goal. Those on the side of the former have been called "social conservationists," while those on the side of the latter have been named "nature preservationists."[4] Those in the latter camp believe that the only way to prevent biodiversity loss (including genes, populations, and landscapes) is to have areas strictly protected from human interference, on the basis that loss of biodiversity is occurring at around a thousand fold higher rate in comparison with estimates of "background" loss due to non-anthropogenic factors.[5] The vision of protected areas as a fortress against the ravages of human interference is much more difficult to sustain in practice due to complex social and political challenges in these areas. Displacements of local, indigenous peoples raised some serious critical voices to such efforts, resulting in an emergence of an alternative rhetoric, namely that of sustainable development, such as that discussed in the Brundtland Report.[6]

For a while there was, it appears, a truce between preservationist and social conservationist perspectives, including an integration of social and economic goals with that of biodiversity conservation.[7] Integrated

4. For a recent review, see Miller et al., "The New Conservation Debate."

5. See, in particular, summaries of overall synthesis reports of the *Millennium Ecosystem Assessment*. Over a thousand scientists were involved in compiling these reports.

6. See Brundtland Report.

7. See The World Conservation Union, *Caring for the Earth*.

Conservation and Development Projects (ICDPs) emerged in the 1990s, and, "are intended to link the conservation of PA [sic protected areas] with the development of better living conditions in local human communities, including programs promoting agroforestry, ecotourism, and various models of sustainable use alongside traditional biodiversity protection in parks."[8] Such attempts, it seems, have largely failed to deliver development and wildlife conservation benefits in tandem; an example is the Ranomafana National Park in Madagascar, where the forest clearing has continued and tourism revenue has not reached the local population.[9] Often it seems that new sources of income from ICDPs supplement that from the exploitation of biotic reserves rather than replace it. Such failed attempts have opened up the old divide between those who are concerned with biodiversity conservation and those more concerned to protect vulnerable human communities.

There is, then, a re-opening of the split between those who view conservation goals as a means to address social ends, such as the alleviation of poverty, economic development, and political participation, and those who view those goals as distracting from the central mission of protecting areas for the sake of biodiversity conservation and human induced species extinctions. For nature preservationists, sustainable development is not just rejected, but a *threat* to the aim of biodiversity preservation. But there is also a wider critique of sustainable development beyond that of PA advocates, in so far as from an indigenous perspective it is viewed as a politically imposed (and some would say colonial) agenda that is perceived behind many sustainable development projects.[10]

Social conservationists (SC) use empirical data to argue against PA as an effective means to protect biodiversity, while those who advocate nature protection point to the failure of combined approaches, and press for greater political regulation of PAs. For Nature Protectionists (NPs) human beings are a threat, while for SC they are effective means to promote conservation efforts. NPs may even go as far as putting the protection of fragile areas above the survival interests of people, as Holmes Rolston III famously argued in his discussion of Nepal's Chitwan National Park, a UNESCO world heritage site that protects endangered and threatened species, including the one horned rhino (*Rhinocereos unicornis*) and tiger (*Panthera tigris*). A malaria eradication program resulted in a higher population density, pushing

8. See Miller et al., "The New Conservation Debate," 950.

9. Ibid.

10. There have been arguments against the view that valuing ecology is a kind of Western imperialism. See Shoreman-Ouimet and Kopnina, "Reconciling Ecological and Social Justice."

the threatened species to near extinction in less than a decade. Rolston asks, "Ought we to save nature if this results in people going hungry? In people dying? Regrettably, sometimes, the answer is yes."[11] In his most recent publication he has not pitched one against the other in quite such a stark manner, but he does suggest the following:

> If it makes any sense to claim that one ought not to kill individuals without justification, it makes more sense to claim that one ought not to extinguish species lines, without extraordinary justification. A shut down of the life stream on earth is the most destructive event possible. In threatening Earth's biodiversity, the wrong that humans are doing is stopping the historical vitality of life.[12]

The argument he is making is, therefore, much the same; the relative harm of shutting down a species is greater than the risk of expending some human lives of an overpopulated species. It is hardly surprising that those writing from an indigenous perspective strongly object to Rolston's position.[13]

What I find particularly interesting in this discussion is that both camps use scientific evidence to support their case, and in this respect I agree with the philosophical analysis of Thaddeus Miller *et al* that a masquerade of empirical disagreement may disguise deeply held philosophical commitments.[14] A more integrated approach that attempts to identify the ethical commitments of different parties has come to be termed, somewhat confusingly in my view, a variety of *ecological ethics*, where those commitments are broader than environmental ethics, including social justice, animal ethics and professional ethics.[15] Yet this model still leaves the presuppositions of the different parties largely intact; it does not attempt to shift the debate one way or another, or generate another narrative that might be helpful in resolving the tensions. Lining up different ethical commitments may bring some clarity, but at the end of the day there will still be significant splits between different parties because the vision of what needs to be done is different.

Miller et al. argue that in the end conservation pragmatism will trump those philosophical differences, as those with different commitments learn more about each other. I am far less convinced that this is sufficient, even

11. Rolston III, "Feeding People versus Saving Nature," 459.
12. Rolston III, *A New Environmental Ethics*, 153–54.
13. See Siurua, "Nature above People."
14. Miller et al., "The New Conservation Debate," 953–54.
15. Minteer and Collins, "From Environmental to Ecological Ethics."

though it has its theological analogues in, for example, the work of theologian Willis Jenkins, who presses for "prophetic pragmatism," as opposed to what he believes are the damaging influences of "worldviews." The basis of his argument is that worldviews changes are too slow, since action is delayed until consensus is reached.[16] But is this reasonable as an assessment? I am rather more skeptical that a worldviews approach is harmful, unless those worldviews lack analysis or depth in terms of theological interpretation. A vision is, it seems to me, preferable terminology to worldview, as it implies a *direction of movement*. Building that vision can provide motivation for action as much as being integrated in a pragmatic community. The two, in fact, need to work together. The art of a good story, though, is not to be naïve but realistic without losing the possibility of an alternative.

Elizabeth Johnson's Reworking of the Scientific Story

Elizabeth Johnson in *Ask the Beasts* has used the story of Charles Darwin's account of natural selection in *The Origin of Species* in order to construct a theological case for ecological ethics, and, to use her terms, "invigorate ethical behavior that cares for them with a passion integral to faith's passion for the living God."[17] That ethical approach remains idealized, though, through her analysis of the nineteenth-century text of *The Origin*. In so far as it creates an alternative cosmology, her account still seems remarkably detached from the practical conservation literature I have been discussing above. Her intention, though, is entirely correct: namely to combine biological accounts of the natural world in all its diversity with a Christian theological vision that serves to inspire practical action.

I do, however, quibble with an aspect of her thesis developed in this book. Her appropriation of necessary evolutionary loss into her overall approach through rendering the suffering of the natural world "cruciform," follows the work of Rolston. I object on a theological basis. Evolutionary suffering is inevitable (it has happened this way), but should not be viewed as strictly "necessary" in a hard sense in the way that Johnson assumes.[18] If

16. Jenkins, *The Future of Ethics*.

17. Johnson, *Ask the Beasts*, xvii.

18. Johnson's objection to my view on this point is that it "conflates the ethical with the biological," but her position unfortunately misses my intention in using such language. It is not that I think that human beings are somehow responsible for all the suffering in the world before humans came along in the way she implies—a view that places a huge burden of guilt on humanity for all the evils that have ever existed. Such a position cannot be sustained. Even though the early church fathers believed that the

we endorse whatever is evolutionary as "necessary" and simply call it 'cruciform' on the basis that this is just the way life has come about, it amounts to a reification of evolutionary naturalism. Hence, I recognize that from our own lights of standard evolutionary science that suffering is inevitable, but I refuse to accept that God could not have done otherwise, that is, that it is strictly "necessary" in an absolute sense.

In addition, and this is important for the argument I am making in the chapter as a whole, newer evolutionary theories put more emphasis on mutual malleability between individual creatures and their environments, thus taking out the sting of fatalism that seems to be associated with strong versions of evolution by natural selection. Ironically, perhaps, given the history of the idea of natural selection, what was in Charles Darwin's time considered a relatively "weak" force that many scientists doubted was sufficient to craft the variety of species on earth, has now become so dominant in the standard scientific and popular literature that natural selection takes on a life of its own, bolstering a particular variety of naturalistic ethics.

Rolston, unlike Johnson, also combines cruciform nature with an ethical preference for other animal lives in a way that does not make sense theologically. It is not that he does not care about the suffering of people; it is rather that the loss of natural species takes *ethical priority*. Johnson has no objection to the possibility of a cruciform world since she believes it is possible to distinguish between how we might act, and the biological "facts" associated with the tree of life; hence, if humans no longer existed, "pain, suffering and death will continue unabated for other species."[19] I agree with her that there is a need to distinguish ethically between what

fall of humanity had cosmic implications, they had no inkling of contemporary evolutionary theories. Perhaps some confusion has arisen in Johnson's interpretation of my position due to the fact that I drew on Reinhold Niebuhr for the terms "inevitable" in relation to "necessary." He originally used these terms to speak about human responsibilities for evil actions that seem unavoidable. He makes a philosophical distinction between two unavoidable human acts, both of which lead to evil consequences. One is caused by the physical, material nature of things, that he calls *necessary*, and the other is that arising as a result of our human transcendental freedom, that he calls *inevitable*. My objection to the language of necessity in the literature about evolution is less about human freedom and more about how we might perceive how *God as Creator* acts. So, while Niebuhr did seem to associate necessity with biological acts in a fatalistic way, an argument for including the possibility of inevitability in evolutionary terms is important and highly relevant, since it (a) portrays agency in the natural world in a way that loosens the contrast between the freedom of humans and all other creatures, and (b) allows for the affirmation of the possibility at least of God's freedom to act in the created order in alternative ways.

19. Johnson, *Ask The Beasts*, 189.

humans have done with respect to species extinction and what happens in evolutionary history. But the sheer extent of suffering and extinction through evolutionary processes alone give pause for further thought. Johnson rather too easily accommodates that evil, rather than insisting, as I do, that another world is, at least theoretically, possible. So, envisaging a world where there is mortality and pain, perhaps, but a lesser degree of what looks to us like cruelty built into the natural processes may be a *future hope*, but it is hope nonetheless, hope that believes in the possibility of the redemption of human sin and what could be termed natural evils.[20] This is not so much a conflation of ethics and biology, as a disavowal of purely naturalistic ethics and a refusal to allow what we observe to be unchallenged or simply incorporated into a theological schema.

For Johnson, the natural world in all its biodiversity reflects the goodness of God, so, "[t]he whole natural world exists by participation in the being of God."[21] While this is true in a very general sense, such inclusivity avoids the issue of conflict of interests between humans and other beings and avoids challenging processes in the natural world that by our lights are violent. For Johnson, God's immanence in the world is profound, so "the natural world bears the marks of the sacred, being itself imbued with a spiritual presence."[22] Hence, while like Johnson I also draw on evolutionary accounts I feel free to object to what could be termed the tenor of how standard evolutionary narratives tell the story about the world. Yes, it is important to engage in evolutionary biology, but the power of so called "real" accounts of that biology Johnson enlists can risk becoming hoodwinks that avoid facing the difficulties with theological accommodation.

One part of that difficulty, perhaps, is that while Johnson recognizes that the questions that theology and biology ask are distinct, her assumption seems to be that the story told by science is a *descriptive* account of reality, rather than a story laden tale in and of itself.[23] This has implications for the way she treats the material she encounters, for, as she acknowledges, the scientific account will become outdated. She believes she is justified in using Darwin as a primary source because natural selection has stood the test of time. To some extent, I think she is correct—evolution by natural selection is largely unchallenged as a central thesis in evolutionary biology. However, as I will explain further below, newer theories such as the extended

20. See Deane-Drummond, *Ethics of Nature*, 235n66.

21. Johnson, *Ask the Beasts*, 150.

22. Ibid.

23. Ibid., 12. Of course, some of Darwin's ideas are now being "rediscovered," but the point is that she does not report on what these discoveries are or what might be significant about them.

evolutionary synthesis are significantly different philosophically compared with evolution by natural selection alone, and this changes the dynamics of the discussion with evolutionary thought. While it is still commonplace to retain a materialistic philosophy in combination with evolutionary theory, it is rendered less likely once newer more interactive theories open up.

The Extended Evolutionary Synthesis

Evolutionary stories have, I believe, gripped the public imagination in a way that is arguably unique. Darwinian thinking has seeped into the cultural milieu of our times almost by stealth and it may be one of the reasons why well-recognized scholars like Elizabeth Johnson take Darwin's original work so seriously. But there are damaging ideas buried in with his science in his approach to the human that also show strong racist influences. The persistence of these ideas in public discussion has given rise to the assumption that race is biologically and evolutionarily determined. It is hard sometimes to distinguish the scientific from the political and even moral; so on that basis it is unsurprising that sections of the American public turn to a facile version of the creation story as a counter to that powerful and seemingly irresistible Darwinian influence. Biologists, though, if they are being honest, will admit that the so-called Darwinian laws are not so much proofs but appealing correlations. For example, take something like the survival of the fittest, which is a core idea in the theory of evolution by natural selection. "Survival" in biological terms means successful reproduction, as does "fittest," so what does the tautology "survival of the fittest" really mean? I am not suggesting that Darwinian theories are necessarily wrong, but the solidity of biological theories will never be of the same order as physical laws, and even these laws are often couched in terms of their probabilities. That is why the language of necessity is so problematic; it seems to go against the grain of contemporary philosophy of biology.

What this amounts to is that we have to accept that many of our passionately held scientific beliefs are powerful stories about the world that, we wager, are connected in some sense with the way the world is. And, importantly, our trust is merited because science works. But, what if stories about evolution were also to take more explicit ecological stories much more seriously? This has actually happened in a shift from the classical neo-Darwinian view to what is now being termed the *extended evolutionary synthesis*. I am not going to go into details of what this means here, except to say that this approach is shifting, in a highly significant way, stories about our own deep social *and biological* historical origins.[24] In the extended evolutionary synthesis there is an awareness that there are "a myriad of entangled agents in the processes of human becoming."[25] Optimal models in human evolution assume "cultural" information as input and behavior as output, rather than taking proper account of the way behavior *both shapes and is shaped by* the ecological and social context, the *bio-socio-cultural niche*. This means that for human beings the genetic, behavioral, epigenetic, and what might be termed symbolic inheritance pathways all contribute to evolutionary change.[26] The important point to make is that rather than viewing evolutionary change working through fixed "traits" that are selected for through the winnowing process of natural selection, the new evolutionary model stresses that the behavior of particular organisms actually influences the natural environment, and it is that which is inherited along with the genetic inheritance. So, if we imagine all organisms interacting in this way, the picture of evolutionary change becomes incredibly complicated. One of the important points in this discussion is that organisms, including humans, were not simply passive in the face of environmental change, but active, and actively influencing the environment in feedback loops. As Bateson and Gluckman note: "By their mobility, in the case of animals, or facility to disperse, in the case of plants . . . organisms often expose themselves to new conditions that may reveal heritable variability and open up possibilities for evolutionary changes that would not otherwise have taken place."[27]

Reflecting upon this bio-socio-cultural niche Jeremy Kendal et al. suggest that "the defining characteristic of niche construction is not the modification of environments per se, but rather the organism-induced changes in selection pressures in environments."[28] Niche construction represents a philosophical shift in understanding the way evolutionary processes work, so that while some have incorporated aspects of niche construction theory (NCT) in their frameworks, a more radical standpoint puts evolutionary questions under the umbrella of NCT, rather than adding it on to previous models.[29] This is particularly interesting in my view as it provides a

24. As clearly represented in Fuentes, "Blurring the Biological and Social."

25. Ibid., 42.

26. Laland and Brown, *Sense and Nonsense*.

27. For a specific discussion of freedom and agency, see Bateson and Gluckman, *Plasticity*.

28. Kendal et al., "Human Niche Construction."

29. The mathematical expression of NCT is straightforward. Standard evolutionary theory assumes an organism's state is a function of the organism and the environment (dO/dt= f(O,E) and changes in the environment are a simply a function of that environment (dE/dt=g(E)). NCT, on the other hand, allows for the organism to be able to

significant bridge between the biological sciences and the human, cultural sciences. In NCT the idea of "causation" becomes problematized. So, the "dichotomous proximate and ultimate distinction" is replaced by "reciprocal causation."[30] In this way niche construction works with natural selection in the evolutionary process in a dynamic interchange. Niches are themselves part of the inheritance process, so that an *interactionist* theory replaces an *externalist* theory. Niche construction theory emphasizes not just genetic and cultural inheritance, but also ecological inheritance as well, in interaction with the first two.[31] However, I would posit that envisioning cultural aspects as separate from ecological inheritance seems too constraining. Ecological and cultural inheritance under a broader "ecological" category carries the advantage of perceiving a developmental context where the physical niche is not separated from the social niche.[32] We can refer to this multi-faceted emergence as entanglement. Entanglement is therefore real and integral to the deep history of our species in relationship with others. How does this new vision of our evolutionary past help us to adjudicate in the Social Conservationist versus Nature Preservationist dispute?

Ecological Ethics

The Nature Protectionists could be said to be aligned almost with a pre-Darwinian model that stresses the intrinsic importance of each species in a given environment. Biodiversity preservation presupposes that an ecosystem, sometime in history, needs protecting. In other words, the reasons for protecting those species do not seem to follow a strict Darwinian logic of change, unless we assume that what exists now, as the outcome of millennia of evolution is given special value. Social conservationists, on the other hand, view the natural environment as somehow "external" to human interests, even if incorporated into that flourishing.

Of course, the reality is that different species are much more intimately entangled and bound up with each other than either NP or SC assume. Human beings, in so far as they are super-cooperators, still interact with the

change the environment, and so can be expressed mathematically as $dO/dt=f(O,E)$ and $dE/dt=g(O,E)$.

30. Kendal et al., "Human Niche Construction," 786.

31. This threefold model of Laland et al. compares with the four dimensions of evolution suggested by Jablonka and Lamb. The difference in this case is a greater emphasis on the ecological aspects; the latter allow for niche construction, but place this in the context of behavioral change and symbolic change as two of the four dimensions of evolution. See Laland et al., "Cultural Niche Construction."

32. Odling-Smee, "Niche Inheritance."

natural environment in such a way so as to re-shape it either consciously or unconsciously. This generates feedback loops in the process of evolution, but that is also true in ecological relationships and in the natural maturation of humans in relation to other organisms as well. Even if human societies have largely distanced themselves from a felt dependence on other living things, symbiotic relationships are still present in the living flora that inhabit human bodies and urban communities.[33]

At this point it is worth noting an important distinction between evolutionary-anthropological-ecological accounts of the world and that according to Christian theology. The former, in so far as they are based on the natural sciences, do not admit to a teleological vision even though it is hard to avoid that language. The conservation of biodiversity is traditionally based on acknowledgement of intrinsic value of each species, or their value to the ecosystem as such, or a more instrumental value to humans. Looking at biodiversity through a deep history lens complicates such categorizations, since humans have been interacting with other species in diverse ways since the dawn of human history.

Perhaps it is worth noting that humans were not always the top of the hierarchy historically; mega fauna roamed the landscape in the Pleicestocene in what to us would seem horrifying and terrifying ways. Human-like creatures then were simply food resources for mega-fauna; it took ingenuity and careful observation of the habits of other species to overcome this threat. Paul Trout believes that predators were crucial to the development of human mythic imagination.[34] It would be a mistake to avoid this phase in human history because it seems unpalatable to our modern sensitivities about animal cruelty. Indeed, lodged in human pre-consciousness there may well be a memory of such a precarious existence with giant carnivores that eventually came to symbolize the divine in the human imagination. Trout argues that it was because of our terrifying history as prey that we quite literally cannot stop killing. While this does not provide an excuse for violence against other animals, and callous indifference to their suffering or even extinction, it may help us understand it rather better. Theologian Gene Rogers believes that the symbolism of blood is crucial to a religious imaginary. While tamed in the Christian tradition, for Catholics at least the heart of faith includes the memory of the bloody and violent sacrifice of the Son,

33. Examples of this association include friendly gut bacteria and also microscopic skin and hair mites adapted to living in human bodies that become parasitic when out of control, such as scabies. Further back in evolutionary history, mitochondria had their origin as prokaryotic cells that took up residence in eukaryotic hosts.

34. Trout, *Deadly Powers*.

the lamb slain for human redemption.[35] Sarah Coakley, on the other hand, uses the language of sacrifice in order to build the case for a new natural theology based on evolutionary theories of cooperation.[36] But she does not touch on the early history of hominins and hardly mentions the significance that such ideas about sacrifice might have for ecological ethics.[37] While it may have been kindled deep in the past, the human mythic and religious imagination is also capable of looking to the future and envisioning other hope-filled worlds. Christianity is important in this discussion as it is both grounded in the material world affirmed through the incarnate Christ, yet, looks to a world transformed, through the life of the Spirit.

The Book of Revelation and Future Theological Visions

So, what might Christian theology offer to this future vision? In order to ground this part of the discussion in a language that is common across Christian traditions, I am going to draw on Richard Woods's contemporary interpretation of the seven bowls of wrath in the Book of Revelation.[38] While the use of biblical texts for ecological purposes has been subjected to some critique in recent decades,[39] it makes little sense for Christian theology to ignore their rich resources. Traditions are always received by particular communities and therefore can be subject to further discussion. The Book of Revelation is contested in American evangelical traditions, providing for some a reason to abandon care for the created world.[40] It is therefore really important to consider the text carefully and argue what it is or is not saying. The use of natural catastrophic imagery was not, Woods argues, merely about metaphorical illustration, but was intended to remind readers of real natural disasters, such as the eruption of Mount Vesuvius in AD 79 and great plagues.

Drawing on a rich wealth of biblical commentaries, Woods states that "while the planetary wounds (*plēgai*) from the "seven bowls of wrath" function as symbolic admonitions, they evince a sophisticated insight into the organic connection that exists among biological and geological systems,

35. Rogers, "Creationist Accounts of Evolution."

36. Coakley, *Sacrifice Regained.*

37. She does, though, engage with John Hare's discussion of the evolution of morality. This is another huge topic outside the scope of this chapter.

38. Woods, "Seven Bowls of Wrath."

39. See Nash, "The Bible vs Biodiversity."

40. Maier, "Green Millennialism."

the consequences of disrupting this balance through human greed, oppression, and malice, and, finally, the compensating divine response to ecocatastrophe."[41] The animal imagery is also striking in one of the two main story lines; the assault of the dragon and the two beasts on the followers of the lamb; alongside a second story line in the plot, namely, the rise and fall of the city of Babylon, representing oppressive political power of Roman imperialism. All seven bowls of wrath are directed against the powers of evil, but result in natural ecological disasters. The seven bowls, administered by angels over the known cosmos, epitomized a liturgy of destruction, conjuring up the sacrificial imagery in Temple ceremonies.[42] The libation bowls pour out destruction (*plēgē*, meaning more than plague, but deep blows or wounds) to all the earth's inhabitants, but especially humans. The portrayal of the destructive wrath of God, and the depiction of Christ in military imagery in this book is disturbing for most Christian sensibilities.[43] Over half the time that passion, *thumos* (related to inner anger or *orgē*), appears in the New Testament is in the Book of Revelation. *Thumos* is not used of the lamb, but only *orgē*, and that only once in Rev. 6:16. And, how might we interpret that anger? Many commentators believe that, in the light of the overwhelming love of God as the primary stance, anger and the plagues are the fruit of the rejection of God's will, rather than God's primary intention. Woods concludes that "Overall it may be granted that the blows of Revelation are primarily meant to move people to repentance, not to harm them or Creation. That they do so results from human impenitence, not divine malice."[44]

The vision, too, in Revelation, is one where the destroyers will be destroyed and there will be eventual healing of the earth. The details of ecological destruction today are different in that we know far more compared with the author of Revelation of the complex intertwining between species and ecosystems. Yet, John of Patmos was right to point to the underlying cause of such destruction in human greed, avarice and political oppression of the most vulnerable members of the human community. It is not enough, in other words, to protect biodiversity on its own without taking account social impacts. The vision of the wounds of creation is appropriate as it implies the need for healing, not least healing in human relationships. As Woods and others have pointed out, we are working for a *renewed* creation, not one

41. Woods, "Seven Bowls of Wrath," 65.

42. Ibid., 67.

43. Hanson, *The Wrath of the Lamb.*

44. Woods, "Seven Bowls of Wrath," 68.

that has been destroyed, hence against those who view current ecological disasters as some sort of necessary prelude to the end of the world.

The consequences of enacting that hoped for future are profound; a working for justice both for those who are vulnerable in society *and* protecting endangered species, especially those that are the most significant for the overall flourishing of an ecosystem. Recent research that tries to understand how other animals have become adapted to human communities is also helpful, since it may give insight into ways of being in the world where both humans and other animals can become better adapted to each other.[45] A difficult task of discernment is evoked when human flourishing and that of other species are perceived as in conflict. I suggest that this requires a re-imagining of what development means—against the business as usual model, and in favor of a deeper appreciation of indigenous socioeconomic needs, working in concert with the interests of other beings in the natural world, rather than against it. Belief in God as creator and redeemer of that world requires that we attempt to do this, rather than refuse to take our responsibilities towards other creatures and ecosystems seriously. I resist, too, a ready romanticism that fails to face the destructive force of lethal organisms; some realism is necessary. So, was it right to clear up malaria in regions close to Chitwan National Park and so put intense pressure on the one horned rhino and tiger populations? Yes, but addressing global health issues cannot be detached from ecological goods; one of the problems is a lack of joined up thinking between different goods by parties with different vested interests. A Christian vision of hope can help to resolve that dilemma by insisting on the good for all and for each, and aim to deepen the combined wisdom and compassion of those making hard choices.

And practical projects do exist that work towards giving hope for people and planet; the Maasai tribe in Kenya, for example, in a CAFOD project benefited from distillation of water from steam vents; a simple technique that helped this community survive in an ecologically fragile landscape.[46] But their acknowledgement of support was translated into the language of praise, that all the blessings they have received come from God. It is this language of praise that is echoed in Pope Francis's encyclical *Laudato si'*; and it is through praise that it becomes possible to garner hope in an alternative. So, I will finish this chapter with a few words from *Laudato si'* that are directed towards the whole human community, and the community of religious believers in particular:

45. Agustin Fuentes, personal communication.

46. I discuss this in Deane-Drummond, "Public Theology."

Triune God, wondrous community of infinite love,

Teach us to contemplate you in the beauty of the universe, for all things speak of you.

Awaken our praise and thankfulness for every being that you have made. Give us the grace to feel profoundly joined to everything that is.

God of love, show us our place in this world as channels of your love, for all the creatures of this earth, for not one of them is forgotten in your sight.[47]

Bibliography

Bateson, Patrick, and Peter Gluckman. *Plasticity, Robustness, Development and Evolution*. Cambridge: Cambridge University Press, 2011.

Brundtland Report of the United Nations at Report of the World Commission on Environment and Development, Our Common Future (Brundtland Report). March 20, 1987. http://www.un-documents.net/wced-ocf.htm. Accessed January 11, 2018.

Coakley, Sarah. *Sacrifice Regained: Evolution, Cooperation and God*. 2012 Gifford Lecture. http://www.giffordlectures.org/lectures/sacrifice-regained-evolution-cooperation-and-god.

Deane-Drummond, Celia. *Ethics of Nature*. Oxford: Wiley, 2004.

———. "Public Theology as Contested Ground: Arguments for Climate Justice." In *Religion and Ecology in the Public Sphere*, edited by Celia Deane-Drummond and Henrich Bedford-Strohm, 189–210. London: Continuum, 2011.

Fuentes, Agustin. "Blurring the Biological and Social in Human Becomings." In *Biosocial Becomings: Integrating Social and Biological Anthropology*, edited by Tim Ingold and Gisli Palsson, 42–58. Cambridge: Cambridge University Press, 2013.

———. *Race, Monogamy and Other Lies They Told You: Busting Myths about Human Nature*. Berkeley: University of California Press, 2012.

Hanson, Anthony Tyrell. *The Wrath of the Lamb*. Eugene, OR: Wipf and Stock, 2010.

Jenkins, Willis. *The Future of Ethics: Sustainability, Social Justice and Religious Creativity*. Washington, DC: Georgetown University Press, 2013.

Johnson, Elizabeth. *Ask the Beasts: Darwin and the God of Love*. London: Bloomsbury, 2014.

Kendal, Jeremy, J. Tehrani, and F. John Odlinget al-Smee. "Human Niche Construction in Interdisciplinary Focus." *Phil. Trans. Royal Society B* 366 (2011): 785–92.

Laland, Kevin, et al. "Cultural Niche Construction and Human Evolution." *Behavioral Brain Sciences* 23 (2000) 131–75.

Laland Kevin, and Gillian Brown. *Sense and Nonsense: Evolutionary Perspectives on Human Behavior*. (Oxford: Oxford University Press, 2011).

47. This is an extract taken from "A Christian Prayer in Union with Creation," which is an addendum to Pope Francis's encyclical *Laudato si'*.

Laland, K. N., J. Odling-Smee, and M. W. Feldman. "Cultural Niche Construction and Human Evolution." *Journal of Evolutionary Biology* 14 (2001) 22–33.

———. "Niche Construction, Biological Evolution, and Cultural Change." *Behavioral Brain Sciences* 23 (2000) 131–75.

Maier, Harry. "Green Millennialism: American Evangelicals, Environmentalism and the Book of Revelation." In *Ecological Hermeneutics*, edited by David Horrell, Cheryl Hunt, Christopher Southgate and Francesca Stavrakopoulou, 246–65. London: T. & T. Clark, 2010.

Millennium Ecosystem Assessment. 2001–2005. http://millenniumassessment.org/en/index.aspx. Acessed January 11, 2018.

Miller, Thaddeus, et al. "The New Conservation Debate: The View From Practical Ethics." *Biological Conservation* 144 (2011) 948–57.

Minteer, Ben A., and James P. Collins. "From Environmental to Ecological Ethics: Toward a Practical Ethics for Ecologists and Conservationists." *Science and Engineering Ethics* 14, no. 4 (2008) 483–501.

Nash, James. "The Bible vs Biodiversity: The Case against Moral Argument from Scripture." *Journal for the Study of Religion, Nature and Culture* 3, no. 2 (2009) 213–37.

Maier, Harry. "Green Millennialism: American Evangelicals, Environmentalism and the Book of Revelation." In *Ecological Hermeneutics*, edited by David Horrell et al., 246–65. London: T. & T. Clark, 2010.

Odling-Smee, F. John. "Niche Inheritance." In *Evolution: The Extended Synthesis*, edited by Massimo Pigliucci and Gerd B. Muller, 175–207. Cambridge, MA: MIT Press, 2010.

Pope Francis. *Laudato si': On care for our common home*. Huntington, IN: Our Sunday Visitor, 2015.

Raworth, Kate. "A Safe and Just Space for Humanity: Can We Live Within the Doughnut?" *Oxfam Policy and Practice: Climate Change and Resilience* 8, no. 1 (2012) 1–26.

Rockström, Johan, et al. "A Safe Operating Space for Humanity." *Nature* 461, no. 7263 (2009) 472–75

———. "Planetary Boundaries: Exploring a Safe Operating Space for Humanity." *Ecology and Society* 14, no. 2 (2009) 32.

Rogers, Eugene. "The Sociology and Theology of Creationist Accounts of Evolution: How Blood Marks the Bounds of the Christian Body." *Zygon* 49, no. 3 (2014) 540–53.

Rolston III, Holmes. *A New Environmental Ethics: The Next Millennium for Life on Earth*. London: Routledge, 2012.

———. "Feeding People versus Saving Nature." In *Environmental Ethics*, edited by Andrew Light and Holmes Rolston III, 451–62. London: Routledge, 2011.

Shoreman-Ouimet, Eleanor, and Helen Kopnina. "Reconciling Ecological and Social Justice to Promote Biodiversity Conservation." *Biological Conservation* 184 (2015) 320–26.

Siurua, Hanna. "Nature above People: Rolston and 'Fortress' Conservation in the South." *Ethics & the Environment* 11, no. 1 (2006) 71–96.

Steffen, Will, et al. "Planetary Boundaries: Guiding Human Development on a Changing Planet." *Science* 347, no, 6223 (2015). http://science.sciencemag.org/content/347/6223/1259855.full. Accessed Feb. 2, 2018.

Trout, Paul. *Deadly Powers: Animal Predators and the Mythic Imagination*. New York: Prometheus, 2011.

White, Merton. "Original Sin, Natural Law and Politics." In *From a Philosophical Point of View: Selected Studies*, 270–83. Princeton: Princeton University Press, 2009.

Woods, Richard. "Seven Bowls of Wrath: The Ecological Relevance of Revelation." *Biblical Theology Bulletin* 38 (2008) 64–75.

The World Conservation Union. *Caring for the Earth: a Strategy for Sustainable Living*. London: Earthscan, 2009.

Phenomenology

3

The Phenomenology of Hope

Nicola Hoggard Creegan,
A Rocha Aotearoa New Zealand

On the banks of the Rhine, a beautiful castle had been standing for centuries. In the cellar of the castle, an intricate network of webbing had been constructed by mysterious spiders who lived there. One day a strong wind sprang up and destroyed the web. Frantically the spiders worked to repair the damage. They thought it was their webbing that was holding up the castle.[1]

—Morris Kline: *Mathematics, The Loss of Certainty*

When we think of hope it is often in terms of stories. A range of modalities and disciplines from narrative therapy through to the narrative emphasis in biblical studies and theology have realized the potential of stories to heal and give hope on the one hand, or to undermine hope and cause despair on the other hand. Stories fill out the emotional landscape; they help us to identify with the characters and take on imaginary lives or virtues. Hope in stories is effected in most cases not by a leap of logic, but indwelling the story, by unconsciously taking on a whole lifeworld that is evoked by the narrative. "A scriptural world," says George Lindbeck "is able to absorb the universe."[2] Hope is a stance, a way of being in the world, a belief that in spite of the logical evidence available, there is another deeper source of ultimate concern. We are called to hope, very often, because we have read and indwelt heroic

1. Kline, *Mathematics: The Loss of Certainty*, 277.
2. Lindbeck, *The Nature of Doctrine*, 189.

stories of perseverance in the face of dreadful odds. Nevertheless, as we are all too aware, stories can be and are constructed out of nothing and with no basis in any other reality. Narrative is a double-edged sword.

In this paper I examine a range of common stories that contribute to an overall orientation to the distant future and what we call the eschaton. I then turn to nature and matter and the sense of depth and vitality that exists in nature—the matter of the castle, as it were—as a necessary adjunct to and foundation of hope in human societies and churches. I argue that our sense of depth in nature is also influenced by our understanding of the evolutionary story. Are our stories about nature ones that see it as just a surface phenomenon, or as having depth and life? The depth of nature funds and undergirds our stories of hope, because in nature we intuit the deeper hidden ultimate concern and love of the divine.

The Stories We Live By

Stories draw on the perceptions and intuitions about life that are often on the periphery. Narrative therapy, for instance, is founded on the idea that we are telling ourselves self-fulfilling self-defeating stories (or listening to inner voices that are disparaging) and a therapist is able to draw on strengths hidden or occluded by the dominant story in order to bring healing.[3]

Scripture is a rich resource for stories of restoration, as is the tradition, ancient literature and popular culture. And storytelling may be a way to approach an edge like death over which we have little we humans can do to make a difference, except in terms of a few years and the prevention of premature demise. But how does the Christian narrative really work when applied to climate change? One might argue that it is counter-productive. The stories of life after death have made people complacent. They have deferred to God what should be taken up by human effort. Inferring that matter is of only penultimate importance, Christian stories have simply allowed Christians—like other contemporary people—to treat the earth as mechanical and as an object for our control and manipulation.

Christians do not agree on the nature of sin, or on human origins. How can we sensibly tackle the theology of disaster? The world of conservationists at large is divided, as Celia Deane-Drummond has mentioned, into those who believe we should concentrate on habitat at the expense of humans and those who think that the climate must be saved primarily for humans. How do Christians navigate between these extremes? How does hope function in this context?

3. See for instance, Maisel et al., *Biting the Hand the Starves You.*

In the *Nature and Destiny of Man*, based on the Gifford Lectures given in 1939 as war was breaking out in Europe, Reinhold Niebuhr talked about whether our religious stories "expect a Christ" or don't expect a Christ. He noted that the Abrahamic religions all expect a messiah.[4] They are stories/religions of hope. He had a point, and one that is important at this time which often again seems so hopeless. The stories we tell one another do give us hope or lead us to despair, either active full-fledged despair or the slow ebbing away or erosion of hope (and faith) so common in the contemporary world. Although Niebuhr was right, there is more to the business of hope than he allows. For even a messiah can divide; a messiah can come only for humans at the expense of all other life, or for only some humans at the expense of others. Eschatology can in fact be bad news for all but a select group of people. And we must admit that eschatological visions have tended toward the apocalyptic. Christians are often in danger of embracing stories that have unpleasant endings, almost as proof that there really is another dimension.

Consider for instance, the well-known and quite widespread premillennial account, popularized by authors such as Hal Lindsey and Tim LaHaye.[5] In these stories Christians have a very pessimistic story of the future of this Earth. It will simply be burned up. It will be destroyed when Christ comes to rescue the elect. Religions may expect a Christ, but what else they expect also matters. Premillennialism gives hope to a few, but only at the cost of hoping for a conflagration. One might think of Christians in the southern states of America in 1991 as they embraced the Gulf War as a harbinger of Armageddon (Islam, of course has similar theological variants). Apparently indeed, "49% of Americans think the severity of recent natural disasters are signs of the end times as described the Bible and not evidence of climate change."[6] On the other hand, secularists don't have a particularly pleasant counter-story; the end occurring as the sun devours the earth (if meteorites, plagues, climate heating, nuclear war, or magnetic shifts have not done it already), albeit in a few billion years' time.

For every story that expects a messiah—and a hope—there is another one that speaks of destruction in the name of Christ, either of other humans or of the earth. For every technological advance and new story of stunning success—whether from the Hadron Collider or the Hubble Space Telescope—there is the deeper story of our eventual demise in the heat death of the exploding sun, and thus the end of all hope for the Earth. For every story

4. Niebuhr, *The Nature and Destiny of Man.*

5. LaHaye and Jenkins, *Left Behind.*

6. Quoted in Miller, "Deep Responsibility for the Deep Future," 445.

of life after death for the individual there is another one of annihilation for all other forms of life. In this volume Philip Church discusses how the story of human dominion can be a harsh pessimistic assumption of superiority or a loving God-intended care for creation. Human dominion can also be rejected entirely in a story that understands humans as merely an unhelpful weed species.

Charles Taylor has captured the intellectual vision of the world with his notion of the "social imaginary."[7] The social imaginary overlaps with the concept of hope and eschatology, because it refers to the way in which people consciously, but mostly unconsciously, collectively imagine the social space, its limits, promise and the dynamics of inclusion and exclusion. The "social imaginary" can almost be considered to be the culture specific niche of a people group or a community. It is created by them and by the slow effects of generations and environments before them, but it also acts back upon them as though it carried the physical properties of water or earth. The social imaginary bubbles up to the surface in tales and common religious and secular stories like the ones above.

This dilemma of hopeful versus fearful stories is related to the perennial problem of the hiddenness of God and the problem of evil.[8] Believers affirm the sovereignty (more or less) of a God who is not easy to experience. When life is good, Christians rejoice and give thanks, and "see" the hand of God. When things go wrong they do not see it as evidence that God is not there, but rather claim that God is present in suffering, and will bring life and new life out of death and darkness, and their stories are expressed this way. Faith, then, is often perilously close to foolishness or inauthenticity. When Christians insist on interpreting their stories as hopeful in spite of manifest evidence to the contrary, it is because experience comes in many layers. While feeling desperate or experiencing despair or betrayal at one level it is nevertheless possible to discern "absolute dependence" at another, or to remember a religious experience from the past.[9] Believers respond to the Spirit in Scripture or to the Spirit in nature. Nature is largely responsible for the feeling of absolute dependence. And it is to this sense of the Spirit in nature that I now turn. For I argue that what we experience in nature and how we interpret that experience will sustain us through the "long dark

7. Taylor, *A Secular Age*, 95, 146–211.

8. For connections between the problem of evil and the problem of the silence of God, see Rea, "Divine Hiddenness, Divine Silence."

9. The sense of "absolute dependence" was famously posited by the great German theologian, Friedrich Schleiermacher, as the basis of all piety and religion. See Schleiermacher, *The Christian Faith*, 8.

night of the soul." Nature and our understanding of nature—our narratives of nature—either fund or undermine our stories of hope.

Evolution as Story

And indeed what we experience in nature is related to another story, that of evolution. Evolution is a narrative of life's existence. There are many stories associated with evolutionary biology. Deane-Drummond has noted in the previous chapter how evolutionary paradigms have been changing. On the one hand natural selection has come to bear an inordinate weight in our understanding of the history of life on earth; on the other hand newer ecological paradigms are now opening up and changing the ancient story in ways that are more compatible with the sacred. As Richard Miller has said:

> While some disciplines in the natural sciences expose us to the possible contours of the deep future, if one holds to a scientific worldview that sees the human being as an accident that came into being through chance, then there is no intrinsic teleological connection between human beings and the earth. There is only an accidental material connection. Without such an intrinsic teleological connection to the Earth the deep future will appear alien and foreign to the human community and thus the imagination will resist contemplating such a future.[10]

In the world of modernity, or post Enlightenment, both Christians and non-believers often act and speak as though the world and matter are mechanical stuff. Even most other life is somewhat mechanical. Hence the experiments done on animals and the persisting assumption that they don't really suffer like we do. Hence the misuse of agricultural land as a commodity. Only the human mind (or in the case of Christians, God's mind as well) soars above this stuff. Hence the emphasis on reason as distinctly human. Within this story our cleverness is used to fight nature. We re-route rivers, defy gravity, kill bugs and so on.[11]

While the control of nature at some level will always be one of the crowning achievements of humanity—and a part of what is meant by dominion in its best sense—many biologists would now disagree with the associated mechanistic understanding of the world. One thinks here of the "extended evolutionary synthesis" and theories of evolution into entangled niches, all of which have been mentioned by Deane-Drummond.

10. Miller, "Deep Responsibility for the Deep Future," 443.

11. See McPhee, *The Control of Nature*.

But vestiges of the mechanistic story persist nevertheless.[12] Secularists have long understood the story of evolution to be one without a goal or purpose. This core dogma of evolution is still thought to be sacrosanct. Something very mechanical and impersonal drives it by a random algorithm. This is not a discarded story even if it is now properly being eclipsed by paradigm changes in evolutionary theory. According to this older yet dominant story of evolution, although humans are tempted to see our emergence as very exceptional we are nothing special, merely one particular endpoint of a giant tree of life. As Deane-Drummond has noted, mega-fauna once ruled the earth, when mammals were still a small insignificant line on the tree of life. To a strict Darwinist, mega-fauna and humans are simply equal end-points on the tree of life. While strong human exceptionalism has had shocking effects on human behavior, so also has this type of Darwinism. In both cases the effect is profound, but mostly unconscious.[13]

So where does this leave us? A multitude of uncommonly pessimistic stories, both religious and secular surround us, and invade us. In the popular imagination these take root as movies and novels of dystopia: think of *Melancholia* (Lars von Trier, 2011), reflecting the deep unconscious "social imaginary" of disaster, and the heroine's brave attempt to weave new stories, even as the inevitable end comes into sight, much like the spiders in the castle, frantically spinning and re-spinning their webs. A similar imagining of the impossible is found in *Station Eleven*.[14] This is not a tale of a climate changed ending, but rather of a particularly severe plague (though we might argue that such plagues will become common as a part of nature out of control as the earth warms and ecosystems are strained). In the end what keeps some humans alive is the retelling of Shakespearian stories because as Star Wars has told us, "survival is not sufficient." *Station Eleven* allows us to imagine what might happen if civilization suddenly disappeared, and with it all technological props. Humans survive, but in a very reduced form.

Although these stories of despair surround us and form us they are contrary to what we know of the Christian God, a God who intends hope and love and harmony and healing and wonder. A garden of delight and

12. For newer evolutionary paradigms, see for instance, Ingold, "Beyond Biology and Culture."

13. Christians who accept evolution also often have several unhelpful strategies. Some will accept the process reluctantly but add a special moment at which humans were separated from the rest of the animal kingdom. They split the sixth day of creation. Perhaps into the first 11 hours and 59 minutes and last minute. Others see design everywhere. Yes the process of evolution happened but it was all designed, again with connotations of a big machine. (Of course, nature is replete with little feedback loops, and design like features, but I am wanting to insist that is not all there is.)

14. St. John Mandell, *Station Eleven*.

plenty begins the Scriptures: the trees for the healing of the nations ends the Bible, as Deane-Drummond has described. God's Spirit is the Spirit of nature, of matter, of interiority. Christ came to share matter and in some transformed way still shares with us this mysterious form called life. Yet this understanding of nature is at odds with the mechanical view of nature, and at odds with the idea of salvation coming always from outside. The conflict between an older enchanted view of nature and the contemporary scientific ones lies not only in surface questions of meaning but at this deeper level of how nature is understood, for nature remains one of the places where God is discerned, in spite of tragedy, and in spite of suffering. If one suspects this place is really the result of mechanical algorithms and forces, then the place of God and the stories of hope are less accessible. A mechanical surface nature does not fund stories of hope. A nature of depth does. The only hope, if nature is mechanical, is that our minds might be above nature, that salvation might come from outside, that our salvation is too somewhere outside where God must lie if God is anywhere[15]

Outside stories offer little hope, however much a messiah (also from the outside) is expected or welcomed. They appear to be less and less plausible when our fate is threatened by the factors surrounding our material existence, and when viewed in an evolutionary perspective. Why would God create by slow and careful incremental steps only to switch it all at the end for a few surviving humans? Why would God go to such pains to become so entangled in matter that observers could not see the divinity in the flesh? The only stories that will offer us real hope are ones that come to terms with our radical embeddedness in and dependence on matter—and with the Incarnation's radical ongoing embeddedness as well. Hope begins as we come to terms with human life as deeply interconnected, as occurring within a depth that is nature, as being emergent, like all nature, in unpredictable ways from within previous life or matter. Human similarities to all nature matter, as does our dependence on nature, and the healing that comes from nature. We hope for a world that is again material but without tragedy—and thus subtly different from this one. In trying to describe this hopeful inner world I turn to two theorists. One is the philosopher David Abram who works with Merleau Ponty.[16] The other is Jane Bennett and her

15. Tanner defines the transcendent as what is above and not competing with finite creatures. God, as transcendent, can become human or indwell us without in any way detracting from our finitude or freedom. Only what is transcendent can interact with what is not transcendent without competition. See Tanner, *Jesus, Humanity and the Trinity*, 3.

16. Abram, "Merleau-Ponty and the Voice of the Earth."

stunning work *Vibrant Matter.*[17] Neither is working as a Christian, but both rediscover what Christians might call the glory of the inwardness of the natural world. They also describe what I argue is the inward world of the psalms and wisdom literature, as well as the glory and anticipation of which Romans 8 speaks. This inner world of nature gives us an immediate and inward connection to the stories of hope we tell as part of our Christian ritual. The inwardness is an important affirmation of narratives of hope, and participation in nature helps us then to connect to God and to be converted to a way of life that embraces all of life on earth.

To summarize, stories and narratives, however popular they have been in terms of reshaping individual lives, and in terms of recovering biblical hope can be received as nothing more than superficial tropes suspended above the real, bleak world. Stories also have the power to feed our dualistic selves; they reassure us that our minds have ultimate power over our truth and reality. As a partial antidote to the superficiality of story, especially in postmodernity, I turn to the substratum of life—the walls of the castle—to find a grounded hope upon which stories can find their inner life. Both phenomenology and evolutionary theory shows us we need to heed the long, long pre-history of humanity. In our animal past can be found a different kind of story, one that shows us the discarded selves of our inward natures. In this long history, cells, mitochondria, molecules and intricate neurobiological networks undergird and make life and consciousness possible. Language and all higher intellectual powers have their origins and prototypes in other forms of life. Humans are deeply embedded creatures, sharing in a multiplicity of kindred life and matter. When hope is funded by these deeper levels of being it is less brittle and more robust.

This turn to nature can be revitalizing. In nature we can again find ourselves and our origins and our vitality. This knowledge can be brought back to our meta-level stories and can inform them, chasten them, and reshape them in light of a deeper knowledge and intuition. In nature and in solidarity with nature are also the first hints of promise and hope. In the end this embedded hope must inform our other stories and our social imaginary. It was Peter Berger who argued that in spite of what we know about social constructions of reality there are also "rumors of angels" that reach deeper still than the surface constructions.[18] These rumors find their way into our common parlance. I will argue that a qualified attention to matter and embeddedness can similarly give us a sense of the transcendent and is anticipatory of a kind of transformation from the inside out.

17. Bennett, *Vibrant Matter: A Political Ecology of Things.*

18. Berger, *A Rumor of Angels.*

I am arguing, then, that there is an underside to the emergence of stories, especially in the domain of life and ecology. We now know that humans inhabit a rich hyper-cooperating community niche that has its roots in our highly social primate and mammalian past. We know that our cooperation permeates our lives, and is as much unconscious as it is conscious. This hyper-cooperation cuts both ways allowing prodigious empathy and also stunning cruelty. The social niche forms us unconsciously and pre-linguistically. From our ancient habits and ways of seeing emerge human language and its associated imagination and mythical and storied ways of being.

Phenomenology

First let us attend to depth. The phenomenologists have taught us that all our abstract thinking and our language has its genesis in our perception of *depth* in nature, and the entanglement that is caused by our sensory reciprocity with the world. They invite us to look further at the very act of making words and language, and constructing stories. At the heart of this process is a long long development of what is called the human niche. Abram says:

> The fluid creativity we commonly associate with the human intellect is an elaboration or recapitulation of a deep creativity already underway at the most immediate level of bodily perception.[19]

He continues, "All subjectivity or awareness, presupposes our inherence in a sensuous, corporeal world."[20] Most important to worldview is that nature itself is depth. Nature as a machine had become more and more shallow. The more we realize that a reductionist grasp of nature fails fundamentally to comprehend anything much about nature, the more we grasp nature's intricate systems and interdependency and depth. Abram continues,

> The experience of depth is not *created* in the brain any more than it is *posited* by the mind. He [Merleau Ponty] showed that we can discover depth, can focus it or change our focus within it only because it is *already there,* because perception unfolds *into* depth—because my brain, like the rest of my body, is already enveloped in a world that stretches out beyond my grasp.[21]

19. Abram, "Merleau-Ponty and the Voice of the Earth," 85.

20. Ibid.

21. Ibid.

In the Western Tradition human language was commonly thought to be an emancipation from the animal natures of the 11 hours and 59 minutes of the "sixth" day of creation. In contrast, Merleau-Ponty recognizes that we respond to the forms and inwardness of nature, and consciously or unconsciously these responses shape our thinking, even or especially, thinking of transcendent and spiritual things. Although Merleau-Ponty based his philosophy on earlier science, phenomenology does cohere with our present evolutionary thinking which understands that language and symbolic thought, however and whenever they emerged, did so gradually as the extension of our animal cognitive abilities as they were shaped by the social domain of our tribal existence. Phenomenology here also grounds us in a way our free-wheeling stories do not.

David Abram, further expanding on Merleau-Ponty, articulates from a phenomenological perspective the way in which our language and thought world starts from our perceptions of being embodied, not above but within an ecology of life. We live within this life and not on top of it, though we have come to think of ourselves as living on the world rather than within it. Although our objectifying consciousness *allows us* to distance ourselves, at a deeper level, at the pre-conscious level of perception we are sensing the underlay of what will become our most abstract thoughts.

This is radical, and has far-reaching repercussions. Our creativity and its most abstract conceptions, begin not only with some transcendent *outside* connection with God, but also with the depth of the living world within which we reside. From a theological point of view, of course, this means that all nature—within which God was and is incarnate and all of which originates in God—speaks to us first. Its interior life, its fractal like tributaries, its concealed formal causes are the beginning of our communicative magic. Nature bears the marks, as Andrew Shepherd will explain, of the energies of God. When we think we are being most transcendent (in mathematics, for instance) most emancipated, we are really most embodied. Nature informs us of depth. This realization also connects us to the animal world. For they too are perceiving nature along these same lines, but without the leap to symbolic language. They inhabit the same intersubjective space; but their whole apparatus of communal life occurs outside the kind of conscious self-reflection and recursion humans experience and express.

What is meant by depth? In part it is an intuitive grasping of nature in all its fullness, and expectation and beauty; nature as anything but a machine. But as a corollary of this depth we might add that it seems to be almost infinite—as we recognize and describe it at one level another level of depth opens up. Nature's depth also results in the emergence of the radically new. There was a time on earth when there were no trees. Before the age of trees, trees must have been unimaginable. There was a time before there was any light in the universe. A time before water. A time before and after mega-fauna. A time before human consciousness. A time before the spoken word. We don't know what else the universe holds in waiting. Only that depth suggests there is always more to come. Depth can be understood objectively by science and imagination. It can also be perceived especially at liminal moments and places. This more to come is typical also of the subjective interior, of personhood.

Depth is also a glimpse of nature's formal causes. On the progressive edge of biology, evolutionary thinkers are now suggesting that evolution has its roots in primal molecules. What looks random at one level is nevertheless inhered by an overarching order, not an imposed design, but rather a dense deep space into which life flows. Similarly Abram says:

> I may notice that the primordial experience of depth is always the experience of a sort of interiority of the external world, such that each thing I perceive seems to implicate everything else, so that things, landscapes, faces all have a coherence, all suggest a secret familiarity and mutual implication in an anonymous presence that subtends and overarches my own. [22]

Nature and our embeddedness within it therefore give us a first indication of personality, and a hint of the connection of all things. Either consciously or unconsciously this suggests that whatever the future of the world, it is tied irrevocably to my own future and that of other humans. Schleiermacher talked about the "race consciousness" (by which he means species consciousness) that would preclude believing in a story that separates some of us from others as an ultimate destination.[23] The sense of depth in nature might give us a deeper intuition still of life and matter consciousness. We are in so deeply together that our ultimate purpose must be together.

Contrast this with the separations and dualities that have become so prevalent in modernity. Humans and other forms of life are at odds, or humans need to control all life. Humans survive death and other animals do not. Some humans are saved and others are damned. Salvation comes from the outside, but through a God-figure who pays an extrinsic price, or appeases the devil. When we have solutions to intractable problems they are frequently by escape from the flesh to the separated mind. Stories of separation thrive in the face of these dualities, as does the violation of the planet.

The recognition of the depth of nature, is an inherent critique of these dualities—giving us a sense of our purpose as one of solidarity and in

22. Ibid., 86.

23. Schleiermacher, *The Christian Faith*, 543.

solidarity with other life and matter. From this life and matter our lives are bequeathed and are dependent. Human life is simultaneously not ours, but also resolutely ours. Humans are dependent, but are also possessing glimpses of freedom. Kathryn Tanner has argued that God and humans are not in competition. It is a part of the definition of transcendence that God can become what God is not.[24] And humans become more truly themselves when aligned freely with this God. I would argue similarly that human stories and human hopefulness are not at odds with the remainder of life. Although there is competition between all levels of life on earth, there is also overwhelming co-dependency. Humans are truly human when we understand that all life is intertwined and interdependent. Humans are not radically free from matter and other life; we are formed out of this life.

Vibrant Matter

Jane Bennett's book is also about matter and its inner vibrancy. It is yet another way of showing that humans are not the only sources of action, and indeed that human action is on a continuum with and dependent upon the myriad sum of actions of matter and other life around us. Moreover matter has in inner vibrancy that has an effect on us and all around it. Bennett claims we have only to examine our reactions to things—a dead bird, a scrap of rubbish—to see that these are not empty of all dynamism. She says,

> This entails, in my case, a willingness to theorize events (a blackout, a meal, an imprisonment in chains, an experience of litter) as encounters between ontologically diverse actants, some human, some not, though all thoroughly material.[25]

Like Abram and Merleau-Ponty all of this requires that we see with different eyes, that we undergo a conversion of sorts in our perceptions of the world. She adds,

> Without proficiency in this countercultural kind of perceiving, the world appears as if it consists only of active human subjects who confront passive objects and their law-governed mechanisms.[26]

She argues, as does Abram, that we have not been anthropomorphic enough. "We need to cultivate a bit of anthropomorphism—the idea that

24. Tanner, *Jesus, Humanity and the Trinity*, 2–3.

25. Bennett, *Vibrant Matter*, 15.

26. Ibid.

human agency has some echoes in nonhuman nature—to counter the narcissism of humans in charge of the world."[27]

But herein lies the crux of things from the point of view of this paper: Matter which often seems to be so dead, and to move inevitably towards death, also has another aspect that can be glimpsed. As Christians we might call this aspect the glory of God. Bennett does not but she says, interacting with Derrida, and pointing to the presence of an implicit trajectory in matter, that:

> In addition to being tied to the idea of efficacy, agency is also bound up with the idea of a trajectory, a directionality or movement away from somewhere even if the toward-which it moves is obscure or even absent . . . Jacques Derrida offers an alternative to this consciousness-centered thinking by figuring trajectory as "messianicity."[28]

She quotes Derrida: "things in the world appear to us at all only because they tantalize and hold us in suspense, alluding to a fullness that is elsewhere, to a future that, apparently, is on its way. . . the straining forward toward the event never finds relief."[29] And yet, this anticipation is what we as Christians might interpret a different way, as hope. We cannot have a true ecological hope without sensing this trajectory within nature. The story of the Christ is then a story of recognition, of the Christ already present with us in the shadows of the logos, the glory of nature's inwardness, the vibrancy of infinitely nesting formal causes, as well as in the spoken words and prayers and psalms of the prophets.

Conclusion

To find hope for and in and with nature we need more than stories that have an ending, more than a messiah who comes from afar. The stories we tell must resonate with life and matter. The life in which we reside, if perceived as depth, may give us reason to hope. Human life as we know it, on this planet, is embedded within a depth of nature, and reflects and resonates with that depth. Humanity has appeared very very late in an ecology that stretches deep into the universe's astral history. Depth is what we might expect if matter is tinged with, and ridden through with transcendence—the Spirit's breath, the energies of God, the whole earth groaning. This is depth

27. Ibid., 32.

28. Ibid.

29. Ibid.

through a number of different filters. Language is only possible through the waves, and trajectories and patterns of this depth. All life—and matter—is deeply indebted to logos, and formal cause. Moreover, that nature, perceived as vibrant and full of depth *is also suggestive of a future.* The depth hides the possible futures, now and still unknown to us except for images of restoration, like those of Isaiah and Romans 8 and Revelation.

But human life that is the conscious self-conscious manifestation of such closely allied other life and matter cannot be expected to survive alone. All matter must be transformed; humans cannot be transformed without it. "The whole creation," says Paul, "waits in eager expectation." Moreover, while we might imagine a final hope that separates us from the rest of nature and sends us off to some sublime existence apart from nature if we are fundamentally different from nature, that is not the case if we are embedded within it. Then the shape of the eschaton, the shape of hope must be inclusive of the community of all life in some way. For even Jesus came embedded within vital matter. As Schleiermacher says, we first meet the supernatural only in the natural.[30] The complexity and the depth of the interiority of matter gives us every reason to think that this is a glimpse of glory that will be fulfilled, but also that it will be fulfilled as a piece, and not by the separation of one species from the rest. This hope for the planet is further endorsed by the hints of a trajectory of promise we are able to glimpse within nature itself. This is a trajectory that could be observed by any sentient observer of life on earth in the last 4 billion years.

We cannot presume, however, to know what post-mortem and post-death-of-the-planet life will be like. We have only the merest hints of what the resurrection from the dead and the ascension of Jesus mean for us now or in the future. We do know there will be a future, and out of this future and its promise we tell stories of redemption and hope. But just as we must not settle for a planet that is being burned and destroyed, nor should we presume that the scientific story of our ending is completely false. Perhaps there are tricks in the equations we don't yet understand. Perhaps what is genuinely new will really be the new heavens and the new earth. Or perhaps the universe will die and be resurrected. We don't know. Hope cannot be linked too closely to either scenario. Hope, as Kathryn Tanner has said, is the presence of God with us now—and experienced now—and the knowledge that even death cannot overcome that life.[31] In the end the spider's webs will be spun in gratitude, as gift, as spinners of love and beauty in the midst of a castle that is already full of surprise and stateliness and history.

30. Schleiermacher, *The Christian Faith*, §13

31. Tanner, *Jesus, Humanity and the Trinity*, 101ff.

Bibliography

Abram, David. "Merleau-Ponty and the Voice of the Earth." In *Minding Nature: The Philosophy of Ecology*, edited by David Macauley, 82–101. New York: Oxford University Press, 2014.

Bennett, Jane. *Vibrant Matter: A Political Ecology of Things*. Durham, NC: Duke University Press, 2009.

Berger, Peter L. *A Rumor of Angels: Modern Society and the Rediscovery of the Supernatural*. New York: Doubleday, 1969.

Fuentes, Agustin. "A New Synthesis." *Anthropology Today* 25, no. 3 (2009) 12–17.

Ingold, Tim. "Beyond Biology and Culture: The Meaning of Evolution in a Relational World." *Social Anthropology* 12, no. 2 (2004) 209–21.

Kline, Morris. *Mathematics: The Loss of Certainty*. New York: Oxford University Press, 1980.

LaHaye, Tim, and Jerry B Jenkins. *Left Behind: A Novel of the Earth's Last Days*. Colorado Springs: Tyndale House, 1995.

Lindbeck, George A. *The Nature of Doctrine*. Louisville: Westminster John Knox, 1984.

Maisel, Richard, et al. *Biting the Hand the Starves You: Inspiring Resistance to Anorexia/Bulimia*. New York: Norton, 2004.

McPhee, John. *The Control of Nature*. New York: Farrar, Straus, Giroux, 1989.

Miller, Richard W. "Deep Responsibility for the Deep Future." *Theological Studies* 77, no. 2 (2016) 436–65.

Niebuhr, Reinhold. *The Nature and Destiny of Man*. Louisville, Westminster John Knox, 1996.

Rea, Michael. "Divine Hiddenness, Divine Silence." In *Philosophy of Religion: An Anthology*, edited by Louis P. Pojman and Michael C. Rea, 266–75. 6th ed. Boston: Wadsworth, 2011.

Schleiermacher, Friedrich. *The Christian Faith*. Vol. 1. Edited by H. R. Mackintosh and J. S. Stewart. New York: Harper & Row, 1963.

St. John Mandell, Emily. *Station Eleven*. New York: Vintage, 2015.

Tanner, Kathryn. *Jesus, Humanity and the Trinity*. Minneapolis: Fortress, 2001.

Taylor, Charles. *A Secular Age*. Cambridge, MA: Harvard University Press, 2007.

4

Spirit, Seabirds, & Sacramentality

Ponderings on Petrels and Pneumatology

Andrew Shepherd,
A Rocha Aotearoa New Zealand

You who live in the shelter of the Most High,
who abide in the shadow of the Almighty,
will say to the Lord, "My refuge and my fortress;
my God, in whom I trust."
For he will deliver you from the snare of the fowler
and from the deadly pestilence;
he will cover you with his pinions,
and under his wings you will find refuge;
his faithfulness is a shield and buckler

—Psalm 91:1–4 (NRSV).

A Being was taking form in the totality of space; a Being with the attractive power of a soul, palpable like a body, vast as the sky; a Being which mingled with things yet remained distinct from them; a Being of a higher order than the substance of things with which it was adorned, yet taking shape within them.

—Teilhard de Chardin "The Spiritual Power of Matter"[1]

1. Teilhard de Chardin, "The Spiritual Power of Matter," 65.

Introduction

It is a stormy night. The trees along the cliffs are in constant motion—blown to and fro by strong gusts of wind. Clouds race across the sky, obscuring the stars. In the semi-dark, hovering above, a high-pitched distinctive sound breaks forth. A dark silhouette passes overhead and soon after there is a crashing sound as an object hurtles into the forest canopy.

The intrepid few witnessing this scene now work their way from the cliff-edge, ducking under low-lying branches, traversing the steep ground, edging carefully deeper into the forest. The dark specter-like shapes that had swooped overhead can now be seen. Illuminated by torchlight, the brown plumed birds stand stunned, gazing upwards at the welcoming party of humans.

Before *homo sapiens* arrived in Aotearoa, birdsong filled the forests that covered eighty percent of the islands, and millions of sea birds returned to these shores each year to breed.[2] The vast coastline was dotted with sea bird colonies and honeycombed with underground burrows. Due to millennia of bio-geographic isolation, Aotearoa, with no mammals except two species of native bats, had evolved into a bird paradise. The rest of the story is well-known: two waves of human migration (Polynesian in 1100–1300 CE, and then Europeans from the late eighteenth century onwards) with their accompanying mammals, had a catastrophic impact on the archipelago's unique ecosystems. Unused to mammalian predation, many ground-nesting sea-birds, like their better-known forest cousins, were extremely vulnerable. Today, New Zealand's mainland sea-bird colonies have been decimated, and the remnants are threatened by these introduced pests—possums, rats, mustelids, domestic cats and dogs.

Grey Faced Petrels (*Pterodroma macroptera gouldi*/*Oi*) are one native species of burrowing sea bird that were once widespread on mainland coastlines. Two features set *Oi* apart from most other sea-birds. First, *Oi* are nocturnal, feeding at night on squid, small fish, and crustaceans approximately 100km off-shore. Second, the *Oi* breeds in winter. It is for this reason that, on stormy winter nights when most sensible people are wrapped up at home beside the fire, you will find volunteers scouring along the cliffs and coastline near the township of Raglan/Whāingaroa, seeking out these inconspicuous and mysterious visitors.

2. http://www.teara.govt.nz/en/map/23596/forest-cover-before-human-habitation (accessed 18/2/2017).

The Karioi Project

This work—monitoring the burrows of *Oi*—is part of the *Karioi: Maunga ki te Moana (Mountain to the Sea) Biodiversity Restoration Project*. Led by Christian conservation organization A Rocha Aotearoa New Zealand, the conservation project is an ambitious undertaking—seeking to restore biodiversity to Mount Karioi (756m) a heavily eroded forested volcanic cone that sits to the south-west of the Raglan/Whāingaroa harbour.[3]

In 2009, at the invitation of the local community, A Rocha began a restoration project on Karioi.[4] Initially, Upper Wainui Reserve, a small area of 10 hectares with good forest bird life and easily accessible to the public was chosen as an area for intensive predator control. And then, in the winter of 2009, almost by accident, it was discovered that across the road from the reserve, along the sea cliffs, *Oi* were present. While it was unclear whether this small remnant colony was successfully breeding, there was awareness that without active pest control the existing population was unlikely to survive. Nine years later, the Karioi project has expanded to the management of 2300+ hectares with the monitoring and protection of this *Oi* population a centerpiece of the biodiversity restoration work.[5] Complementing this restoration work, A Rocha also runs a range of educational and advocacy activities around the Karioi project, engaging both the local community and domestic and international visitors and students.

Karioi, while with its own unique identity and regional significance, is merely one of hundreds of community conservation projects across Aotearoa New Zealand. Each week many thousands of volunteers—from Christian faith backgrounds, other faith traditions, and many who espouse no faith—devote considerable time and energy into these conservation efforts. In light of the rediscovery in the twentieth century of *Missio Dei*—the

3. Mount Karioi is the most northerly mountain in the country having an unbroken vegetative transition from the sea to an altitude that supports a montane forest flora and is the second largest coastal forest between Taranaki and Auckland. The mountain is covered by podocarp/hardwood and montane forest including some species considered rare on the North Island West Coast.

4. Mount Karioi has special cultural, environmental, and historical significance to the Raglan/Whāingaroa *tangata whenua* (local indigenous Māori tribe), who are the *kaitiaki* (guardians and conservers) of the mountain and its *taonga* (resources, treasures) for future generations. *Oi,* like other mutton-bird species around the country, were once harvested for food by the local *hapū* (local Māori sub-tribe). A rapid decline in their numbers has meant that this cultural practice no longer takes place.

5. The Karioi Project now involves management of all public land on the mountain and also involves predator control and biodiversity work on a further 700 hectares of privately owned and Māori land around Karioi. See http://www.arocha.org.nz/projects/karioi-maunga-ki-te-moana/.

belief that all mission is primarily God's work—it is worth considering in what way these human conservation activities participate in God's work in the world. What is the relationship between our human conservation activity and God's grace-filled empowering presence seeking to "reconcile" all things?[6] How and where is God present in the conservation activities undertaken on Karioi, around Aotearoa New Zealand, and globally?[7]

An Age of the Spirit

We live in a so-called "post-modern" age where themes of "spirit" and "spiritualities" are back in vogue. The rationalism and intellectualism of "modernity" has been partially replaced by a new thirst for experiential/mystical/spiritual knowledge. Our epoch, some commentators suggest, is an "Age of the Spirit."[8] Protestant theologian Mark I. Wallace, reflecting on this renewed interest in "spirit," writes:

> Practitioners of nature-based religion, from native peoples to neopagans, claim that a reverence for the Spirit in all life-forms, from people and animals to trees and watersheds, is the most promising response to the threat of global ecological collapse . . . There appears to be an emerging sentiment that the topic of pneumatology is the right focus for an ecumenical theology that speaks to the spiritual hopes and desires of our age.[9]

If this is the case, if we live in an age of the Spirit, how might a pneumatological perspective, that is an emphasis on the Spirit, assist us to reflect specifically on the role of hope in the conservation activity of A Rocha within New Zealand society, but also more broadly?

6. Colossians 1:15–20

7. While *Karioi: Maunga ki te Moana* is the "flag-ship" project of A Rocha Aotearoa New Zealand, other local A Rocha groups around the country are involved in a range of smaller-scale conservation activities including wetland, native bush and stream restoration, a native tree nursery, sustainable transport ventures, and educational and advocacy initiatives. A Rocha Aotearoa New Zealand is part the global A Rocha family working in twenty countries around the world. See http://www.arocha.org/en/.

8. On the emergence of "spirituality" in the Western world, see Tacey, *The Spirituality Revolution*. Harvey Cox contends that this same emphasis on "spirit" is also apparent in contemporary Christianity. The last fifty years, Cox believes, are best seen as the emergence of the "Age of the Spirit." Christians, Cox argues, are now less concerned with institutional forms of religion and dogma and more focused on spirituality and praxis. Cox, *The Future of Faith*.

9. Wallace, "The Wounded Spirit," 51–52.

The Promise of Pneumatology

How and where is the Spirit of God present in the world around us? Arguably one of the problems with contemporary Western expressions of Christianity is an inadequate pneumatology. Many sections of the Protestant Church offer a pneumatology which either implicitly or explicitly encourages a spirituality which devalues embodiment and which disconnects the faithful from their createdness and from the rest of creation. Likewise, within contemporary Western Protestant Christian faith, the scope of the work of the Spirit is often primarily understood in anthropocentric and individual-therapeutic terms with lack of attention given either to community-corporate dimensions, or the Spirit's presence within the rest of the created order.

Mark I. Wallace suggests that one of the difficulties within the Western Christian tradition has been the translation of the *Holy Spirit* as *Holy Ghost*. Wallace contends that such language means that we conceive of God's invisible presence in creation as a "spook," "unreal," and "immaterial."[10] Wallace is one of a number theologians who over recent decades has offered explicit eco-pneumatologies. Whether Australian Catholic theologian Denis Edwards's "Biocentric Spirit," US feminist-theologian Sallie McFague's "Hopeful Spirit" or Mark Wallace's emphasis on a "Wounded Spirit," each of these pneumatologies is influenced to a certain degree by Moltmann's kenotic pneumatology, or what Moltmann refers to as the "the unspeakable closeness of God" to creation in the Holy Spirit.[11]

In *Finding God in the Singing River* Wallace seeks to retrieve what he argues is a "central but neglected Christian theme—the idea of God as carnal Spirit who imbues all things."[12] For Wallace, "[t]he Spirit is not a heavenly phantom—immaterial and unreal (and perhaps a bit scary as well!)—but God's all pervasive presence and energy within the universe"; God's Spirit is the "enfleshed presence of God in all things."[13] In developing his panentheistic theology Wallace contends that throughout Scripture, "[t]he Holy Spirit is a wholly enfleshed, avian life-form made up of the four primitive

10. Wallace, *Finding God in the Singing River*, 7–8.

11. Edwards, *Breath of Life*; McFague, *A New Climate for Theology* (esp. chap. 9); Moltmann, *Spirit of Life*, 12. Other significant eco-pneumatologies include the ongoing work of Celia Deane-Drummond—and in particular her engagement with Orthodox thinking regarding Sophia: see Celia Deane-Drummond, *Creation through Wisdom*, 113–52. For the development of an eco-pneumatology from within the Pentecostal tradition, see the work of Yong, *The Spirit Poured out on All Flesh*, 267–302; and Yong, *The Spirit Renews the Face of the Earth*.

12. Wallace, *Finding God in the Singing River*, 6.

13. Ibid., 6–7.

elements—wind, water, fire, and earth—that are the key components of embodied life as we know it."[14]

The idea of an avian pneumatology is particularly evocative in light of the ecological history of Aotearoa New Zealand as a bird paradise. How may such an avian pneumatology offer a lens with which to understand the conservation work taking place on Karioi? And how may conceiving of the character and function of the Spirit of God in avian terms provide broader insights into ecological action and practice within Aotearoa New Zealand and globally?

Avian Pneumatology

Avian imagery of the Spirit appears frequently in the Christian Scriptures and within the Christian theological tradition. Saint Basil of Caesarea in the fourth century, commenting upon the presence and activity of the Holy Spirit in the creation accounts of Genesis 1 states that the Spirit:

> cherished the nature of the waters as one sees a bird cover the eggs with her body and impart to them vital force from her own warmth. Such is, as nearly as possible, the meaning of these words—The Spirit was borne: let us understand, that is, prepared the nature of water to produce living beings: a sufficient proof for those who ask if the Holy Spirit took an active part in the creation of the world, and above all ensouled life.[15]

Basil's imagery here of an avian Spirit hovering over waters is particularly apt in reflecting upon the Karioi project. Ecological theology often focusses on the inter-relatedness and interdependence of life, and indeed, the way in which the presence of birds/Spirit is critical to the flourishing of all life is very evident on Karioi. A friend of mine—a forest ecologist—often reminds me that all forest ecologists, in truth, study soil. The composition and diversity of a forest is always dependent upon the soils that nourish it. In the case of Karioi, the *Oi* plays a critical role. Over millennia, the *Oi*, in its activity of burrowing to create nests, has mixed the nutrients from the guano of millions of sea-birds into the rich volcanic soil. The dense coastal forest exists due to the fertilizing functions performed by this *ecological engineer.*[16] Is it possible for the *Oi* to be viewed

14. Ibid., x. On the same page, he writes of the Spirit as a "sacred animal."

15. Basil of Caesarea, *On the Six Days of Creation* II.7.

16. This phrase is taken from Department of Conservation sea-bird expert, Graeme Sinclair, with permission.

not merely as a keystone species—essential to the web of life on Karioi and its environs, but also, pneumatologically, as the very breath of God which nurtures and animates life?[17]

While finding Wallace's writing deeply evocative, there are I believe some significant weaknesses in his eco-pneumatology—in particular, his romanticizing of nature, an inadequate ontology, and the lack of relationship between pneumatology and Christology. In what follows I will address each of these areas of concern and in so doing seek to develop an avian-pneumatology that provides a firmer foundation for hope-filled action.

Firstly, like many eco-theologians, Wallace's theology appears to offer an overly "romanticized" view of nature. Wallace argues for a "belief in God as Earth Spirit, the compassionate, all-encompassing divine force within the biosphere who inhabits earth community and continually works to maintain the integrity of all forms of life."[18] The Spirit, Wallace contends "is an earthen being who infuses all things with the power for growth, change, and renewal. Nature itself in all its many manifestations is to be understood as the primary mode of being for the Spirit's work in the biosphere."[19]

But, how does this understanding of the Spirit as "compassionate," as "a wholly enfleshed life form who engenders healing and renewal throughout the abiotic and biotic orders" cohere with some of the realities of biological principles at work in ecosystems?[20] If the Spirit is "embodied through natural processes" then how does one understand competition, predation, animal suffering and species extinction? Are these natural processes part of the "compassionate" and "healing" work of the Spirit or are they moral anomalies? While recent theories in the fields of biological and ecological sciences have advocated for an awareness of the role that mutuality and cooperation play in ecosystem health, there are nonetheless aspects of the natural world that for Christians who believe in a loving and "compassionate" God are morally troubling. If such "violent" natural processes are "the primary mode of being for the Spirit's work in the biosphere," does this mean the inevitable sacralization of such suffering and death?[21]

17. See, in particular, the work of Catholic theologian Edwards, *Breath of Life*.

18. Wallace, *Finding God in the Singing River*, 6.

19. Ibid., 9.

20. Ibid., 8.

21. The broader discussion on how evolutionary thinking impacts both ecological ethics and theodicy are beyond the scope of this chapter. For contrasting perspectives on such topics, see the work of Rolston III and Deane-Drummond. Also see Sideris, "Writing Straight With Crooked Lines," 77–101; and Hoggard Creegan, *Animal Suffering and the Problem of Evil*.

Secondly, while sympathetic with Wallace's panentheistic approach, I am not entirely convinced that that he is able to successfully hold the balance between God's transcendence and immanence.

Wallace contends for a theology in which "the waters and winds and birds and fires will not be regarded only *as symbols* of the Spirit but rather as sharing in her very *being* as the Spirit is enfleshed and embodied through natural organisms and processes."[22] But such a statement immediately raises two further questions. Firstly, when Wallace speaks of the waters and winds and birds and fires sharing in the very *being* of the Spirit what is the ontological status of this *sharing of being*? Is he suggesting that these *created* elements share essence with the *uncreated* Spirit? And if so how? And secondly, what is the relationship between *symbol* and *being*? Inherent here within Wallace's logic seems to be the idea that *symbolism* and *real presence* are mutually exclusive. But is it possible to perceive of an avian Spirit as both a *symbol* and as sharing in the very *being* of the Spirit? It is here that an Orthodox understanding of sacramentality offers greater richness to the development of an avian pneumatology.

Sacramental Ontology and Symbols

In his *For the Life of the World,* Alexander Schmemann contends that the world in its entirety is "sacrament." For Schmemann, the problem the world faces is the "fundamental rejection of 'epiphany': the primordial intuition that everything in this world and the world itself not only have *elsewhere* the cause and principle of their existence, but are *themselves* the manifestation and presence of that *elsewhere*."[23] For Schmemann, Western theology is grounded upon an underlying dichotomous mode of thinking in which the "symbolic" and the "real" are seen as mutually exclusive.[24] In contrast to such thinking, in the ontological sacramentality that is integral to Orthodox

22. Wallace, "The Green Face Of God," 310–31.

23. Schmemann, *For the Life of the World*, 124.

24. Schmemann traces the origins of this dichotomous thinking to the Lateran Council of the twelfth century. In refuting Berengarius of Tours's assertion that because the presence of Christ in the eucharistic elements is "mystical" or "symbolic," it is not real, the Council simply reversed this formula, arguing that "since Christ's presence in the Eucharist is *real* it is not '*mystical*.'" For Schememann the fatal error here is the underlying thinking in which "mystical/symbolic" and "real" are seen as mutually exclusive. Schmemann argues that such thinking involves "the collapse of the fundamental Christian *mysterion,* the antinomical 'holding together' of the reality of the symbol, and the symbolism of reality. It was the collapse of the fundamental Christian understanding of creation in terms of its ontological s*acramentality*." *For the Life of the World*, 129.

theology, "'symbolic' here is not merely not opposed to 'real,' but embodies it as its very expression and mode of manifestation."[25]

There is, Schmemann asserts, a critical distinction here between what he argues is a patristic ontology (still present in the Orthodox tradition) and post-patristic Western theology. Western theology, Schmemann argues, is concerned with *knowledge about* the world and understands "symbol" in semantic (A *means* B), causal (A *is the cause of* B), or representative (A *represents* B) terms. In contrast, for Schmemann, that the world is "symbolic" is a statement about its ontological status. Accordingly, in a sacramental ontology, a "symbol" is not merely a mode of perceiving and understanding reality, "a means of cognition, but also a means of *participation*."[26] Such a relationship, Schmemann contends is an *epiphany*. 'A *is* B' means that the whole of A expresses, communicates, reveals, manifests the 'reality' of B (although not necessarily the whole of it) without, however, losing its own ontological reality."[27] Historically this discussion on the relationship between "symbolic" and "real" stems from a discussion around the sacraments—and in particular the sacrament of Eucharist. But is the power of such a sacramental ontology to be confined to the area of eucharistic theology and discussion on the nature of the elements? If as Scripture contends the earth is full of God's glory (Isa 6:3) then is it possible to understand not just the body and blood of Christ in the Eucharist but also birds as *"symbols, images,* and *mysteries*." If this is the case, then to apply Schmemann's logic, while a Petrel (A) "communicates, reveals, manifests the reality of the Spirit" (B) it does so while not blurring the ontological distinction between the Spirit (*uncreated)* and the Petrel (*creature*).

Of course within Western logic to suggest that the God's Spirit is *present* in a bird is seen as opening the door to polytheism. Again Orthodox theology allows us to move beyond this impasse. A central principle of Orthodox theology is the belief that there is a real distinction between the essence (*ousia*) and the energies (*energeia*) of God.[28] Thus to affirm that God's Spirit is present in a particular bird is not to say that this bird *is* the Spirit in its essence and totality. Rather, the particular bird is a manifestation, an expression of the energies of God's Spirit. Within sacramental ontology all bread and wine are gifts of the Creator, as are all the elements of the created order, to be received and given thanks for. And yet, as with the

25. Ibid., 139.

26. Ibid.

27. Ibid., 141.

28. This distinction between the essence and energies of God finds its origins in the work of fourteenth-century Orthodox theologian Gregory Palamas.

Eucharist where *particular* elements become epiphanic mysteries could it be that there are occasions when the *particular* presence (*energeia*) of God's Spirit embodies a particular bird (or other creature)?

In contrast to this Orthodox distinction between the essence and energies of God, Wallace seeks to ground his pneumatology upon an ontology informed by Christian animism. Wallace contends that authentic Christian faith is a form of Christian animism. For Wallace, "Christianity's transcendentalist animist identity consists of a twofold belief that all of nature is infused with God's presence, on the one hand, and that God is not collapsed into nature without remainder, on the other."[29] Elsewhere he contends that "God continually enfleshes Godself through the Spirit in the embodied reality of life on Earth."[30] But in stressing the closeness of God's Spirit within creation, what happens to otherness? How does creation have a relationship with Spirit if the uncreated Spirit is bound up so closely with creation? Is not a relationship of freedom and love dependent upon otherness?[31]

Further, Wallace's eco-theology with its strong emphasis on animism would seem to contend that *all* birds are an expression, manifestation of God's Spirit. Herein lies the strength and the weakness of such an approach. Scripture does indicate that all living creatures are dependent upon the animating breath of God's Spirit.[32] However, if all birds (and indeed all species) become expressions and manifestations of God's Spirit then pragmatic questions about how one engages in conservation activity become deeply problematic.[33] Again, a theology which affirms that all creatures are dependent upon the life-giving breath of the Spirit but also recognizes that at specific moments the *energies* of God's Spirit may be present in *particular* individual creatures allows us to move beyond such a conundrum.

This understanding that the presence of the Spirit becomes manifest in *particular* birds/creatures at specific times is not only the testimony of Christian Scripture and tradition but also one that resonates with our human experiences. Many of us will remember experiences where an

29. Wallace, *Finding God in the Singing River*, 16.

30. Ibid., 23.

31. See Zizioulas, *Communion and Otherness.*

32. Genesis 6:17; 7:21–22; Job 12:10, 27:3 32:8,33:4, 34:14–15; Ps 104:29–30, Isa 42:5, 57:16.

33. This is particularly the case in Aotearoa New Zealand where a significant aspect of conservation involves the killing of other introduced "pest" species. But even in other contexts where non-lethal force is being used, active conservation management still involves a form of triage as one determines which species will be prioritized. Even those guided by a biocentric philosophy who advocate "do nothing and let ecosystems do their own thing," through their non-action, are thus still implicated in questions of the survival of both individual creatures and species.

encounter with a bird (or other creature) has not merely fostered a sense of awe and wonder, but more than this, we have in some sense felt as though we were in the very presence of the Divine. In the context of Aotearoa/New Zealand where due to both their uniqueness and often threatened status native birds are regarded as national treasures (*taonga*) and where Māori spirituality has shaped attitudes towards nature, it is not unusual for people to understand the presence of particular birds as an experience of the Spirit's presence. I have a friend who has a particular affinity and fondness for *kererū*—New Zealand's native wood pigeon. Recently, she shared with me about a specific encounter with a *kererū*/Spirit. In a particularly tumultuous period of life that involved significant energy output, the friend had become overwhelmed and one day after a miscommunication led to a "huge meltdown" she broke down in tears. Deciding that a walk to a nearby hill may "aid recovery," she climbed and sat down on a grass bank overlooking the city. The friend recollected that: "as I sat I heard the familiar and very clear *whoosh whoosh* of the *kererū*. It plummeted right down in a straight vertical line in front of me, maybe twenty meters out in front of me. It then perched in a tree and sat and I felt the words: 'you know how to watch and pray, but I'm telling you, don't do that right now. Don't watch, rest. Don't pray, I'll pray for you.'" She noted that this moving encounter as well as "helping me hugely" in the moment also continued to sustain her during a particularly difficult period of life as she later began a "cancer pilgrimage."[34]

A Wounded Spirit?

A final aspect of Wallace's avian-pneumatology which to my mind requires some modification is with regard to his emphasis upon a "Wounded Spirit."[35] Influenced by Moltmann's affirmation that Christ's death creates "a deep division in God himself,"[36] opening the Godhead to the pain and suffering of human existence, Wallace contends that likewise, the Spirit's suffering within creation brings suffering to God. Wallace writes "as Jesus" death on the cross brought death and loss into Godself, so the Spirit's suffering from persistent environmental trauma engenders chronic agony in the Godhead . . . as the God who knows death through the cross of Jesus is the cruci-

34. Contained within this personal story are both elements familiar with the Pentecostal tradition—an emphasis on the the intimate and personal experience of the Spirit—and also an echo of Rom 8:26–27—that the Spirit intercedes with "sighs" (or in the case of the *kererū*, cooing). Quotations taken from personal correspondence.

35. Wallace, "The Wild Bird Who Heals," 15, and note 9, above.

36. Moltmann, *The Crucified God*, 244.

fied God, so also is the Spirit who enfleshes divine presence in nature the wounded Spirit."[37]

If one follows Wallace's trajectory and recognizes birds as in some ways an enfleshment and embodiment of the Spirit, then the evidence of this wounded Spirit in Aotearoa New Zealand is not difficult to find. Like large numbers of the native birds of Aotearoa, *Oi* live a challenging life. At sea they face the trials of declining food-sources and the perils of long-lines. Returning to the coast, that they nest in burrows makes them particularly susceptible to mammalian predators—in particular stoats and rats and in areas close to human populations, domestic cats and dogs. To work in conservation within Aotearoa is, in the well-known words of Aldo Leopold, to be both conscious of and proximate to a "world of wounds."[38] A triumphalistic pneumatology is strikingly dissonant when one witnesses the destruction that can be wreaked in a sea-bird colony in one night by a single predator.

And yet to my mind something is amiss with this pneumatological emphasis. Wallace, following a Moltmannian trajectory, offers a kenotic pneumatology, but also one with almost no relationship to Christology. Wallace writes:

> The hope of Christianity is the promise of God's omnipresent Spirit to till the earth with power and love so that all of God's creatures, human and non-human alike, can be brought into healing and restorative relationship with the truth . . . We live in the age of the Spirit in a time when the Spirit expands Jesus' work into the full expanse of the whole created order . . . this earth-centered doctrine of the Spirit—reminiscent of Jesus' love for all creatures testified to in the Gospels—is the best grounds for hope and renewal . . . [39]

But what is Jesus's work? Wallace's *Finding God in the Singing River* is almost completely devoid of any Christological discussion. I am left wondering what is the relationship between Wallace's "Wounded Spirit," present in creation, and the Spirit of Christ that raises Christ from the dead?[40] Further,

37. Wallace, *Finding God in the Singing River*, 132–33.

38. Leopold, "The Round River: A Parable," 165.

39. Wallace, *Finding God in the Singing River*, 33.

40. The christological basis for Wallace's pneumatological hope is "Jesus' love for all creatures testified to in the Gospels." While sympathetic with Wallace's intentions, one must be honest with the actual brevity of passages describing Jesus's interaction with non-human creatures. The gospel writers clearly see considerable significance in Jesus's interaction with creation—evident in his actions of stilling of storms, the feeding of multitudes and physical healing and exorcisms. But arguably, the breadth of Christ's love and hope for all creation, the cosmic scope of salvation, while hinted at in the Gospels,

central to New Testament thought is not the suffering of the Spirit, but rather the resurrection power of the Spirit. In Romans 8 it is not the Spirit which as a "wounded Spirit" is groaning in pain, but rather the whole of creation itself which is doing the groaning. And this groaning of creation is not akin to the cries of dereliction stemming from emotional torment and physical pain that issue from the lips of Jesus in the garden of Gethsemane or while he hangs on the Cross.[41] For Paul, this groaning is not due to wounding but rather is the result of labor pains. For Paul, humanity and all of creation have an eschatological hope that the Spirit who raised Christ from the dead is at work in Creation and is bringing redemption to our material bodies. The imagery in Romans 8 is not of a wounded Spirit, but rather of the Spirit as a midwife who accompanies creation and urges us to look beyond our current pain and struggles to the hope of new life. In contrast to Wallace's contention that "an earth-centered doctrine of the Spirit—reminiscent of Jesus' love for all creatures testified to in the Gospels—is the best grounds for hope and renewal . . . ,"[42] the Apostle Paul contends that we find our hope in the resurrection power of the Spirit—the Spirit who both animates and sustains life in this world, but who also in raising Christ from the dead gives us the first glimpse of a new order—one in which pain, suffering and death are overcome.[43]

And yet, herein lies the paradox of the Christian story. To develop an avian-pneumatology perhaps assists us in finding the balance between an overemphasis on a wounded Spirit and at the other extreme a form of triumphalistic pneumatology. The avian Spirit, as *Oi*, through its activity of burrowing and fertilizing enriches the soils of the *Maunga*—"the Spirit enfleshed and embodied through natural organisms and processes" is the life-giving Spirit through whom all life "lives and moves and has its being" (Acts 17:28). And as noted above, this life-giving Spirit also lives a fragile and exposed, one could say even a *wounded* existence. But this woundedness and vulnerability is neither the totality of the Spirit's nature or work, nor the basis for the hope which empowers the conservation activity taking place on the Karioi Maunga. It is the *Oi* soaring in full flight, a symbol participating and pointing towards resurrection life and glory which is the vision of hope which inspires and motivates human ecological action. Such

is more explicitly stated in other New Testament writings. For the significance of Jesus's interaction with wild creatures, see Bauckham, "Jesus and the Wild Animals," 3–21.

41 Whether Jesus's cries from the cross are primarily those of dereliction is itself a debatable point.

42. Wallace, *Finding God in the Singing River*, 33.

43. Gunton's assessment of Moltmann applies here to Wallace's thinking too. "God does not suffer history, he moves it." Gunton, *Christ and Creation*, 87.

a pneumatology—one that gives flesh (& feathers) to the life-giving, vulnerable, yet soaring nature of the Spirit summons human communities not to merely gaze in wonder at the Spirit in full flight but also to venture out to the steep cliffs—to the places of vulnerability and danger.

One is reminded here of perhaps the most striking episode from Scripture in which the Spirit is portrayed in avian-terms—the brief account of the baptism of Jesus given in Mark 1:9–13. Heading out to the Jordan river, Jesus's public ministry begins with the very public manifestation of God's Spirit. Rising out of the water, the Spirit/dove descends upon Jesus accompanied by an audible voice of commendation. This mystical experience is not one of disembodiment or disengagement from creation. Indeed, Jesus's baptism by what Wallace would term the "carnal Spirit"[44] is now followed by this same Spirit forcibly driving Jesus into the wilderness. Empowered by the Spirit, Jesus does not retreat from nature but rather heads deeper into it. It is in the wilderness, pushed to his physical, psychological, emotional and spiritual limits that Jesus experiences the fullness and paradox of the human life—facing temptation, encountering physical danger, experiencing grace. Led by the Spirit, Jesus is not immune from the precarious and exposed nature of life but rather experiences the angelic presence of God alongside other creatures.[45] An avian-pneumatology does not deny that filled by the Spirit we will be led to contexts where we encounter and participate in Christ's suffering and thus are wounded. But this woundedness is not the *telos* of a Spirit-filled life, but rather as the Apostle Paul states: "we suffer with him so that we may also be glorified with him" (Rom 8:17).

This understanding of creation as a place inhabited by the Spirit where humanity and non-human creatures together delight in the presence of God occurs throughout Scripture. The vision of the Karioi project, of humans and sea-birds living in communion on a sacred mountain, is a powerful one resonating with other voices from across the ages. The Psalmist declares:

> 1 How lovely is your dwelling place,
> O Lord of hosts!
> 2 My soul longs, indeed it faints
> for the courts of the Lord;
> my heart and my flesh sing for joy
> to the living God.
> 3Even the sparrow finds a home,

44. Wallace, *Finding God in the Singing River*, 27.

45. For an ecological interpretation of this passage, see note 40 above.

and the swallow a nest for herself,
where she may lay her young,
at your altars, O Lord of hosts,
my King and my God.
4Happy are those who live in your house,
ever singing your praise.[46]

Avian Pneumatology & Global Realities

Finally, as well as offering a lens with which to interpret and understand the presence of God in the Karioi story, could conceiving of the character and function of the Spirit of God in avian terms also offer hope in light of the global ecological realities we now face?

While less present in contemporary Western theology, the conceiving of the Spirit in avian terms is not confined purely to history or Scripture. C.S. Lewis offers a vivid account in one of his Narnia chronicles, *The Voyage of the Dawn Treader*. Nearing the Dark Island the Narnian crew of the Dawn Treader take on board a stranger who immediately warns his rescuers of their imminent danger: "Fly! Fly! About with your ship and fly! Row, row, row for your lives away from this accursed shore . . . This is the Island where Dreams come true."[47]

Lewis's narrative focuses here on humanity's internal brokenness. To delve into our own deepest, darkest dreams, Lewis explains through the words of King Caspian, is to encounter "some things no man can face."[48] Immediately the crew seeks to turn the ship and head to safety. Lewis's allegorical theology can be read, not merely psychologically, but also ecologically. Our ship is indeed on a dark course. Human civilization heads into uncharted waters—dark and foreboding. The human dream of late modern capitalism—of progress and limitlessness[49]—has become the nightmare of climate change, mass extinctions and ecological devastation.

However, even in the midst of this darkness, God's wounded yet life-giving Spirit which nurtures and sustains human and intra-species community continues to be present. Lewis continues:

46. Psalm 84:1–4 *NRSV*. Such imagery finds its climax in Rev 4–5 where humanity and living creatures join together in worship before the throne of God.

47. Lewis, *The Voyage of the Dawn Treader*, 140.

48. Ibid., 141.

49. On the theme of limitlessness and the vice-like grip this asserts upon our imaginations, see Berry, "Faustian Economics," 35–42.

> Lucy leant her head on the edge of the fighting top and whispered, "Aslan, Aslan, if ever you loved us at all, send us help now." The darkness did not grow any less, but she began to feel a little—a very, very little—better . . .
>
> "Look!" cried Rynelf's voice hoarsely from the bows. There was a tiny speck of light ahead, and while they watched a broad beam of light fell from it upon the ship. It did not alter the surrounding darkness, but the whole ship was lit up as if by searchlight. Caspian blinked, stared round, saw the faces of his companions all with wild, fixed expressions. Everyone was staring in the same direction . . .
>
> Lucy looked along the beam and presently saw something in it. At first it looked like a cross, then it looked like an aeroplane, then it looked like a kite, and at last with a whirring of wings it was right overhead and was an albatross. It circled three times round the mast and then perched for an instant on the crest of the gilded dragon at the prow. It called out in a strong sweet voice what seemed to be words though no one understood them. After that it spread its wings, rose, and began to fly slowly ahead, bearing a little to starboard. Drinian steered after it not doubting that it offered good guidance. But no one except Lucy knew that as it circled the mast it had whispered to her, "Courage, dear heart," and the voice, she felt sure, was Aslan's, and with the voice a delicious smell breathed in her face.[50]

The blended imagery here of breath/wind and a bird that Lewis employs, is reminiscent of the flood narrative in Genesis 8. Noah and the inhabitants of an ark experience together the deluge that turns the face of the earth once again to watery chaos. It is the breath of God which sweeps over these waters (8:1) and a dove whose future is inextricably tied up with the future of humanity. Sent out into the world, the dove returns, its presence of peace required by the ark dwellers as they look out to the watery chaos that surrounds them. The second time the dove returns with a token—a freshly plucked olive leaf—a symbol of new life, an emblem of hope for those on the ark. And then, on the third time of being sent, the dove doesn't return but rather ventures forth, summoning humanity into the newly emerging world.

For those in Raglan/Whāingaroa, the *Oi* is a symbolic presence. Connected to the *Oi* and with dreams of a restored mountain the community is looking with hope toward the future. Like this community we too are summoned to be grounded, to burrow ourselves into our own

50. Lewis, *The Voyage of the Dawn Treader*, 142–43.

ecological communities. And then, filled by the resurrection power of this life-giving, wounded Spirit, we are invited to take flight—working collaboratively and in partnership with others to participate in God's redeeming work of all creation.

Bibliography

Basil of Caesarea. *On the Six Days of Creation: A Translation of the* Hexaemoron *by R. Grosseteste*. Translated by C. F. J. Martin. Oxford: Oxford University Press, 1996.

Bauckham, Richard. "Jesus and the Wild Animals (Mark 1:13): A Christological Image for an Ecological Age." In *Jesus of Nazareth: Lord and Christ: Essays on the Historical Jesus and New Testament Christology*, edited by J. B. Green and M. Turner, 3–21. Grand Rapids: Eerdmans, 1994.

Berry, Wendell. "Faustian Economics: Hell Hath No Limits." *Harper's Magazine*, May 2008, 35–42.

Cox, Harvey. *The Future of Faith*. New York: HarperOne, 2009.

Deane-Drummond, Celia. *Creation through Wisdom: Theology and the New Biology*. Edinburgh: Clark, 2000.

Edwards, Denis. *Breath of Life: A Theology of the Creator Spirit*. Maryknoll, NY: Orbis, 2004.

Gunton, Colin E. *Christ and Creation*. Carlisle: Paternoster, 1992.

Hoggard Creegan, Nicola. *Animal Suffering and the Problem of Evil*. New York: Oxford University Press, 2013.

Leopold, Aldo, "The Round River: A Parable." In R*ound River*, edited by Luna B. Leopold, 158–65. Oxford: Oxford University Press, 1993.

Lewis, C. S. *The Voyage of the Dawn Treader*. London: Fontana Lions, 1980.

McFague, Sallie. *A New Climate for Theology: God, the World, and Global Warming*. Minneapolis: Fortress, 2008.

Moltmann, Jürgen. *The Crucified God: The Cross of Christ as the Foundation and Criticism of Christian Theology*. Translated by R. A. Wilson and John Bowden. Minneapolis: Fortress, 1974.

———. *Spirit of Life: A Universal Affirmation*. Translated by Margaret Kohl. Minneapolis: Fortress, 1997.

Schmemann, Alexander. *For the Life of the World*. Crestwood, NY: St. Vladimir's Seminary Press, 1973.

Sideris, Lisa. "Writing Straight with Crooked Lines: Holmes Rolston's Eco-Theology and Theodicy." In *Nature, Value, and Duty: Life on Earth*, edoted by Holmes Rolston III, Christopher Preston, and Wayne Ouderkirk, 77–101. Dordrecht: Springer, 2006.

Tacey, David. *The Spirituality Revolution: The Emergence of Contemporary Spirituality*. Sydney: HarperCollins, 2003.

Teilhard de Chardin, Pierre. "The Spiritual Power of Matter." Translated by Gerald Vann. In *Hymn of the Universe*, 53–69. New York: Harper & Row, 1961.

Wallace, Mark I. *Finding God in the Singing River: Christianity, Spirit, Nature*. Minneapolis: Augsburg Fortress, 2005.

———. "The Green Face of God: Christianity in an Age of Ecocide." *Cross Currents*, 50, no. 3 (2000) 310–31.

———. "The Wild Bird Who Heals: Recovering the Spirit in Nature." *Theology Today* 50, no. 1 (1993) 13–28.

———. "The Wounded Spirit as the Basis for Hope in an Age of Radical Ecology." In *Christianity and Ecology: Seeking the Well-Being of Earth and Humans*, edited by Dieter T. Hessel and Rosemary Radford Ruether, 51–72. Cambridge, MA: Harvard University Press, 2000.

Yong, Amos. *The Spirit Poured out on All Flesh*. Grand Rapids: Baker Academic, 2005.

———. *The Spirit Renews the Face of the Earth: Pentecostal Forays in Science and the Theology of Creation* Eugene, OR: Wipf and Stock, 2009.

Zizioulas, John. *Communion and Otherness: Further Studies in Personhood and the Church*. Edited by Paul McPartlan. London: T. & T. Clark, 2006.

5

Listening in the Landscape of Aotearoa New Zealand

Sue Burns,
St John's College, Auckland

An Affirmation

You, O God are supreme and holy.
you create our world and give us life.
Your purpose overarches everything we do.
You have always been with us.
You are our God.

You, O God are infinitely generous,
good beyond all measure,
You came to us before we came to you.
You have revealed and proved
your love for us in Jesus Christ,
who lived and died and rose again.
You are with us now.
You are God.

You, O God, are Holy Spirit.
You empower us to be your gospel in the world.
You reconcile and heal, you overcome death.

You are our God. We worship you.

A New Zealand Prayer Book / He Karakia te Mininare o Aotearoa[1]

1. Anglican Church, *A New Zealand Prayer Book (ANZPB).*

I WORK IN THEOLOGICAL education at the College of St John the Evangelist—*Te Whare Wānanga o Hoani Tapu te Kaikauwhau i te Rongopai*, the Anglican theological college for Aotearoa, New Zealand and Polynesia. The Anglican Church here is constituted in three Tikanga (partners)—Māori, Pākehā and Polynesia. United in Christ we are enriched by the differences the Tikanga bring to our common life; we endorse each Tikanga to order practices and ministry that embody each culture. At St John's College students and staff worship, live and study together in a residential community.

I responded to God's love, becoming a follower of Christ, while a student of biblical hermeneutics at Sheffield University. Ever since then I have been fascinated by language and text. More recently I have been exposed to social constructionist theory making connections with theology and new paradigms for ministry and mission. I am sensitive to what we say and how we say it, mindful that conveying meaning from one place to another is not straightforward, particularly if it has to cross time, human and/or geographical landscapes.

I am a migrant to Aotearoa. I benefit from the hospitality of two covenants, one the new covenant offered to us in Christ, the second offered by Māori—*tangata whenua*/"the people of the land," expressed through the Treaty of Waitangi.[2] The Treaty gives me a place to stand here. Sometimes when travelling this physical landscape I am positioned as "Stranger," "Other," "Coloniser." Discomfort pushes me to reflect on attitudes and ideas that have given me privilege, and I acknowledge that I have been blind to the cost of this privilege to God, to Land and to the People of this Land.

The gift of discomfort has called me to be a listener—listening with "reverent expectancy"[3] attentive to contexts that shape me as an embodiment of the Gospel God's work in the world. In the company of others, I seek to discern ways that respect the land through which I journey and the people with whom we travel.

This short piece is but a story of listening to a landscape. I listen as a Christian, a Pākehā, female migrant. I offer this account and my personal reflection to you, reader/ listener, hoping that it may contribute to your journey. In my listening to the land, and to the Māori interpreters of the

2. The Treaty of Waitangi was a treaty made between the British Crown and most New Zealand Maori tribes in 1840. Its meaning and interpretation have been controversial. Since the establishment of the Waitangi Tribunal in 1975 both the legal significance of the Treaty and its role in shaping a genuine bicultural partnership within Aotearoa New Zealand has deepened.

3. Thiselton identifies the impossibility of being a neutral observer. He links the approach to biblical text and pastoral listening as listening with respect, with agape. Thiselton, *Interpreting God*, 64.

land, I critique some of the language Westerners have brought to the task of the gospel in this country. I end with an image of fire as a better and more hopeful symbol of our connected being in this land.

The Mountain

August is a pivotal month. Mud reveals the effects of restless animal feet and persistent winter rain. Watery sunshine gains strength that begins to warm the earth and nurture spring growth. Maungakawa is a hill on which I pray. It overlooks the Waikato, a region in the North Island of New Zealand—*Te Ika a Maui o Aotearoa*. One August morning looking over a winter landscape my eye picked out the line from one surveyor's mark to another cut across the ancestral lands of *Ngati-Haua* (the local Māori tribe) by the colonial government in 1865 as part of the boundary of 1.2 million acres of land confiscated from Waikato Māori. Land confiscation inflicted economic ruin on Māori and closed down the possibility of resistance. Waikato Māori speak of this confiscation as *raupatu,* or a fatal blow. I thought of other landscapes in Taranaki, the Bay of Plenty, South Auckland, Hauraki, Te Urewera, Hawke's Bay and Tai Rawhiti/ the East Coast scarred by these lines—scarred by injustice.

The winter mist lifted further and I recognized the richness of the land giving up plenty in agricultural cultivation and human settlement. I recalled that at the time of the confiscation Māori nurtured the land providing for their own needs and trading with the burgeoning settlement of *Tamaki-Makaurau*/Auckland to the north. Immediately after the raupatu/ confiscation militia were gifted land. Later people crossed the world to seek a better future, to work hard, to get ahead. I acknowledged their courage and hope. These later settlers may have not known that "their" land had been taken illegally however expansionist ideology informed the actions of government and expectations of the settlers that included the expectation of militia protection from Māori. The intertwined histories of Māori and Pākehā, of deprivation and struggle, of struggle and hope were in front of me carved in the landscape; overlooked and unvoiced. Within the Waikato, in prayer, I was troubled by their voices: How do we attend to them as we are formed as God's work? How do we speak and live in this context?

In the last two decades, new ways of engaging in mission and ministry that connect with our context have been crossing the world in many directions. Distinctive method, theology and spirituality have been taking shape. In the UK, these new ways are articulated as "mission shaped practices" to form "pioneer ministers." On that day, on that hillside, in that "thin place" where God was so close, I was deeply stirred. How could the church force that language into the soil of Aotearoa? How could Christian ministry be called "pioneer" in these landscapes, by a church that purports to seek justice and partnership, when colonial pioneers had done so much to damage the land and Māori society?

As I struggled I remembered a conversation from another hill, Panekiri in Te Urewera, towards the East Coast of the North Island. This conversation focused on how Māori carried a piece of smouldering fungus, *puku tawai/putawa*, as they travelled to start a fire to ensure warmth, food, sustenance and hospitality. Fire *provided space for* life. Pioneers had brought violence. My spirit glimpsed how problematic "pioneer" is as a description of the work of God's love here; I wondered if ministry in Aotearoa could find a better fit with nurturing the spark of God. I picked my way down the hill, the sun strengthening. I fancied that I saw a shimmer of green on the immigrant, skeletal trees stretching across the Waikato.

Pioneers

The "trouble" that morning was multi textured. Elaine Wainwright writes of doing theology in twenty-first century looking both ways or in multiple directions. "Hermeneutical philosophy . . . has brought many theologians to the awareness that interpretation of the past, of its texts and its traditions is always undertaken from some particular vantage point, stance or perspective in the present."[4] Reflecting on this event invites me to consider post-colonial, historical and social histories, biblical metaphors, missiology, liberation and eco-theology from my location. It is well beyond the scope of this chapter to do these at appropriate depth. I have narrowed the sights to these questions and trust that my attention to them creates space for others to continue this journey. I ask: What are the tensions in calling Christian ministry "pioneer ministry" in this land, Aotearoa? Would the practice of fire-carrying offer a less oppressive and more hopeful metaphor for ministry and mission in Aotearoa where people and land are interwoven?

The language of "pioneers" is biblical. Jesus is described as *archēgos* in the letter to the Hebrews (Heb 2:10; 12:2). Alternative translations of the *archēgos* are "author" and "pioneer." Jesus is *archēgos* of salvation (Heb 2:10) and faith (Heb 12:2). Hebrews describes Jesus's humanity richly in contrast to Paul's letters. Jesus struggles, suffers, feels pain, is tempted, weeps and learns obedience. These human experiences are central to Jesus's role as representative high priest. Through total identification with humanity Jesus is

4. Wainwright, "Looking Both Ways," 127.

both author and pioneer of salvation and faith, offering a path through life and, as the perfecter of faith, through death to open the way for humanity. The energy of the language invites energy in response. The translation "author/ originator/ beginner" is well balanced with perfecter-as-finisher but the energy of "pioneer" matches the active verbs of laying aside and running that Jesus has energetically carved out by his struggles and victories. As the author of the letter to the Hebrews says:

> Therefore, since we are surrounded by so great a cloud of witnesses, let us also lay aside every weight and the sin that clings so closely, and let us run with perseverance the race that is set before us, looking to Jesus the pioneer and perfecter of our faith, who for the sake of the joy that was set before him endured the cross, disregarding its shame, and has taken his seat at the right hand of the throne of God. (Heb 12;1–2)

The Eucharistic Liturgy *Thanksgiving for Creation and Redemption* links these ideas from Hebrews succinctly.

> It is right indeed to give you thanks most loving God, through Jesus Christ, our Redeemer, the first born from the dead, the pioneer of our salvation, who is with us always, one of us, yet from the heart of God. [5]

The concept of Jesus as pioneer is embedded in our liturgies and praxis.

How do we fare when we transfer the descriptor from Jesus as pioneer to ourselves as "pioneers" in mission, especially given all the ambiguity around pioneering in the ecology and social structure of Aotearoa? This naming is well established in the Church of England; it has been used since the publication of *The Mission Shaped Church* in 2004; since then division of ministry discernment and training has been developed to form pioneer ministers. The Church of England's House of Bishops passed legislation to provide for ministry units that were not linked to parishes, thus offering space for fresh expressions as part of dioceses. The Diocese of Wellington in New Zealand adopted similar measures in 2006 offering hospitality to Urban Vision led by Justin and Jenny Duckworth.[6]

In this discourse, what marks a person as a pioneer? There is no one-size-fits-all but some common themes emerge. Pioneer ministers are called by God and have a clear vocation in Christ that pushes them to the edge rather than the centre of existing churches or faith communities. Pioneer

5. The Anglican Church, *ANZPB*, 467.

6. For examples, see Duckworth and Duckworth, *Against the Tide;* Baker and Ross, *The Pioneer Gift.*

ministers are called into the missionary activity of God in Trinity recognizing that God is already active; they are called and empowered by the Holy Spirit into innovation and imagination. The varieties each person brings in response to the call of God are clear in the richness of the communities that are growing. Pioneers work collaboratively and seek transformation for people, communities, and society through the working of God. They are variously described sometimes as entrepreneurs and by others as new prophets. Cathy Ross writes,

> It may be that pioneers have the awkward gift of not fitting in, that we experience a kind of theological homelessness, that we are learning anew to live on other people's terms; but we have hope because we have ancestors who have been before us, and because we have the message of hope, we have the promise of life.[7]

Pioneers are formed by their living faith in Christ, scripture and theology, spiritual disciplines, contextual analysis and community skills.[8] Pioneers are not loners; the intention for pioneers is to gather communities that express the life of God in contemporary contexts, connecting often with those on the edges of society who are close to the heart of God (Luke 4:18–20) How do pioneers know how to start?

Stephen Croft names listening as foundation skill in evangelism. He identifies three levels demonstrating the place of each and the transformative potential of the third. "I listen in order to gain the right to speak; I listen in order to tailor my message to what you say; I listen in order to learn from your wisdom and insight."[9] How do we speak about ministry in Aotearoa if we take this seriously and learn from the land's "wisdom and insight"? Without doubt, there is a great deal in the language of the "pioneer" that is positive and hopeful. Our language has not prevented nor eclipsed God's work in Aotearoa New Zealand; in places in which Christians are listening with people and context, varieties of faith communities have flourished, but my concern is that naming these as "pioneer" endeavors deadens the voice of our history, whitewashes the record of colonial violence, and continues its assaults on *Tangata Whenua*. That assault disempowers us all in the bicultural context of Aotearoa.

7. Ross, "Pioneering Missiologies," 36.

8. Church Missionary Society. https://pioneer.churchmissionsociety.org/.

9. Croft, "Transforming Evangelism," 133.

The Reflection of Hope

How do Māori relate to the land? Pa Henare Tate, in *He Puna Iti i te Ao Mārama* (*A Little Spring in the World of Light*), seeks to create a foundation for indigenous Māori theology. He names the purpose of the book arising "from the desire of Māori people for Christian faith, and thus theology, to be more culturally relevant for Māori in Aotearoa New Zealand. This desire may be described as the desire to rekindle and reclaim their own culture, while at the same time embracing their own forms of Christian faith and life."[10] Pa Tate establishes the principle that is at the heart reclaiming ministry and theology in our times, that theology can no longer be "received." Faith needs to be formed from within Māori.[11]

In the first chapter Pa Tate presents the pressing requirement for this work to be done. He presents his understanding of indigenous theology, the *kaupapa* (principle) of the book and foundational concepts. *Atua, Whenua, Tangata,*—God, Land and People are each inter-related. These three sets of relationships cannot be divided, therefore a Pākehā (person of European descent) action or languaging that effects a separation tramples respect which is foundational to listening incarnationally.

Whenua/Land cannot be divided from *Atua*/God and *Tangata*/ People. European understandings of land from colonial times are fundamentally different from these Māori concepts, yet Māori not only give us another perspective, but bring us much closer to the biblical framework of land and divinity. At its most basic, European notions of owning land are deeply oppositional to Māori's dependence on land for sustenance, identity and belonging. In "A Three-Way Relationship: God, Land, People: A Māori Woman Reflects," Tui Cadogan writes that Māori could not sell land because it was not *tika*, rightly ordered, right response to sell one's mother."[12] This gives voice to the disturbance I experienced on the hillside when I viewed the confiscation line. It is not merely an historical marker it is an open wound in the body of the people of the land. The pain is repeated whenever language is carelessly used. Pa Tate refers to the *raupatu*, confiscation as *whakanoa*—"a violation of tapu (holiness) and mana." He

10. Tate, *He Puna Iti I te Ao Marama*, 16.

11. I offer the following reflection as a Pākehā woman, a beneficiary of the Treaty of Waitangi that gives me a place to be in Aotearoa. I refer respectfully to values but recognize I cannot convey from within to Māori listeners or readers. Nevertheless, I offer this because I recognize that our language as Pākehā ignores and disrespects Māori values. I speak knowing that my language falls short of being the carrier of hope in this land of Aotearoa and the people of the land.

12. Cadogan, "A Three-Way Relationship," 30.

describes "*noa* as the state of diminishment and disempowerment that is the result of violation."[13] This diminishment is a weakening of the people in their relationships with their Land and their People. It is profoundly experienced and has far reaching consequences. Dean Mahuta attends to the implications of *raupatu in* Waikato and the devastation of *ahi kā,* the home fires. Mahuta explains that *ahi kā* is established where there is continuing presence because they connect the People with the Land through *whakapapa* (geneology) and occupation.[14]

Cadogan makes the connection that Māori understood the Treaty of Waitangi as a covenant, a sacred agreement that was negotiated by the missionaries who brought the new religion, Christianity. This covenant offered Māori ongoing sovereignty of the Land. Cadogan explains that without Land, Māori have no identity, no connection to genealogy, no place to return for burial, no connection with ancestral land. She writes:

> At times, for no apparent reason the Māori person in "foreign" territory will be overwhelmed by a need to return home. This feeling cannot be fulfilled through encounters with people. Even family visitors. The call is from "*whenua*"; it is a deep spiritual longing to stand again on ancestral lands and hear the voice of *tipuna* call a welcome on the winds. If unattended, it will cause sickness and at its height can result in death. No diagnosed medical condition can account for the event. Such is the strength of the spiritual relationship between *tangata* and *Whenua.*[15]

Cadogan describes the link between *Atua* God and *Whenua* Land that requires Māori to cultivate and harvest from land with respect for God, harvesting sustainably, always recognizing these intrinsic connections. Land is the foundation from which people express hospitality, manaakitanga, that establishes and enhances relationships, order and mana of the people. Without Land all these are diminished.

If I, as Pākehā, have ears to hear Māori voices shout out in answer to my question, "What are the tensions in calling Christian ministry 'pioneer ministry' in this land, Aotearoa?" Whichever interpretation we lay on the word "pioneer," the idea of breaking new ground is integral to it. There is an implicit assumption that in the mid to late nineteenth century the land in Aotearoa was, as it were, waiting to be broken in. This assumption inflicts pain on Māori today and is problematic for Pākehā. Our brief excursion into Māori concepts of *Whenua* demonstrate that when pioneering settlers

13. Tate, *He Puna Iti te Ao Mārama,* 42; see also 162–64.

14. Mahuta, *Raupatu,* 179.

15. Cadogan, "A Three-Way Relationship," 34.

arrived the Land was not vacant nor a void, the Land had mothered a people, sustaining Māori and given them life for generations.

The Land cannot be separated from the People of the Land nor from God, the three interwoven in life. Pākehā settlement interrupted this equilibrium. Pioneering with its Pākehā history of hope and struggle carries with it a back-story and on-going associations with exploitation and disruption for Māori. If we are committed to God's mission and to listen contextually why would we want to adopt a description that is sullied by our colonial past and repeats our offence against Māori?

Fire Carrying and *ahi kā*

I return to my wondering: would the practice of fire-carrying offer a metaphor for ministry and mission in Aotearoa where people and land are interwoven? Spirituality for our contexts and emerging Christian communities needs to be incarnational and relational. I suggest that the metaphor of fire carrying is both of these as it connects to this particular land of Aotearoa, sustains community in many different ways, and can engender hope.

Fire appears in both the Hebrew Scriptures and New Testament as a sign of God's presence. The angel of the Lord appears to Moses in a flame of fire. Moses is called to lead a people and Yahweh reveals himself from the fire—"I am who I am" (Exod 3:1–12). After the Exodus from Egypt, Yahweh "went in front of them in a pillar of cloud by day, to lead them along the way, and in a pillar of fire by night, to give them light, so that they might travel by day and by night" (Exod 13:21).

Travelling forwards across other references, time and places I recalled Paul's words to the young Timothy when he was facing tough times. "For this reason, I remind you to rekindle the gift of God that is within you through the laying on of my hands; for God did not give us a spirit of cowardice, but rather a spirit of power and of love and of self-discipline. (2 Tim 1:6–7).[16] In *A New Zealand Prayer Book/he Karakia Mihinare o Aotearoa* this passage is an optional reading in the ordination service for a bishop. Are these words only for the ordained, particularly bishops? Is rekindling an exhortation for all of us?

When Paul reminds us that "the gift" is the Spirit of "power and love and self control" who is gifted to "us" (v 7) in Christ we are encouraged that this gift is not for particular people nor is it one particular "spiritual" gift. At Pentecost when the Holy Spirit comes there is the appearance of tongues

16. The author acknowledges there is scholarly controversy over the authorship of 2 Tim.

like fire over the apostles (Acts 2:1–4). This evocative account resonates with John the Baptist's description of Jesus as the one who will baptise "with the Holy Spirit and with fire." (Matt 3:11; Luke 3:16). The Presentation in each ordination tells us "By the Holy Spirit all who believe and are baptized receive a ministry to proclaim Jesus as Saviour and Lord, and to love and serve the people with whom they live and work."[17] None of us is excluded.

The instruction to rekindle the Spirit does not presuppose Timothy's weakness, but recognizes that opposition and/or circumstances can obscure God's potential within. Paul prays with confidence that the Spirit will burn with renewed intensity in Timothy because he knows the heritage of faith that Timothy has through his mother and grandmother (vv. 1–5); and he knows the faithfulness of God in Jesus (vv. 8–11). Our own spiritual heritage in Scripture and Liturgy uses fire as a vibrant metaphor of God's presence with and within us to enrich our living. We pray together that "we whom the Spirit lights may bring light to the world."[18]

I suggest that kindling fire resonates in a particular way in Aotearoa. Rebekah Fuller in her Masters research *Mātauranga Māori o Ngā Harore* or *Māori traditional knowledge surrounding fungi*, researched ethnographic records, historical records and Matauranga Māori.[19] She identifies *puku tawai/putawa* as the fungus that was carried from place to place to create new fire, new community. The carrying task was not restricted to a particular individual, nor does the role have a name—it was a general practice. Philip Cody writes that in Māori mythology fire represents mana, "fire that is constantly alive"[20] He links *ahi* with the fire of the Spirit and *ahi kā* as the place that Christians gather. The fire in each person must be kept alive, being nurtured in relationships. Paul is not explicit in his encouragement to Timothy as to how to rekindle the gift within him. Cody tells us that mana is hidden within a person and waits for others to acknowledge it for it to be sustained.[21] I suggest that rekindling happens most effectively through relationship in Christian community. In sharing bread and wine we have a grounded reminder that we are interrelated in the body of Christ, united by one Spirit to live out God's work in the world. This is the heart of our identity. Cody continues "Fire is the symbol of love and the Spirit. It is through the love of God and the Spirit living in Christians that their mana is

17. The Anglican Church, *ANZPB*, 890.

18. Ibid., 428.

19. Fuller, "Maori Knowledge of Fungi."

20. Cody, *Seeds of the Word*, 84.

21. Tate, *He Puna Iti I te Ao Marama*, 75–102.

nurtured."[22] Cody likens the indwelling of us as individuals and community to *ahi kā* "'the home fire' that gives a Christian a place to live."[23]

Fire is central for gathering community. Relationships around the fire are multi-layered. Let's visit two related narratives gathered round a fire. The first, in the high priest's house (John 18:15–18) where Peter is confronted by a woman and denies Jesus. The second, on a beach where Jesus confronts and restores Peter (John 21:1–19). Setting a fire opens space for conversations, devastations and reconciliation. The fire with its unpredictability opens space for honest truth telling while also offering a nurturing presence that draws people together. If Pākehā could wait to be called into these grounded, hospitable spaces with Māori we might find opportunities to address our history and thus open ourselves to the cleansing fire of God?

Might Pākehā reconsider our approach to the land itself walking forward in different ways in respect rather than domination? This would entail walking with the land and in the land so that the land and the people who dwell here first might live with justice and peace.

Continuing the Journey

I have noticed that when assessing an idea or product people are interested in whether it works. Do the concepts and practices that fire evokes—life in the Spirit, a grounded place of gathering, hospitality, conversation with stranger and friend, truth telling and doing life together—contribute to being the people of God in Aotearoa in 2016? All these ideas have been identified as integral to spirituality for contextual mission and ministry. I seek to embody these ideas in my approach to ministry practice as an educator and facilitator in the New Zealand Dioceses. It is for others to evaluate that worth. I recognise that "pioneer" captures the imagination of the entrepreneur, the energy of youth and I give thanks for the many expressions of faith that have emerged across the country, but I sit with my disquiet and sensitivity to the voice of this land and *tangata whenua*. This being so I think the pioneer label needs to be reviewed for this country. Aotearoa offers many metaphors and images from our place. Kath Rushton, in this volume, draws on living waters from the braided rivers in Te Waipounamu; Andrew Shepherd took us soaring with the Holy Spirit on the wings of the petrels off the Raglan Coast. These are invitations to further conversations.

The theme of the book is hope. Nicola Hoggard Creegan has reminded us that hope in our environment is multi textured, deeply connected. I have

22. Cody, *Seeds of the Word*, 84.

23. Ibid.

heard hope described as a "practice" not an emotion. I am committed to listening to unearth and discern hope. Listening in this way is God-breathed. In his poem *The Rain Stick* the Irish poet, Seamus Heaney, writes:

> You are like a rich man entering the kingdom of heaven
>
> Through the ear of a raindrop. Listen now again.[24]

I have sought to listen to God, the Land and People of Aotearoa that we might begin our practices of restoration by recognizing the violence of the past and seeking to move forward by a different way. May this personal reflection be an invitation to watch what we say and what we miss, to join a renewed journey in ways of justice and peace for Aotearoa and all who inhabit the Land of the Long White Cloud.

> Praise to God who has given us life.
>
> Whakamoemititia te Atua, te Kai-homai i te ora.
>
> Blessed be God for the gift of love.
>
> Kia whakapainga te Atua, mo tana o te aroha.
>
> Praise to God who forgives us our sin.
>
> Whakamoemititia te Atua, e muru nei i to tatou hara.
>
> Praise to God who kindles our faith.
>
> Whakamoemititia te Atua, te ahi ka o te whakapono.
>
> Blessed be God, our strength our hope.
>
> Ka whakapainga te Atua,to matou kaha, to matou tumanako.
>
> The Liturgy of Baptism[25]

Bibliography

Anglican Church in Aotearoa, New Zealand and Polynesia. *A New Zealand Prayer Book/ He Karakia Mihinare o Aotearoa*. Christchurch: Genesis Publications, 2005.

Baker, Johnny, and Cathy Ross, eds. *The Pioneer Gift: Explorations in Mission*. London: Canterbury, 2014.

Cadogan, Tui. "A Three-Way Relationship, God, Land, People: A Maori Woman Reflects." In *Land and Place: Spiritualities from Aotearoa*, edited by Helen Bergin and Susan Smith, 27–40. Auckland: Accent, 2004.

24. Heaney, "The Rain Stick," 1.
25. The Anglican Church, *ANZPB*, 387.

Cody, Philip. *Seeds of the Word: Ngā Kākano O Te Kupu: The Meeting of Maori Spirituality and Christianity*. Wellington: Steele Roberts, 2004.

Croft, Steven. "Transforming Evangelism." In *Evangelism in a Spiritual Age—Communicating Faith in a Changing Culture,* edited by Steven Croft et al., 126–47. London: Church House, 2005.

Duckworth, Justin, and Jenny Duckworth. *Against the Tide, Towards the Kingdom*. Eugene, OR: Cascade, 2011.

Fuller, Rebekah, et al., "Māori knowledge of Fungi / Matauranga o Nga Harore." In *Introduction to Fungi of New Zealand* edited by E. H. C. McKenzie, 81–118. Hong Kong: Fungal Diversity, 2004.

Heaney, Seamus. "The Rainstick." In *The Spirit Level*, 1. London: Faber, 1996.

Mahuta, Dean Patariki Smeatham. "Raupatu: A Waikato Perspective." *Te Kaharoa* 1 (2008) 174–82.

Ross, Cathy. "Pioneering Missiologies." In *The Pioneer Gift: Explorations in Mission,* edited by Johnny Baker and Cathy Ross, 20–38. London: Canterbury, 2014.

Tate, Pa Henare. *He Puna Iti I te Ao Mārama: A Little Spring in the World of Light*. Auckland: Libro, 2012.

Thiselton, Anthony. *Interpreting God and the Post-Modern Self: On Meaning Manipulation and Promise*. Grand Rapids: Eerdmans, 1995.

Wainwright, Elaine. "Looking Both Ways, or in Multiple Directions: Doing/Teaching Theology into the Twenty-First Century." *Pacifica* 18, no. 2 (2005) 123–40.

Text

6

The Animal in Derrida's Bible

Yael Klangwisan,
Laidaw College

If the animal moving toward us
so securely in a different direction
had our kind of consciousness
it would wrench us round.
But it feels its life as boundless, unfathomable
and without regard to its own condition:
pure like its outward gaze.
And where we see the future
it sees all the time
and itself within all time, forever healed.

—Rainer Maria Rilke, *The Eighth Duino Elegy*[1]

Genesis 2/Gilgamesh I:110

I came awake in the dirt, in the mud, as if thrown down. Lips upon my nose. My body was alive with sensation. All around was green and new. The air, the sensation of toes and feet on the dry ground. I was as shaky and wide-eyed as a new born foal. I waded into cool waters, the very source of the Pishon river, to wash the stain of clay from my skin and hair. A herd of gazelle lined the bank, drinking in the twilight. I placed my hand on a warm furred flank and drank too.

1. Rilke, *The Selected Poetry of Rainer Maria Rilke*, 195.

As in the extract from Rilke's 'Eighth Elegy' that begins this essay, the other-than-human in the world is an object of curiosity, mystery and denigration. Derrida's 1997 Cerisy lectures "L'animal que donc je suis [à suivre]" aligns itself with Rilke's mood in its desire to be *with* or for rather than in spite of the animal.[2] In his first lecture, Derrida speaks of the difference between nudity and animal non-nudity. He speaks of the beginnings of the civilized world. The beginnings of literature and of language. He reveals his shame. He speaks of cats in literature; and of poetry and passion. He speaks of sacrifice.

Derrida's survey of the question of the animal in Genesis penetrates into the heart of animal theology. Much of the Western theological tradition has interpreted the hierarchical distinction between the animal and the human as ratified and limned with divine authority in the first pages of the Judeo-Christian sacred text. Thus in Derrida's rewriting and re-interpretation of Genesis, he is firstly recognizing the power of these texts that are lodged at the heart of the question of the animal and then offers an "other" reading that deconstructs this dominating theological narrative and the ways in which it is made manifest. Likewise, in the Western philosophical tradition the animal has been an invisible and mute companion—easily set aside—and, as Derrida will claim, the historic span of this consequential monologue about the animal has done little except to further underline the false dichotomy of the human-animal relation. In this situation Derrida offers a reading of hope: a new relation, and this means looking into the face of *l'animal* as a divine moment.

Initially, the question of the animal is one of difference, insurmountable distinction. The animal is considered as one not: "capable of consciousness, of language, of a relation to death . . . incapable of the phenomenological . . . a relation to the other as other".[3] Humanity is defined over and against the animal. Derrida's return to Genesis and to the first animal is a search for the animal face.[4] It is a search for the animal subject denied in philosophy and that has shaped animal lore/law:

2. Derrida's Cerisy-la-Salle 1997 lectures on the question of the animal, *L'Animal autobiographique*, were later published in French as *L'Animal que donc je suis* (Paris: Galilée, 2006) and then in English as Derrida, *The Animal That Therefore I Am*. The title of the book was taken from the title of Derrida's first lecture.

3. Derrida, "Eating Well," 255–87.

4. Derrida introduces the notion of coming face to face with the animal as a signal of his intention to challenge Levinas, whose philosophical project involved a radical and relational engagement of alterity (for humans). He will critique Levinas, among others (such as Heidegger, Kant, and Lacan) regarding ways in which their philosophical projects have contributed to the human/animal hierarchy.

> That would be the law of an unperturbable logic, both Promethan and Adamic, both Greek and Abrahamic . . . Its invariance hasn't stopped being verified all the way to our modernity.[5]

Like Rilke, Derrida seeks to encounter the animal, and to look it squarely in the face, and to do this naked, removing the clothing that blinds western philosophy. He plays in the possibility of humanimality and divinanimality. He searches for a place where human and animal share a border.

This engagement of the question of the animal is not an obscure cause for Derrida. He made a life's work of deconstructing phallocentric or anthropocentric othering or silencing such as that that silences woman and of injustices endemic in sexual difference.[6] For Caputo, Derrida's theological offering is one of justice: "for a justice to come that will count our every tear"[7] from a God whose name constitutes a call "for the other, that calls from the other, the name that the other calls, that calls upon us like Elijah at the door, and that calls for something new."[8] In animality studies, Derrida sounds this call for a new relation by making a "turn toward the animal gaze"[9] in the most surprising of ways.

> I often ask myself, just to see, who I am—and who I am (following) at the moment when, caught naked, in silence, by the gaze of the animal, for example the eyes of a cat, I have trouble, yes, a bad time overcoming my embarrassment.[10]

This beginning of Derrida's lecture recalls the words of Rilke's Eighth Duino Elegy, "Oder daß ein Tier, ein stummes, aufschaut, ruhig durch und durch./ Dieses heißt Schiksal,/ gegenüber sein und nicht als das und immer gegenüber./"[11] [And yet sometimes, a silent animal looks up at us and silently looks through us. We call it Fate to be in opposition. Nothing but that. Forever opposite.][12] And Derrida's key points [or *punctum*] are all here in these first few lines of his lecture just as they are in Rilke's *Eighth*: seeing, the body, language and shame. The question for Derrida is whether it is truly fate to be in such opposition as Rilke suggests. Humans and animals share this garden of a world, thrown here together, surely there is another way of

5. Derrida, *The Animal That Therefore I Am*, 20–21.
6. Kearns, Foreword to *Divinanimality*, ed. Moore, xiii.
7. Caputo, *The Prayers and Tears of Jacques Derrida*, 113.
8. Ibid.
9. Moore, Introduction of *Divinanimality*, ed. Moore, 1.
10. Derrida, *The Animal*, 3–4.
11. Rilke, *Selected Poetry*, 195
12. Rilke, *Duino Elegies*.

being here together. Humans and animals share much of the experience of vitality: pleasure, bodily sensation if not the Heideggerian fullness of Being, and as Derrida asks, what of the possibility then of friendship. Could the animal not be "the voice of the friend"?[13]

Genesis 2/Gilgamesh I:195

I had been happy in my herd. Running with the gazelle, a part of the gazelle world. I was humanimal. The herd did not shy from me. Yet I yearned for something more. I yearned for language. I yearned for a way out of silence. I heard a sound. I heard an echo from another border. The world so wide, so open.

Genesis 2:4 to 4:1 is an ancient Semitic narrative which presents profound philosophical questions with deceptive simplicity.[14] As is common in Ancient Hebrew literature it is embedded into the discursive space of Near Eastern Mythology. It shares therefore an uncanny kinship to the Epic of Gilgamesh which, according to Andrew George, is a very existential writing that explores humanity's fear of death: "in examining the human longing for life eternal, it tells of one man's heroic struggle against death—first for immortal renown . . . then for eternal life itself; of his despair when confronted with inevitable failure . . . "[15]

The Genesis text is a text of transitions. Like the figure of Enkidu in the *Epic of Gilgamesh*, Adam's story is one of dynamic and essential change or as Derrida puts it, "the crossing of borders between man and animal."[16] This threshold is not one readily surrendered to in philosophy nor in conservative theological discourse where the *mechitza* between human and animal must remain divinely absolute. This fear of the "betwixt and between state" (between humans and animals) is seen in myth where the travesty or reminder of human "animality" is swiftly and gloriously put to death, such as Perseus's heroic slaying of Medusa and Bellerophon's vanquishing of Chimaera.[17] Adam's story in Gen 2:4 is one of liminality, and a change of state or being, and just as it is for Enkidu in the *Epic of Gilgamesh*, sexuality is the catalyst, and this is, at once, in the fatalistic form of a woman, the man's salvation and doom. The woman in both these texts signals the end of

13. Derrida, "'Eating Well,'" 278.

14. LaCocque, *The Trial of Innocence.*

15. George, *The Epic of Gilgamesh*, xiv.

16. Derrida, *The Animal*, 3.

17. Renger, *Oedipus and the Sphinx*, 38; see also Derrida's engagement with the Chimaera myth, *The Animal*, 45.

innocence and immortality. Whether knowingly or in a divine naiveté, she is, for all intents and purposes, the personification of mortality.

In these texts we have time for Derrida/Adam/Enkidu, cat/creature/gazelle but not yet for woman. In Genesis 2 she is last to come, appearing after both Adam and animals (Gen 2:22). The Feminine blurs the borders between man and animal in these texts. In the *Epic of Gilgamesh* and *Genesis* it takes a woman to bring man across the animal-human divide, "the journey of nights from the herds to the cities of men".[18] She is "other" and yet is "same." In the *Epic* she initiates the man into the mysteries of the body, she cares for, feeds and clothes him, and makes it possible that he might be leader and friend to other men, but the cost of this is that the animal is no longer kin and no longer "friend" (VIII: 4). In the writings of the ancients, woman was a symbolic doorway and yet the transition through that doorway simultaneously brought both civilization and defilement to man. Masculine innocence was signified by its affinity with wilderness and animality, and that primordial time is immortalized in legend as a time of purity and strength.[19] In Eden too, at the beginning of Genesis 2 woman doesn't yet exist but will come. Adam is there in the garden, with the creatures, his friends, innocent and pure. In Genesis, in the liminal space of Adam's innocence, the question of the animal is bared, unveiled, but just as quickly put away, as is the question of woman. Via a route of veiling (exclusion and invisibility) both questions are entombed and lost to the garden. The animal has not been "seen" again, according to Derrida, and perhaps (in another discourse) neither has woman. Civilization, the Proper and Law, always already takes first place in discourse and sees only itself. It has done so from the beginning of literature, signified in the world's oldest epic tale.

Adam's first encounter with the animal is one of innocence. As opposed to Derrida's embarrassment, Adam has awoken via the breath of life in the Garden of Eden molded from the very clay of the ground (Gen 2:1–4). This place in which he finds himself is a place of wealth, not only in water and food resource but in materials of civilization and royalty: gold and precious stones (Gen 2:8–14). Adam is surrounded by unsullied creation and begins to make his place there. Law enters. God commands that the fruit of the tree of the knowledge of good and evil must be left (Gen 2:16–17) and that to eat this fruit will mean certain death.[20] With the weight of the law and the

18. Klangwisan, "Countersigning," 229.

19. LaCocque, *The Trial of Innocence*, 128.

20. Gen 2:17 *mot tamut* in the infinitive absolute. An irony in that death is already definitive. *Mot tamut* (or similar), elsewhere in Scripture refers to execution by decree, a violent death (1 Sam 14:39, 44), though in Adam's case the death sentence was commuted to exile.

possibility of death on his shoulders, all around him the world of animals thus comes into being (Gen 2:19). It is God that forms them, and it is for the purpose of finding Adam a mate as he is alone. Lonely. *Levado* (Gen 2:18). God is not his peer, and neither are the animals. Adam finds himself unable to relate to either. He demonstrates this by naming. God does not name. Adam names the animals (Gen 2:19), and will finally name woman (Gen 2:23). Society begins on this antecedent in which it has long since continued. He who names rules, and he who rules defines being.[21]

It is not surprising that Derrida evokes the story of Genesis and the animal in *L'animal* in the questioning of the monologue about animals in western philosophy to this point. Genesis 2 returns us to that first encounter: Adam's animal parade. In the literary universe of Genesis 2 the primordial beginning of human relation to the animal is established. Derrida's scene is set here, as if the story of Adam and his animal encounter holds the invariable phallogocentric monologue that forever since shapes our thinking (that and his moment of startlement in the bathroom with Lutece). For Calarco, the suspicion that underscores Derrida's engagement with both the text of Genesis and western philosophy in *L'animal* (evidenced by his description of Heidegger's "violent" discourse of the animal) is its ontotheological presumption (the relation between being and Being). In other words, the question of the animal is stymied by religious humanism and an implicit anthropocentrism that is facilitated by binary and hierarchical thinking.[22] What Derrida seeks to do, is not to conflate or homogenize the relation between human and animal but to draw the animal into a framework of ethical concern. Derrida wants to question the anthropocentric and absolute responsibility to God with respect to its traditional erasure of an ethical responsibility to the animal and the accompanying denigration of the possibility of animal suffering.

Gen 2:21/Gilgamesh I:190:

She came towards me, my own kind. I saw her, and suddenly there was no one else. She spoke with me, and suddenly there was no other language but one. Touching her was like touching my own skin. And in her eyes I saw both my children and my death. The world that was, became the world that will be. The herd turned away in fright. I discovered I was naked and I wept in my grief.

21. See Irigaray, Kristeva, and Cixous on Lacan around the Lacanian notion of "Father, Word, and Law" and the sexual politics of language. For an overview, see part II of Moi, *Sexual/Textual Politics*.

22. Calarco, *Zoographies*, 104.

> I have trouble repressing a reflex of shame. Trouble keeping silent within me a protest against the indecency. Against the impropriety that can come of finding oneself naked, one's sex exposed, stark naked before a cat that looks at you without moving, just to see.[23]

In Genesis 3:7 Adam and Eve discover they are naked. This nudity was irrevocably related to sight. Their eyes were opened, the text says, and they are startled by their nakedness. They are embarrassed and feel ashamed. To hide the shame they grasp at fig leaves to cover themselves but this only partially eases their emotional pain. What are they hiding and what do they hide from?

Calarco reminds us that Nietzsche's explanation of human discomfort with one's *deshabille* is not that it reveals "the animal" but that the animal revealed is so ignoble.[24] Clothing in this case becomes an insufficient cover, a deflection or sublimation of shame. Human uniqueness is thus signified by a poorly constructed cover up. LaCocque notes of Adam and Eve: "Clothes do not just hide their nakedness but, by hiding, they simulate, dissimulate, and stimulate . . . clothing has been both an art and artifice."[25] Clothing in this light is a volatile simulacrum, poorly veiling the truth beneath. This necessary traverse towards civilization (as per the *Epic of Gilgamesh*) and away from the animal is then compounded. The relation to the animal is irrevocably torn when in Gen 3:21 fig leaves (man's first textile) are replaced with animal skins. This most explicit symbol of human difference to the animal stands upon the death of the animal. The skins and furs of the innocent utilized to cover the shame of the Open ones (the ones with "open" eyes). Derrida, naked in his bathroom before the eyes of his cat, Lutece, becomes the second Adam. In giving us the cat's eye view of him exiting the shower wearing nothing but his skin he makes a messianic return to the Garden, a movement of redemption, of *tikkun olam*, a removing of the skins and leaves that obstruct our empathy and courage to meet the animal gaze.

> Still I have been wanting to bring myself back to my nudity before the cat, since so long ago, since a previous time, in the Genesis tale, since the time with Adam, alias Ish, called out the animals' names before the fall, still naked but before being ashamed of his nudity.[26]

23. Derrida, *The Animal*, 4.
24. Calarco, *Zoographies*, 122.
25. LaCocque, *Trial of Innocence*, 171.
26. Derrida, *The Animal*, 3.

It is both Derrida's awareness of his nudity—his startled sense of shame in response to meeting the gaze of his cat—that he emphasizes. In this he may well be drawing on Sartre's fascinating reflection on "being seen" in *Being and Nothingness*. Here, Sartre asserts that the existential apprehension of being held in someone's/something's gaze precipitates a fall, The Fall, all over again: "I see myself because somebody sees me".[27] This phenomenon of being looked at presents the horrifying notion of the existence of other subjects and this notion functions as a kind of alienation of self and of possibility.[28] The experience of being objectified by Lutece, as Derrida writes in *L'animal*, presents a crack in the façade of his humanity: ". . . a lapsus, a fall, a failing, a fault, a symptom," an "*échéance*."[29] Becoming self through a look is akin to complete alienation, as per Sartre, " . . . my original fall is the existence of the Other. Shame—like pride—is the apprehension of myself as a nature although that very nature escapes me and is unknowable . . ."[30] The artifice of clothing veils and makes invisible (except for its trace) the question of the animal by preventing or limiting such a devastating gaze. But, the human experience of shame before the animal, makes possible the notion of an animal subject. Our transcendence is transcended by the witness.

> It is as if I were ashamed, therefore naked in front of this cat, but also ashamed for being ashamed. A reflected shame, the mirror of a shame ashamed of itself, a shame that is at the same time specular, unjustifiable, and unavowable.[31]

For Derrida, the animal's gaze is a mirror that reflects back Derrida's own shame. In his experience of shame he reveals his implicit blindness. He can't meet the eyes of the animal, and to be drawn into that space of truly seeing it. The animal subject in that moment sees everything, without comprehending it, and through this specular gateway it causes Derrida to comprehend and to see his failure, to apprehend the moment of his own fall. In the moment he sees himself in the mirror of the animal's eyes, he sees only himself, his shame, and in that existential moment the animal itself is erased. The animal is not naked, yet through its eyes Adam becomes so. Like Rilke's poem quoted by Bruns, "ihr Gesicht und mitten in das deine;/ und da triffst du deinen Blick im geelen,/ Amber ihrer runden Augenstein

27. Sartre, *Being and Nothingness*, 284.

28. Ibid., 286.

29. Derrida, *The Animal*, 4.

30. Sartre, *Being and Nothingness*, 286.

31. Derrida, *The Animal*, 4.

unerwartet wieder" [she turns her face to yours;/ and with a shock, you see yourself, tiny,/ inside the golden amber of her eyeballs/ suspended].[32]

The animal regards the human without shame and without consciousness of it. It is careless in its non-nudity and without knowing what it is doing offers a gift: that of being. The animal is sensible to neither modesty nor immodesty yet nudity and shame underline humanity's self-knowledge.[33] Humans are able to conceptualize immodesty and via Adam's shame, humanity is made affective.[34] What is the truth of human being? For Nietzsche, humanity's beastly nakedness is veiled by clothes as one kind of truth or flag. In the tale of Enkidu in Babylon and perhaps also in Genesis, clothing has another function. It becomes a forgotten sign of mourning; mourning that veils a lost relation to the animal.[35]

As opposed to the animal, it is humanity that is dumb and blind to the question that presents itself through every animal face—in the glassy, myopic gaze of every cat. And it seems a fact of life that the animal never responds (though Derrida does ask this question) and thus the question goes unanswered and unexamined. The animal unassailably bound as it is by its silence and mystery, "pure like its outward gaze".[36] This law that guards the human-animal divide seems unassailable in its mundane erasure. Humanity's eyes are opened to nudity and shame but closed to the suffering and mute sacrifice of the animal. The blood of the animal runs in rivers from the Temple. Who holds whom captive? And what if the animal should respond? For Derrida, this question is a matter of life and death, of fear and of theology.

> It is the dizziness I feel before the abyss opened by this stupid ruse . . . whenever I run away from the animal that looks at me naked. I often wonder whether this vertigo before the abyss of such an "in order to see" deep in the eyes of God is not the same as that which takes hold of me when I feel so naked in front of a cat, facing it, and when, meeting its gaze, I hear the cat or God ask itself, ask me: Is he going to call me, is he going to address me? What name is he going to call me by, this naked man, before I give him woman, before I lend her to him in giving her to him, before I give her to him or before he gives her to himself by

32. Bruns, "Derrida's Cat: Who Am I?," 408.

33. Derrida, *The Animal*, 5.

34. Guerlac, "Derrida and His Cat," 696.

35. Derrida, "A Silkworm of One's Own," 49–50.

36. Rilke, *Selected Poetry*, 195.

> taking it upon himself, from under him, from at his side [*à ses côtés*]? Or even from his rib [*de sa côte*]?[37]

Through the animal gaze, God speaks, questions, and causes the philosopher to rethink himself. Perhaps the philosopher might then surrender to the questions of both animal and woman, and one day the question of God. Surrender is the high cost of this question. In the text of Genesis 2, we are all yet living creatures, prior to speech and prior to naming. Thus the tête-à-tête between Derrida as Adam and his cat as *l'animal*, is conceived as surrender as one living creature to another.

> Gen 5:5/Gilgamesh VII:145
>
> *Is it possible to be a friend? To see them, finally, as before. I sit and stare. Alone . . .where once there were gazelles all around me . . . now carcasses on the fire pit. I too am nearly gone. And my loved ones mourning my passing will grieve, hair matted and beating their hands on their chests. I see a door before me. Its ancient wood is a memory of paradise. It beckons me through. Perhaps once more, to touch its bark, and eat its fruit. Once more to drink the water of the Pishon with my herd. Once more to be innocent.*

It is with a view to hope that Derrida poignantly recreates the scene of Garden of Eden in his home in Ris-Orangis as a way to deconstruct the animal blindness that is threaded through philosophy and theology like an mist wrapped barrier.[38] As Caputo fondly avers, Derrida here is like an "angry Jewish prophet"[39] who seeks to disturb the present because, in the words of Blanchot, "justice cannot wait".[40] Derrida is a messianic Adam coming with a second law, a law of love for the animal.

> Messianic time is prophetic time; the time to come is the time of the justice to come, that disturbs the present with the call for justice, which calls the present beyond (au-delà) itself. For the most unjust thing of all would be to close off the future by saying that justice is present, that the present time is just, "to pretend that the last word is spoken, time completed, the Messiah come at last."[41]

37. Derrida, *The Animal*, 17–18.

38. "The most constant aspect of Derrida's concern with the question of the animal is evident in his efforts to underscore the anthropocentric dimensions of ontotheological humanism." Calarco, *Zoographies*, 104.

39. Caputo, *Prayers and Tears*, 203.

40. Ibid.

41. Ibid., 81.

Derrida disturbs the present by a fait accompli, by taking the reader there and placing the reader face-à-face with the animal other. The reader is made to look into the eyes of the cat. Mesmeric. Amber globes. Owlish blinking. Wholly other.[42] In this ancient gaze, readerly subjectivity and freedom finds itself "withering in the presence of the other".[43] The pre-nude Adam and the non-nude cat face-à-face and the scene of naming arrives, language instituting and shaping the boundary. And yet:

> Since so long ago, can we say that the animal has been looking at us?[44]

Derrida invokes in the reader, the question, "Who am I?" and "Who am I following?" The reader becomes "naked, in silence"[45] caught in the gaze of these animals that come. The reader is brought by stealth to a time, before shame, and before the calling of names, when Adam was "naked as a beast" and did not know it.[46] As I have written before, this is a moment of vertigo when the sudden awareness of the chasm in-between makes one feel momentarily vulnerable and exposed, as if falling into its depths. This exposure lies in stark relief next to the potently poignant silence of *l'animal*. Apprehension of this terrifying silence—pouring out of the abyss—screeches, roars and howls at this universally human blindness.[47] Derrida's work intensifies that sense of falling, that loss, and that trace of mourning until we are led to ask, like Derrida, "Who was born first, before the names?"[48]

> For thinking concerning the animal, if there is such a thing, derives from poetry . . ."[49]

For Derrida, the poetic is the only way to think the animal because philosophy with its ontotheological presumption has failed the task. The poetic plays on the edge of language and is a gateway to the beyond. This is a space where with the imagination at work, a new way of thinking about the animal might be possible. Derrida argues that poetry provides a way to take on the "address" of the animal (sans language), and even then, of course not fully, and not before the designation "human" slowly but surely obscures

42. Rowe reminds us that our relation to the Wholly Other is divine in "The Divinanimality of Lord Sequoia," in *Divinanimality*, ed. Moore, 102–3.

43. Wood, "Thinking with Cats," 131.

44. Ibid.

45. Derrida, *The Animal*, 3.

46. Ibid.

47. Klangwisan, "Countersigning," 235.

48. Derrida, *The Animal*, 18.

49. Ibid., 7.

the gaze once more. It is poetry that for Derrida disturbs the present, that jars the reader, that calls with the voice of a friend, for justice, in the present time, that makes it for a moment possible to imagine the animal point of view. This is the hope that Derrida presents in *L'animal.* He hopes that we will become disturbed enough to consider a new ethical responsibility to the animal, our forgotten friend who calls to us. He hopes we will be disturbed enough by the question put to us by God through the animal's amber eyes, to upset the pre-established order. For a moment we might just forget ourselves and look again:

> . . . nothing will have ever given me more food for thinking through this absolute alterity of the neighbor or of the next(-door) that these moments when I see myself seen naked under the gaze of a cat.[50]

In Derrida's bible, we return to the scene of a first death and we present ourselves in surrender in order to make retribution, to find relief from our mourning. Redemption comes with the possibility of a new relation; to imagine a new and just relation to each irreplaceable one. The emphasis is not what makes us same or other, but what binds us. Thus Derrida makes the traverse back to the biblical animal's side, back to Paradise. It is not a new law that he brings, at the end of the day, but the desire for a new way to think: "The animal looks at us and we are naked before it. Thinking perhaps begins here."[51]

> And how bewildered is any womb-born creature
>
> that has to fly. As if terrified and fleeing
>
> from itself, it zigzags through the air
>
> the way a crack runs through a tea-cup. So the bat
>
> quivers across the porcelain of the evening.
>
> Rainer Maria Rilke, *Eighth Elegy.*[52]

Bibliography

Alter, Robert. *Genesis.* New York: Norton, 1996.

Atterton, Peter, and Matthew Calarco. *Animal Philosophy: Ethics and Identity.* New York: Continuum, 2012.

50. Ibid., 29.
51. Ibid.
52. Rilke, *Selected Poetry*, 195.

Bruns, G. L. "Derrida's Cat: Who am I?" *Research in Phenomenology* 38 (2008) 404–23.

Calarco, Matthew. "On the Borders of Language and Death: Derrida and the Question of the Animal." *Angelaki: Journal of Theoretical Humanities* 7, no. 2 (2002) 17–25.

———. *Zoographies: The Question of the Animal from Heidegger to Derrida*. New York: Columbia University Press, 2008.

Caputo, John D. *The Prayers and Tears of Jacques Derrida*. Bloomington: Indiana University Press, 1997.

Cixous, Hélène, and Jacques Derrida. *Veils*. Stanford, CA: Stanford University Press, 2001.

Derrida, Jacques. *The Animal That Therefore I Am*. Translated by David Wills. New York: Fordham University Press, 2008.

———. "'Eating Well,' or the Calculation of the Subject." In *Points: Interviews 1974–1994*, edited by Elizabeth Weber and translated by Peggy Kamuf, 255–87. Stanford: Stanford University Press, 1995.

———. "A Silkworm of One's Own." In *Veils*, by Hélène Cixous and Jacques Derrida, 49–50. Stanford, CA: Stanford University Press.

George, Andrew. *The Epic of Gilgamesh*. London: Penguin, 2003.

Guerlac, Suzanne. "Derrida and His Cat: The Most Important Question." *Contemporary French and Francophone Studies* 16 (2012) 695–702.

Klangwisan, Yael. "Bereshît: Countersigning Maria O'Connor's Equus Ashes with Derrida's 'L'Animal.'" In *The Bible and Art: Perspectives from Oceania*, edited by Caroline Blyth and Nasili Vaka'uta, 255–87. London: Bloomsbury, 2017.

LaCocque, André. *The Trial of Innocence: Adam, Eve, and the Yahwist*. Eugene, OR: Cascade, 2006.

Moi, Toril. *Sexual/Textual Politics*. London: Routledge, 2008.

Renger, Almut-Barbara. *Oedipus and the Sphinx*. Chicago: University of Chicago Press, 2013.

Rilke, Rainer Maria. *Duino Elegies*. Translated by Stephen Cohn. Evanston, IL: Northwestern University Press, 1998.

———. *The Selected Poetry of Rainer Maria Rilke*. Edited and translated by Stephen Mitchell. New York: Vintage, 1989.

Rowe Terra S. "The Divinanimality of Lord Sequoia." In *Divinanimality*, edited by Stephen Moore, 109. New York: Fordham University Press, 2014.

Sartre, Jean-Paul. *Being and Nothingness: An Essay on Phenomenological Ontology*. Translated by Hazel Estella Barnes. London: Routledge, 2008.

Wood, David. "Thinking with Cats." In *Animal Philosophy*, edited by Peter Atterton and Matthew Calarco, 129–44. London: Continuum, 2004

7

Waterlings from Water

Exploring a Cosmological, Eschatological Reading of "Living Water" in John 4:4–42 amidst the Braided Rivers of Canterbury, Aotearoa New Zealand

Kathleen P. Rushton,
Nga Whaea Atawhai Sisters of Mercy

IN THIS CHAPTER I interpret the "living waters" of John 4:4–45 through the reading lens of the cosmological, eschatological framework of the prologue (1:1–18). My hope is to offer a scriptural voice among the many voices raised in Canterbury, Aotearoa New Zealand where water "rights," its use and storage are contested. My interpretation is set within contemporary approaches of ecological hermeneutics. However, I understand a cosmological framework, which incorporates ecological concerns, is necessary for John's gospel and for my earth-quake affected context of the city of Otautahi Christchurch.[1] I shall consider my context which influences my approach to water. Next, I shall explain my cosmological, eschatological methodology outlining how it links with Johannine symbolism. Then, living water is considered in the light of (i) Shechem having been an area of conflict related to water; (ii) an early Christian fresco, and (iii) the Jacob traditions and two terms used for water: "still water" as from a well (John 4:11–12 *phrear*) and "living water" as from a spring (vv. 6, 14 *pēge*). In the light of new insights that emerge and the interconnected hopes for ethical action in *this* world that underpin the Johannine eschatological, cosmological vision,

1. Between 4 September 2010 and 7 April 2012, this region experienced four major earthquakes and 10,292 aftershocks. See Rushton, "On the Crossroads," 57–72.

I shall then look briefly at the issue of groundwater and water as a human right locally and internationally.

The Braided Rivers and Plains of Canterbury

My reflection on "living water" in John 4, is influenced by my having lived most of my life at one or other end of the extensive Canterbury Plains, Aotearoa New Zealand across which flow braided rivers. Nowadays, I lose my bearings because the pine forests which lined parts of State Highway 1 have disappeared as have thousands of acres of crops and flocks of sheep. Now gigantic irrigators provide pasture for dairy herds.[2]

Over thousands of years, the greywacke rock of the Southern Alps, which stretch along the western boundary of the Canterbury Plains, has been ground down, washed out to sea, hardened and lifted up above the oceans many times. All the soluble materials have been removed so Canterbury's water is very pure.[3] In interconnected spaces, the waters move downhill. Some of this water surfaces as springs and rivulets which feed the braided rivers. The rest, as groundwater, moves towards the sea taking a century or more.[4] The groundwater-filled spaces are the habitat of and filtered by an estimated 500 species of minute invertebrate stygofauna.[5]

Cosmic Understandings of Water

The Canterbury Plains originated about 70–80 million years ago, when the Tasman Sea opened up in Gondwana Land and Aotearoa New Zealand moved out to sea.[6] The story of water, however, began about 13.7 billion years ago in the first fractions of the second after the Big Bang when

2. For photographs of braided rivers, dairying and a description of the journey from hardship and uncertainty to irrigation-led confidence and wealth in the regions surrounding my birth place, Ashburton, see Macfie, "Rivers of Gold."

3. See Clark, "Water Anguish," C5.

4. Jarvis, "Geopolitics of Groundwater," 437–71. Just 3 percent of the Earth's water is non-saline. Of this 3 percent, most is not in liquid form. Two-thirds are in solid form in glaciers, ice caps of polar regions, and high mountains. Of this 3 percent of freshwater (non-saline), a little more than 1 percent is liquid fresh—of this fresh water less than 3 percent is in rivers, swamps, and lakes; the other 97 percent of liquid fresh water is underground. See ibid., 437.

5. Clark, "Water Anguish," C5.

6. For an overview, see the helpful diagram, *The Press*, "The Creation of New Zealand." 10.

hydrogen nuclei emerged and eventually formed primal stars.[7] Millions of years later, oxygen emerged. When hydrogen and oxygen met finally in the folds of stellar remnants, water came into the Universe and with it new possibilities of creativity.[8]

Water enables the birth of the stars, contributes to the formation of planets, the forming and cooling of earth. Enveloped by water, Earth's creativity flourishes. In its vaporous state, water permeates the atmosphere. In its liquid state, water forms the clouds of the atmosphere, falls as rain and covers most of the earth with oceans. In its solid state, frozen water falls as snow and sleet, covers mountains and forms polar caps. Water permeates every cell of every living being. Water maintains life by moving nutrients and energy within each living cell and between the cells of a whole organism. Water washes all beings constantly. Humans, like other mammals, are about 70% water. Vital systems function because of water within each of the trillions of interconnected cells of the human body.[9] The interaction between the cellular and intercellular fluids allows wellbeing. The same life force enabled by water is replicated in every living being: plant, animal and human.

Use of Water Contested

In Canterbury, the desire for water for agricultural irrigation increases pressure on the rivers and groundwater aquifers for irrigation.[10] The lowering and polluting of the aquifers has an effect on the stygofauna.[11] The right to "living water" is contested. In 2010, the New Zealand government sacked the citizens elected ECAN (Environment Canterbury Regional Council) which was entrusted with environment responsibilities and had a crucial role in determining water allocation. The Environment Canterbury (Temporary Commissioners and Improved Water Management) Act 2010 installed unelected, government-appointed commissioners for a three year term after which there would be a return to democratically elected commissioners. This undemocratic arrangement was extended not only until 2016 but yet

7. Kandel, "Water and Cosmos," 39–63.

8. On the early universe and origins of water, see Ball, *Life's Matrix*. For an overview, see Gibler, *From the Beginning*, 3–11.

9. On the essential role of water in the human body, see Milani, *Biological Science*.

10. On the mistaken perception that ground water is a renewable resource, see Jarvis, "Geopolitics of Groundwater," 443.

11. Clark, "Water Anguish," C5.

again until 2019.[12] Here, as in the Samaria region where the story of Jesus and "living water" is set and elsewhere, conflict results over water.[13]

It is on the basis of this brief overview of a cosmological and contested understanding of water that I now turn to apply an eschatological, cosmological reading of aspects of the water motif in John's gospel.[14] The framework provided by the eschatological cosmology of the Prologue evokes biblical and Hellenistic cosmologies as well as biblical eschatologies. Further, the divine, the cosmic, the flesh (*sarx*) and "all things" (*panta*) are interconnected in this framework which functions as a lens through which to interpret the Gospel that follows. This interconnection in the prologue, as I have argued elsewhere, has the potential to resonate with readers informed by twenty-first century cosmologies and evolutionary biology.[15] Thus, possibilities are opened up to inspire transforming spiritualties which lead to ethical action in the face of the urgent ecological concerns of the present day.

My Eschatological, Cosmological Framework

The prologue of John is a cosmology which establishes a framework through which the rest of the Gospel is read. How, therefore, the genre of cosmology itself was most likely understood in its ancient context is essential for understanding the cosmological framework of the prologue and the Gospel that follows.[16] This is also necessary to counter anthropocentric and Christocentric interpretations which accentuate personal individual redemption and tend to separate this from creation and the cosmic.[17] My hermeneutical lens of an eschatological, cosmological framework is informed, first, by Rémi Brague whose study of ancient cosmologies traces "how the idea of the world, beginning with its Greek formulation as *kosmos*, implied a particular anthropology" which developed in Antiquity and the Middle Ages into a cosmological anthropology or an anthropological cosmology. This

12. For an overview, see Palmer, "Democracy Neglected," A19.

13. For chronological lists, timelines and maps on conflicts over water from 3000 BCE–2015 CE, see Gleick, "Water Conflict."

14. Koester describes the water motif as "like a stream on a hillside . . . readily conforming to the contours of the narrative through which it flows." Koester, *Symbolism*, 176. In this chapter, I am unable to deal with the wider Johannine water motif; see my unpublished paper, "Towards Reading 'Living Waters.'"

15. Rushton. "Cosmology of John," 137–45.

16. On the dangers of being anachronistic, see ibid., 138.

17. Habel, "An Ecojustice Challenge," 76–94.

connection was lost by western culture in the modern era. He speaks of the "totality" of "the *experienced cosmology* of pre-modern humanity" which: 1) articulates the link between cosmology and the human person; 2) considers "the world" as the resting place for humanity; 3) links cosmology to wisdom; and 4) leads to contemplation (*theōria*) as the precursor to ethical action.[18] Cosmology, in this sense, allows for reflection whereby humanity achieves what they are to become through wisdom: "a worldly wisdom."[19] Human action was believed to be related to the reality of the goodness and the beauty of the cosmos. Wisdom understood in this way is a "wisdom of the world which connected closely to contemplation (*theōria*), the precursor to ethical action.[20] There was a dimension, therefore, to ancient cosmology which saw correspondence between the physical world and the moral which led to ethics. Although Brague does not use the term, ancient cosmology was rhetorical because it functioned to advocate a particular ethic or way of seeing and being on the earth. In other words, there is reciprocity in the relationship between anthropology and cosmology.[21]

Second, my hermeneutical lens of an eschatological, cosmological framework is informed by biblical eschatologies, as explained by Donald Gowan, which promote "a worldly hope" for ethical action in *this* world through the transformation of human society, the human person and nature. I have attempted to bring together this overlooked ethical dimension of both cosmology and eschatology which underpins the Johannine *this* world theological vision.[22] Gowan suggests avoiding the term "eschatology" and rather using phrases like "promises concerning a better future" and "a future with significant discontinuities from the present."[23] In the interplay between the sense of radical wrongness and the radical changes,

18. Brague, *Wisdom*, 4–6, 228. See my "Cosmology of John," 139–43, for a fuller discussion of my approach. The connection between cosmology and anthropology links also with Elaine Wainwright's attention to the ecological texture of the biblical text. She argues that utilizing the category of habitat and the way this is encoded in the biblical text enables the interpreter to view the human and habitat as inseparable, see Wainwright, "Images," 280–304.

19. Brague, *Wisdom,* 2, 121.

20. Ibid., 121–26.

21. On ecological concerns at the expense of the human community, see Deane-Drummond, *Creation through Wisdom*, 144.

22. It is beyond the scope of this article to deal with the Johannine tradition in which two differing eschatological perspectives are integrated. On "divergent world-views *side by side* within the Gospel," see, Wahlde, "C. H. Dodd, the Historical Jesus," 150, 155. For a fuller discussion of hopes found in biblical eschatologies and ancient cosmology, see my "Implications of the Cosmology," 37–54.

23. Gowan, *Eschatology,* 1.

four types of hope for the future emerge, which I would understand as forming the biblical background and origins of what is called Johannine realized eschatology. There are:

1. hope for a restoration of the political, military and economic life of the people
2. hope for a more just and equitable kind of human society
3. hope for the transformation of the individual person
4. hope for the transformation of nature.[24]

Consequently, certain influences in the prologue have the potential to create new nuances in its eschatological cosmology which value *the present*, the *now* in *this world*, as the arena in which God's future is already present and underway.[25] The prologue sets up a framework of an eschatological cosmology which leads to ethical action to inspire a transforming spirituality and ethical action which values the materiality of Earth. The eschatological cosmology framework of the prologue alerts the reader to "the centrality of creation as the context from which the evangelist will tell his story of Jesus"[26] and is underpinned by an eschatology which "understands our human nature not only in terms of what we are, but of what we may be."[27]

For John Painter, the foundation of Johannine symbolism is in the creation of "all things" by the Logos, for the "world is a storehouse of symbols which can become bearers of the revelation if they are *seen* to point beyond themselves to the revealer and through him to God."[28] This symbolic function is dependent on how the human person sees the created element which in itself is important "because some aspect of it is applied analogically to that which it symbolizes."[29] Symbols, in this instance, the symbol of water, "force themselves on [the human person's] consciousness in [his or her] experience of the world."[30] Water, like other symbols, in John is universal because it is necessary for human existence and the search

24. Ibid., 2, names a threefold transformation: human society, 21–58; the human person, 59–96; and nature, 97–120. I follow Wahlde, "C. H. Dodd, the Historical Jesus," 151, who divides hope for human society into two categories.

25. My eschatological cosmology framework brings into focus certain terms which I explore elsewhere in a reflection upon the prologue. See my "The Cosmology of John 1:1–14."

26. Browne, "Creation's Renewal," 277.

27. Soskice, "Imago Dei," 296.

28. Painter, "Johannine Symbols," 40.

29. Ibid.

30. Ibid.

for life. Painter sees such symbols as being cosmic in origin as does Lee who talks of "its cosmic appeal."[31] Wai-Yee Ng argues that in the Gospel of John the water symbol must be interpreted in its multiple contexts and its multifold meanings expounded.[32] Water, then, is more than a symbol in John because in the cosmology of the prologue, the spiritual and physical are earthed for the Word takes on the flesh (*sarx*) of all living creatures and through the Word "all things" (*panta*), including water, come into being.[33] In considering the multiple contexts and multiple meanings of water, with which I began this paper, the play on words which Phyllis Trible captured in her translation of earth creature from the earth to preserve the link between *ādām* from *ādāmah* (Gen 2:7) is helpful.[34] She suggests "groundling from the ground" or "earthling from the earth." In a cosmological understanding of water, I suggest that we, and everything that is, are waterlings from water for as Linda Gibler summarizes: "Creation is water-drenched. All living beings on Earth are born of water—in oceans or ponds, within eggs, seeds or wombs."[35]

Background of Ancient Conflict

Samaria has been a region of conflict.[36] To Jesus's request for a drink, the woman, whom I shall call Photini,[37] replies: "How is it that you, a Jew, ask a drink of me, a woman of Samaria?" (John 4:9). Behind her words are centuries of hostile separation between their peoples. The spring-fed well of their common ancestor was to provide "living water" for all. Yet, over centuries land made valuable because of this water was held in tribal, or what now would be called private ownership.

31. Lee, "Quenching Thirst," 65–87.

32. Ng, *Water Symbolism*, 98.

33. On the cosmological understandings of *sarx* and *panta*, see my "The Cosmology of John 1:1–14," 146–50. On water being more than a symbol, see Ayre, "Water, More Than a Symbol," 49–61.

34. Trible, *God and the Rhetoric of Sexuality*, 76–78.

35. Gibler, *From the Beginning*, 2.

36. As Fitzmyer, explains in *Luke*, 829, the origins of the conflict between Samaritans and Jews is "shrouded in mystery and explained differently by each group . . . from Hellenistic time on the sharp division of Jews and Samaritans is clear: the Samaritans developed their own form of Pentateuch . . . their own liturgy . . . and their own liturgical literature in both Hebrew and Aramaic."

37. As in the Orthodox Liturgy on the Feast of St Photini and St. Phota, 26 February; see also Yamaguchi, *Mary and Martha*, 32–33; Westcott, *St. John*, 68, records that in later legends she was called Photina.

The ancient town of Sychar "near the plot of ground that Jacob had given to his son Joseph" (John 4:5) was called Shechem from the Hebrew: "I now give to you one portion (*shekem*) more than your brothers" (Gen 48:22; cf. 33:19; Josh 24:32). Some traditions tell of Jacob's peaceful coming to Shechem.[38] Others tell of livestock, property and trade leading to breakdowns in the relationships between his clan and the clan from whom he purchased the land. This region is dotted with natural aquifers deep under the Earth which surfaced in springs and met the needs of nomads.[39] Jacob bought a field which had a well or a spring or he may have dug a well. Genesis accounts, however, do not record that Jacob ever dug a well or gave a well to his sons. Jacob is recorded as having bought and then given Shechem to Joseph (Gen 33:19; 48:22) which is where Jacob's well was situated (John 4:5).[40] Nevertheless, at some stage, Jacob asserted his rights over this water source in a way which excluded others. In other words, Jacob's actions foreshadow today's practice: the privatization of water.

An Overflowing Well and Standing in Flowing Waters

One of the earliest themes in Christian art is the encounter between Jesus and Photini. The woman at the well became a symbol for baptism and the "living water" which Jesus promised.[41] Four representations, for example, are found in the ancient Christian cemeteries in Rome.[42] One of the least sophisticated images, and probably the earliest of these, is in the third-century Roman Catacomb of St. Callistus.[43] Both the figures of Jesus and the woman are symbolic. Without the well, it would be impossible to identify them. Photini is bucketing water from an *overflowing* well and standing in its *flowing* waters. What might the early Christians associated with the painting of this fresco have been evoking?

38. Biblical Shechem, 2 km east of Nablus and about 63 km north of Jerusalem, is near the archaeological site of Tell Balata, close to the entrance to a mountain pass between Mounts Gerizim and Ebal.

39. Murphy-O'Connor, *Holy Land*, 372–73; Frumkin, "Water-Supply Network," 267–77. For a modern map that shows Nablus to be at the conjunction of two groundwater resources, see Figure 3 in Zeitoun, "Environmental Geopolitics," 58.

40. Neyrey points out that the well in John 4:12 may be known as Jacob's well because it is in the territory of Jacob at Shechem, see Neyrey, "Jacob Traditions," 422.

41. Norfleete, *Woman at the Well*, 61. See 46–49, for illustrations.

42. Hill, *Johannine Corpus*, 157–58.

43. Level 2, area 1, cubiculum A3, south wall, east end. See Hill, *Johaninne Corpus*, 157. For a colored copy, see Bourguet, *Early Christian Art*, 31.

First, excavations of what may be Jacob's well show it was very deep so as to reach a hidden spring.[44] Early Christians seem to have known about the Jewish targumim and legends which tell of Jacob's well *flowing* as gift to offer life to all.[45] One tells of its water overflowing when Jacob removed its stone covering. According to another tradition, so much water was flowing from this well that it flowed into the wilderness to keep the people and their animals alive in their wandering. Traditions associate Jacob not with any particular well but with the travelling well tradition (see 1 Cor 10:4). When Jacob leaves his father's house "*the well went with him*." On another occasion, when he left Bethel, it recorded that he "*left the well*" there.[46]

Second, *flowing water* picks up on a significant textual factor in John 4 which is related to two different understandings of water. When Photini describes the well (*phrear*), the word means "still water" (vv.11–12) which had been separated from its source by being collected and stored in a cistern or pool. "Living water" was wild water from a river or spring. "Spring" (*pēgē*) is used twice (v.6) to refer to Jacob's well and while Jesus was sitting by this well, and again, when he spoke of "living water" (v.14).[47] This distinction, between these two types of water, is lost to those twenty-first-century readers who live in situations where access to water is through the conveniences of complex systems of plumbing and sanitation. The reality of the sources and materiality of water, which are hidden and unacknowledged by such people today, were known in ancient times as illustrated by Augustine's homily on John 4 preached in 407 CE:

> Water issuing from a spring is what is commonly called living water. Water collected from rain in pools and cisterns is not called living water. It may have originally flowed from a spring; yet if it collects in some place and is left to stand without any connection to its source, separated, as it were from the channel of the spring, it is not called "living water." Water is designated as "living" when it is taken as it flows. This is the kind of water that was in that fountain.[48]

44. Murphy-O'Connor, *Holy Land*, 387.

45. On stories and sources, see Neyrey, "Jacob Traditions," 419–37, especially 421–25. On the welling up of water and the well as a gift, see Neyrey, *Gospel of John*, 91; and see Neyrey, "Are You Greater," 106–12.

46. The traveling-well tradition is associated with Miriam in targumim on Num 21; see, Neyrey, "Jacob Traditions," 422.

47. On the rhetoric of these distinctions of water, see Sawicki, "Spatial Management," 15–18.

48. Augustine, *Tractates on the Gospel of John* 15.12, 15 (trans. Elowsky, 149–50).

When attention is given to the historical and hydrological context of this story, the distinctions between the two types of water, known and experienced in the dry arid land of its geographical setting new insights open up for present day readers. Jesus and Photini engage in an exchange which plays on this distinction known to both of them—the distinction between flowing water and standing water. Traditional interpretations make much of Photini's confusion. But, initially, to her, it is Jesus who is clearly confused. How can Jesus ask for "living water" (v10) when he is seated beside a well with "still water"? Having restored John 4 to its historical and hydrological context, I turn now to its cosmological setting.

"Experienced Cosmology" Leading to Wisdom

Alan Cadwallader exposes how Photini has been removed from the materiality of earth in "an overarching dualistic framework of earth and heaven" and how others read from the perspective of so much water yet omit her context.[49] The biblical imagery evoked by "living water" and the spring of water in John 4 are integral, as we have seen above, to the geography and climate of Samaria and wider the biblical regions.[50] Underground sources of water are valued because external sources are precarious. I seek to extend the materiality of water which Cadwallader highlights in order to draw attention to the three tiered ancient cosmology suggested by the grammar of phrases like "the fountains of the deep" (Gen 7:11; 8:2; Job 38:16) which fed the oceans. This understanding underpins the water imagery. The Deuteronomist saw Israel as a "land with flowing streams and underground waters welling up in valleys and hills" (Deut 8:7). God is the "fountain of living water" (Jer 17:13). The two understandings of water are contrasted as in "my people . . . have forsaken me, the fountain of living water, and dug out cisterns for themselves, cracked cisterns that can hold no water" (Jer 2:13). Springs are "abounding with water" (Prov 8:24); their "waters never fail" (Is 58:11); and they "gush forth" (Ps 104:10). The water Jesus promises in John 4:14 is described in terms of the leaping of (*hallomai*) something of life.[51]

49. Cadwallader, "Give the Girl a Drink," 97–100; for an earlier study on dualisms in John 4, see Moore, "Are the Impurities," 279–99.

50. The many aspects of water is beyond the scope of this paper; for a summary, see Ryken, *Dictionary of Biblical Imagery*, 929–32.

51. Usually applied to the quick, leaping movements of human beings (Acts 3:8; 14:10), see Moloney, *Gospel of John*, 123; Westcott, *St. John*, 70. In Koester, *Symbolism*, 191, this expression is used to refer to the effect of the Spirit on Old Testament characters (Judg 14:6; 15:14; 1 Sam 10:10; cf. Acts 2:38; 8:20; 10:45; 11:17; Heb 6:4).

Further, in ancient Mediterranean, as in biblical cosmology, human building and filling of houses "with wisdom" was a metaphor for cosmic creation.[52] In other words, human actions were used to explain the divine action and, vice versa, to underscore that the order inherent in the divine was to inform human order. In particular, water was often linked with wisdom and symbolic of Divine Wisdom (Prov 13:14; 18:4) which, in Israel, is concerned chiefly with the organization of the distribution of water and setting limits on chaotic waters as shown in Ps 104.[53] As Brague holds, there was a link between cosmology and anthropology which lead to a "worldly wisdom" which led to contemplation (*theōria*) and then to moral or ethical action. There was a correspondence between the physical world and the moral which led to ethics.

Releasing Living Water

By giving attention to both the materiality of water which arises from the harsh conditions of life in the arid land surrounding Shechem and the cosmology which is assumed in this story, the symbol of living water is released. Photini, too, is freed from interpreters who speculate about her morality but obscure her materiality and plight as a poor woman working as water carrier (John 4:7, 11, 15, 28) in an arid region carrying water over a great distance (v.8) for the benefit of others. According to Augustine:

> This is what she longed for, to lack nothing and to be spared her hard labor, because she was coming to that fountain day after day, burdened with that heavy load on her shoulders that was supposed to supply what she lacked . . . Her poverty obliged her to work beyond what her strength could handle.[54]

In her female role of water carrier, she is caught in a system which demands hard physical work.[55] This is the lot of poor women today.[56] The

52. Van Leeuwen, "Cosmos," 67–90.

53. Ibid., 70. Other examples include: Job 38:8a, 10–11; Ps 65:9–13; Jer 5:22; Prov 8:24, 27–29.

54. Augustine, *Tractates on the Gospel of John* 15.15, 17 (trans. Elowsky, 154).

55. Schrottoff, "The Samaritan Woman," 165–67; Peppard, *Just Water*, 179–80. The only commentary I have found that mentions she is poor because she draws water is Westcott, *St. John*, 68.

56. For examples, see Peacock. "Water of Struggle," 20–21, where he states that in Asia "to meet the needs of families an average a rural woman walks 14,000 kilometres a year just to fetch water."

encounter between this Jew and this Samaritan released water for the thirsty.[57] Photini responds to Jesus' presence and act of requesting. The water is freed from economic and legal ownership restrictions. Restrictions imposed are released. The universal human right of access to clean water takes precedence over private ownership.

Interconnected Hope

Attention to the cosmology of the text has released water from economic restrictions. This brings us now to the overlooked ethical dimension of both cosmology and eschatology which underpins the Johannine *this* world theological vision. I outlined above that I consider biblical "eschatology" to be concerned with "promises concerning a better future" and "a future with significant discontinuities from the present." I want now to return to four types of hope for the future which emerge in the interplay between the sense of radical wrongness and the radical changes which I would understand as forming the biblical background and origins of what is called Johannine realized eschatology. The first hope is for a restoration of the political, military and economic life of the people. The second hope is for a more just and equitable kind of human society. The third hope is for the transformation of the individual person, while the fourth hope is for the transformation of nature. To deal adequately with these interconnected hopes is beyond the scope of this chapter, but I shall look now briefly at some aspects of the "living water"—particularly that of the issues of groundwater and water as a human right.

Locally, in Canterbury, the recent attempt of the Ashburton District Council to sell Lot 9 which has resource consent to bottle 1.4 billion liters of artesian water each year to an overseas company caused such outrage and widespread opposition that the sale failed.[58] This controversy highlighted the fact that while this proposal concerned the largest volume of water yet to be taken, eleven other consents that allow water bottling in Canterbury already existed.[59] No register exists in this country of companies that have privatised water in this way. What I have sketched briefly here concerning drawing on aquifers for bottled water, and earlier in this chapter on irrigation for dairying, is a microcosm of what is happening internationally for, as I noted previously, over 97 percent of liquid fresh water is underground.[60]

57. Cadwallader, "Give the Girl a Drink," 107–10.

58. O'Neill, "40,000 Urge Council."

59. Mitchell, "Second Canterbury Property."

60. On bottled water, see Salzman, *Drinking Water*.

Todd Jarvis explains how groundwater as common property presents many challenges because of the difficulties with assessing its extent and boundaries. He points out that there is a "general lack of institutional capacity to accommodate groundwater management and governance at the international and local level."[61]

The underlying question here is whether water is a fundamental and universal human right which should be available to all at no charge, or whether water is a commodity able to be owned and traded for profit. In the mid-1990s, one of the loan conditions by which the county of Bolivia secured a development loan from the World Bank was that the water supply in several municipalities would be privatized.[62] Aguas del Tunari, a subsidiary of the huge global corporation Bechtel, with the support of the Bolivian dictatorship and its military enforcement, took over the management, distribution and pricing of the fresh water supply along with infrastructure repairs and development.[63] After days of peaceful protest in Cochabamba, a mountain town, a seventeen year old protester, Victor Hugo Daza was shot dead. Through the Internet, public global consciousness rallied. Christiana Peppard draws on this South American example to show how "water wars" will "shape the political and economic landscape of the twenty-first century."[64] Not long after, in 2002, the United Nations Committee on Economic, Social and Cultural Rights promulgated a non-binding General Comment which "affirmed that access to adequate amounts of clean water for personal and domestic use is a fundament human right of all people," adding that "the human right to water is indispensable for leading a life in human dignity. It is prerequisite for the realization of other human rights."[65]

The global outcry led Aguas del Tunari to withdraw from Bolivia because of damage to its public image. The Bolivian government was then sued by Bechtel for breach of contract. Similar international pressure led Bechtel to drop their lawsuit. In 2006, Evo Morales was elected the first indigenous president of Bolivia on a platform that included that the natural resources of Bolivia are for the Bolivian people not for transnational profit. In early 2010, he convened the "People's Conference on Climate Change and the Rights of Mother Earth." A declaration was issued which included that

61. Jarvis, "Geopolitics of Groundwater," 444–46; 457–62.

62. In what follows on the conflict over water in Bolivia, I draw on Peppard, *Just Water*, 46–48.

63. On corporations having undue influence at the UN and the World Bank, see Barlow, "Report—Our Right to Water," 12.

64. Peppard, *Just Water*, 47.

65. United Nations Department of Public Information, "International Year of Freshwater 2003."

"Mother Earth and the beings of which she is composed have . . . inherent rights" including "the right to water as a source of life." Later that year on 28 July, the United Nations passed a General Convention recognizing access to water and sanitation as universal human rights. The then Bolivian Ambassador to the United Nations introduced the motion. Two months later, the United Nations Human Rights Council went further in adopting a second resolution declaring that "The right to water and sanitation is a human right, equal to all other human right, which implies that is justifiable and enforceable."[66] In "Our Right to Water Report" Maude Barlow in her The Council of Canadians review of the intervening five years outlines "many signs of progress in the struggle to realise the human rights to water and sanitation" and sees good reasons for hope in three main areas: at the United Nations, inside governments and the courts, and against corporate control and abuse of water.[67] Much, however, remains to be done, as still at least 780 million people lack access to safe water. In describing the challenge ahead Barlow asserts: "Water will be nature's gift to humanity to teach us how to live more lightly on the Earth." She sees that the priorities ahead fall into three categories: 1. Use the recently recognized rights to water and sanitation to push governments and the courts; 2. Put human right to water and sanitation at the center of ecological struggle to protect water; and 3. Fight for a just global economy.[68] In his encyclical, *Laudato si'*, Pope Francis objects to the privatization and commodification of water and declared that access to safe, drinkable water is a basic and universal human right and a condition for the exercise of all other human rights.[69]

I Thirst

The interconnected hopes that underpin the Johannine theological visions resonate with brief glimpses I have sketched above of the hopes of people thirsting and acting together locally and internationally for ethical action in relation to "living water" known as groundwater and water as a human right. Water is coterminous with life. Water sustains all life. When thirst is concerned proprietary rights and separation must give way. Reading from the perspective of thirst, Jesus the fountain/spring of "living water" cries out in severe pain out just before his death: "I thirst" (19:28). This is the second

66. Barlow, "Report—Our Right to Water," 4.

67. Ibid., 5–9

68. Ibid., 14–18.

69. Francis, *Laudato si'*, paragraph 185; for an overview of Catholic Social Teaching on water as a right to life issue, see Peppard, *Just Water*, 52–67.

time in the gospel according to John, that Jesus is recorded to have spoken such words. The first time, as we have seen, was when he asked Photini for a drink (4:8).[70]

Conclusion for Waterlings from Water

Arguably the Johannine Christians and the later community or artist(s) of the fresco in the Catacomb of St Callistus knew not only the Jacob traditions of overflowing water but also, knew implicitly there was link between their cosmology (how they understood the world), and their theological anthropology (that is, how they understood their relationship to God and humanity). This knowledge led to a "worldly wisdom" which led to contemplation and thus to moral or ethical action. These early Christian communities, I would contend knew the interconnected hopes of biblical, eschatological, cosmology which value *the present*, the *now* in *this world*, as the arena in which God's future is already present and underway and in which they were to live ethically. Consequently, Photini is presented in this gospel and in the early third-century fresco as transcending the privatization of water because of the flowing water and the traditions of overflowing water in which she stands.

The link between water and creation, between descriptions of the eschatological restoration of Israel, is often connected with "idyllic descriptions of easily accessible water sources and dependable rain patterns"[71] (Isa 35:7; 41:18; 49:10; Zech 10:1). Evoked are the good and fertile land which has an abundant supply of water (Deut 8:7) and the experience of divine leadership during the wilderness wanderings. In addition, the motif of water in the wilderness (Exod 15:25; 17:1–6; Num 20:8–11) echoes the creation link to water. The connection between the providing of water and creation is found in John 4:10, 13–14 when Jesus speaks of himself as the divine water giver evoking these biblical motifs. The one drinking of the living water is transformed and becomes "a spring of water gushing up to eternal life" (John 4:14).

Water symbolism in John 4, which is derived from its historical, hydrological and cosmic origins in the arid context of the early Johannine hearers/

70. There is a further link between these incidents for Jesus is recorded as meeting with Photini "at the sixth hour" (usually translated as "noon") and this seems to be linked with the time of his crucifixion at "the sixth hour" (4:6; 19:14). And further, in 4:23, Jesus speaks of "the hour" thus foreshadowing "the hour" in which he "handed over the Spirit."

71. Klingbeil, "Water," 821.

readers, connects with readers today who informed by interconnections of twenty-first-century cosmologies of water and by evolutionary biology know themselves as waterlings from water in multiple contexts which have manifold meanings. The distinction between "still water" (John 4:11–12 *phrear*) and "living water" (vv. 6. 14 *pēge*) is applicable in the context of the Canterbury Plains of Aotearoa New Zealand. The debates rage between those who see it is their right to draw "living water" from the aquifers below the plains and those who advocate the storage of "still water" during times of plenty such as snow melt and flood-fed rivers. In addition, water is largely invisible for Canterbury users, and for the privileged of the world, because plumbing and sanitation infrastructure obscure the materiality and sources of water.[72] Privilege, too, masks the complexity and instant availability of how water flows out fresh and clean when a tap or shower is turned on.

Like ancient cosmologies, twenty-first-century cosmologies have a "worldly wisdom" of the interconnections of all things which could lead to contemplation and ethical, ecological action in the footsteps of biblical ancestors.[73] Living water—gift (4:10), wonder and necessity nurturing all interconnected life yet privatised, bottled and endangered. Jesus's cry: "I thirst" echoes through time. His sisters and brothers cry out: "I thirst." Those who have encountered the life-giving *flowing* waters which Jesus releases are summoned to respond to these cries. The ecological implications of this narrative are an ongoing work for Jesus's contemporary followers.

Bibliography

Augustine. "Tractates on the Gospel of John 15.12 and 15.15". In *John 1–10 Ancient Commentary on Scripture. New Testament, 4a*, edited by Joel C. Elowsky, 150. Downers Grove: InterVarsity, 2006.

Ayre, Clive W. "Water, More Than a Symbol." In *Water: A Matter of Life and Death*, edited by Norman Habel and Peter Trudinger. *Interface* 14, no. 1 (2011) 49–61.

Ball, Philip. *Life's Matrix: A Biography of Water*. Berkeley: University of California Press, 2001.

Barlow, Maude. "Report—Our Right to Water: Assessing Progress Five Years after the UN Recognition of the Human Rights to Water and Sanitation." http://canadians.org/publications/report-our-right-water-assessing-progress-five-years-after-un-recognition-human-rights.http://canadians.org/sites/default/files/publications/report-rtw-5yr-1115.pdf.

Bourguet, Pierre du. *Early Christian Art*. Translated by Thomas Burton. New York: Morrow, 1971.

72. Peppard, *Just Water*, 176–77.

73. For example, see Delio, *Unbearable Wholeness*.

Brague, Rémi. *The Wisdom of the World: The Human Experience of the Universe in Western Thought.* Translated by Teresa Lavender Faga. Chicago: University of Chicago Press, 2003.

Browne, Jeannine K. "Creation's Renewal in the Gospel of John." *CBQ* 72 (2010) 275–90.

Cadwallader, Alan. "'Give the Girl a Drink': Reading John 4 from a Dry, Parched Land." In *Water: A Matter of Life and Death*, edited by Norman Habel and Peter Trudinger. *Interface* 14, no. 1 (2011) 95–110.

Clark, Wallie. "Water Anguish." *The Press Christchurch*, 8 May 2010, Mainlander, C5.

Deane-Drummond, Celia E. *Creation through Wisdom: Theology and the New Biology.* Edinburgh: T. & T. Clark, 2000.

Delio, Ilia. *The Unbearable Wholeness of Being: God, Evolution, and the Power of Love.* Maryknoll, NY: Orbis, 2013.

Fitzmyer, Joseph A. *The Gospel according to Luke (I–IX).* AB 28. Garden City, NY: Doubleday, 1981.

Frumkin, Amos. "The Water-Supply Network of Samaria-Sebaste." In *The Aqueducts of Israel. Journal of Roman Archaeology Supplementary Series*, edited by David Amit, et al., 46:267–77. Ann Arbor: University of Michigan Press, 2002.

Gibler, Linda. *From the Beginning to Baptism: Scientific and Sacred Stories of Water, Oil, and Fire.* Collegeville, MN: Liturgical, 2010.

Gowan, Donald E. *Eschatology in the Old Testament.* 2nd ed. Edinburgh: T. & T. Clark, 2000.

Gleick, Peter. "Water Conflict." http://worldwater.org/water-conflict/. Accessed 11 August 2016.

Habel, Norman C. "An Ecojustice Challenge: Is Earth Valued in John 1?" In *The Earth Story in the New Testament*, edited by Norman C. Habel and Vicki Balabanski, 76–94. Earth Bible 5. Sheffield: Sheffield Academic, 2002.

Hill, Charles E. *The Johannine Corpus in the Early Church.* Oxford: Oxford University Press, 2004.

Jarvis, Todd. "Geopolitics of Groundwater." In *A History of Water*, edited by Terje Tvedt et al., II/3:437–71. New York: Tauris, 2011.

Kandel, Robert. "Water and Cosmos: From the Big Bang to the Creation of Water and Earth." In *A History of Water*, edited by Terje Tvedt and Richard Coopey, II/1:39–63. New York: Tauris, 2011.

Klingbeil, Gerald A. "Water." In *The New Interpreter's Dictionary of the Bible*, edited by Katharine Doob Sakenfield, 5:818–21. Nashville: Abingdon, 2009.

Koester, Craig R. *Symbolism in the Fourth Gospel: Meaning Mystery, Community.* 2nd ed. Minneapolis: Fortress, 2003.

Lee, Dorothy. "Quenching Thirst: The Symbol of Living Water." In *Flesh and Glory: Symbol, Gender, and Theology in the Gospel of John*, 65–87. New York: Crossroad, 2002.

Macfie, Rebecca. "Rivers of Gold: Water Is Creating Lots of Dairy Millionaires, But at What Cost to Our Environment?" *New Zealand Listener*, May 22, 2014.

Milani, Jean P. et al., eds. *Biological Science: A Molecular Approach.* Lexington, MA: Heath, 1990.

Mitchell, Charlie. "Second Canterbury Property with Water Extraction Rights up for Sale." *Stuff*, April 6, 2016. http://www.stuff.co.nz/business/78561853/second-group-shopping-pure-canterbury-water-to-bottling-companies. Accessed 11 August 2016.

Moloney, Francis F. *The Gospel of John*, Sacra Pagina 4. Collegeville, MN: Liturgical, 1998.

Moore, Stephen. "Are the Impurities in the Living Water that the Johannine Jesus Dispenses? Deconstructionism, Feminism, and the Samaritan Woman." In *The Interpretation of John*, edited by John Ashton, 279–99. 2nd ed. Edinburgh: T. & T. Clark, 1997.

Murphy-O'Connor, Jerome. *The Holy Land: An Oxford Archaeological Guide from Earliest Times to 1700*. 4th ed. Oxford: Oxford University Press, 1998.

Neyrey, Jerome H. "'Are You Greater Than Our Father Jacob?': Jesus and Jacob in John 1:51 and 4:4–26." In *The Gospel of John in Cultural and Rhetorical Perspective*, 87–122. Grand Rapids: Eerdmans, 2009.

———. *The Gospel of John*. New Cambridge Bible Commentary. Cambridge: Cambridge University Press, 2007.

———. "Jacob Traditions and the Interpretation of John 4:10–26." *CBQ* 41 (1997) 419–37.

Norfleete, Janeth Day. *The Woman at the Well: Interpretation of John 4:1–42 in Retrospect and Prospect*. Leiden: Brill, 2001.

Ng, Wai-Yee. *Water Symbolism in John: An Eschatological Interpretation*. Studies in Biblical Literature 15. New York: Lang, 2001.

O'Neill, Helena. "40,000 Urge Council to Drop Water Deal." *Stuff*, June 30, 2016. http://www.stuff.co.nz/the-press/news/mid-canterbury-selwyn/81629782/40000-urge-council-to-drop-ashburton-water-deal. Accessed 11 August 2016.

Palmer, Geoffrey. "Democracy Neglected." *The Christchurch Press*, 21 December, 2012, A19. http://www.legislation.govt.nz/bill/government/2015/0060/15.0/d56e2.html. Accessed 11 August 2016.

Painter, John. "Johannine Symbols: A Case Study in Epistemology." *Journal of Theology for Southern Africa* 86, no. 6 (1979) 26–41.

Peacock, Philip. "Water of Struggle—Water of Life." *Journal of Theologies and Cultures in Asia* 11 (2012) 11–29.

Peppard, Christiana Z. *Just Water: Theology, Ethics, and the Global Water Crisis*. Maryknoll, NY: Orbis, 2014.

Pope Francis. *Laudato si' On Care for Our Common Home: An Encyclical Letter on Ecology and Climate Change*. Strathfield, NSW: St Pauls, 2015.

The Press. "The Creation of New Zealand." *Your Weekend*, 3 October 2009, 10.

Rushton, Kathleen P. "The Implications of the Cosmology of the Prologue for Johannine Eschatology." *InterfaceTheology* 1, no. 1 (2015) 37–54.

———. "On the Crossroads between Life and Death: Reading Birth Imagery in John in the Earthquake Changed Regions of Otautahi Christchurch." In *Bible, Borders, Belonging(s): Engaging Readings from Oceania*, edited by Jione Havea et al., 57–72. Atlanta: SBL, 2014.

———. "The Cosmology of John 1:1–14 and Its Implications for Ethical Action in this Ecological Age." *Colloquium* 45, no. 2 (2013) 137–53.

———. "Towards Reading 'Living Waters.' Unpublished paper given at Aotearoa New Zealand Association of Biblical Studies Conference. 11 December 2012.

Ryken, Leland, et al. *Dictionary of Biblical Imagery*. Downers Grove, IL: InterVarsity, 1998.

Salzman, James. *Drinking Water: History*. London: Overlook Duckworth, 2013.

Sawicki, Marianne. "Spatial Management of Gender and Labor in Greco-Roman Galilee." In *Archaeology and The Galilee: Texts and Contexts in the Graeco-Roman and Byzantine Periods*, edited by Douglas R. Edwards and C. Thomas McCollough, 7–27. Atlanta: Scholars, 1997.

Schrottoff, Luise. "The Samaritan Woman and the Notions of Sexuality in the Fourth Gospel." In *"What is John?,"* edited by F. F. Segovia, 2:157–81. Atlanta: Scholars, 1998.

Soskice, Janet Martin. "Imago Dei and Sexual Difference: Toward an Eschatological Anthropology." In *Rethinking Human Nature: A Multidisciplinary Approach*, edited by Malcolm A. Jeeves, 295–306. Grand Rapids: Eerdmans, 2011.

Trible, Phyllis. *God and the Rhetoric of Sexuality*. London: SCM, 1992.

United Nations Department of Public Information. "International Year of Freshwater 2003 Backgrounder: The Right to Water." February 2003. Doc. No. DPI/2293F. http://www.un.org/events/water/TheRighttoWater.pdf.

United Nations Office of the High Commissioner for Human Rights. "General Comment No. 15 'The Right to Water' (Arts. 11 and 12 of the Covenant)." www.refworld.org/pdfid/4538838d11.pdf.

Van Leeuwen, Raymond C. "Cosmos, Temple, House: Building and Wisdom in Mesopotamia and Israel." In *Wisdom Literature in Mesopotamia and Israel*, edited by Richard J. Clifford 67–90. Leiden: Brill, 2007.

Wahlde, Urban C. von. "C. H. Dodd, the Historical Jesus, and Realized Eschatology." In *Engaging with C. H. Dodd on the Gospel of John: Sixty Years of Tradition and Interpretation*, edited by Tom Thatcher and Catrin H Williams, 149–62. Cambridge: Cambridge University Press, 2013.

Wainwright, Elaine M. "Images, Words and Stories: Exploring their Transformative Power in Reading Biblical Texts Ecologically." *BibInt* 20 (2012) 280–304.

Westcott, B. F. *The Gospel according to St. John*. London: Murray, 1903.

Yamaguchi, Satoko. *Mary and Martha: Women in the World of Jesus*. Maryknoll, NY: Orbis, 2002.

Zeitoun, Mark. "Environmental Geopolitics and Hydro-Hegemony: The Case of Palestine and Israel." In *A History of Water*, edited by Terje Tvedt et al., 3:49–77. New York: Tauris, 2011.

8

God So Loved the Cosmos

Stephen Pattemore,
Bible Society of New Zealand

> For God so loved the *kosmos* that he gave his only Son, so that everyone who believes in him may not perish but may have eternal life.
>
> —John 3:16, NRSV (modified)

That God's love for the κόσμος (*kosmos*, world) in John 3:16 can and should be read as referring to divine love, not just for humanity, but for the whole created order, is taken by many ecologically-sensitive Christians as self-evident. However, there are many other Christians, and in particular evangelicals, who reject such an interpretation, because it appears to challenge the anthropocentric theology of salvation, for which John 3:16 is the widely recognized and much loved summary. In what follows, I hope to argue for the broadest interpretation of *kosmos* in this verse. But it should be clear that I am not throwing stones from afar. I live in this particular glasshouse. I am arguing from my own location within the evangelical corner of the Christian world. I take seriously the concerns regarding this key text because I believe its interpretation has important consequences. There are consequences for evangelical Christians if this central "salvation" text can be seen to have implications for the world as a whole, because it then locates care of the environment as a central Christian occupation, rather than a peripheral and optional concern. And this in turn has consequences for the ecological movement, and for the earth itself, if evangelical Christians were to become more active in fulfilling the mandate "to serve and to guard" the earth (Gen 2:15)—and most particularly so in those parts of the developing world where the evangelical church is strong and growing and the ecological crisis is most acute. These are hope-full consequences which, I believe, amply justify a little exegetical effort.

The Problem Revisited

I have more than a casual interest in this topic, however. There is a story to be told, which like all good tales has a beginning and middle, though I doubt if it yet has an ending.

My interest in reading John 3:16 ecologically began many years ago. I had invited a fresh-water ecologist friend to speak at my home church—an independent, middle-of-the-road evangelical congregation—about the Christian responsibility to care for the world around us. Unfortunately, I wasn't there at the time, and returned to find something of a controversy because the aforesaid ecologist had suggested in the course of his sermon that John 3:16 affirmed God's love for the entire created order. This seemed to have offended the anthropocentric soteriology of some people in the church. I was rather bemused by this reaction because, although I hadn't thought about this verse previously as a "green text," my instinctive response was "well, yes, of course."

A year or so later I was asked to present a keynote paper at the Society of Biblical Literature's Bible Translation section, on "Relevance Theory and Biblical Exegesis."[1] Among the several passages that I treated by way of example, I decided to look in more depth at John 3:16 to find out whether the freshwater ecologist had good grounds for his assertion or whether the congregation was right to have serious doubts. My conclusion, which I will rehearse briefly in a moment, was to support the ecologist. However, the principal respondent to the paper at SBL, Professor Julius Wong Loi Sing of Moody Theological Seminary, thought otherwise. He returned a largely negative verdict on my conclusion. Beyond the usual thinking-on-your feet rebuttal, I didn't follow up the critique at the time but the issue of whether or not God, according to John 3:16, loved the *kosmos* has continued to simmer at the back of my mind. So, last year I wrote to my respondent, who graciously provided me with a written copy of his response at SBL. Professor Wong Loi Sing's criticism of my treatment of John 3:16 was good-natured, but included some serious exegetical considerations. Prejudicial bias regarding either methodology or subject matter, however, did not play a part.

1. The SBL Annual Meeting in New Orleans, November 2009.

Julius is open to and interested in Relevance Theory, and is committed to sustainable development and living off the grid! His substantive critiques were not knee-jerk reactions but were based on exegesis of the text. And so I am now able to go back to my own exegesis, and include a consideration of his most telling objections—namely suppression and prolepsis.

But first, let me consider an objection that I believe was behind the controversy in my church and which was made explicit, albeit tongue-in-cheek, by Professor Wong Loi Sing. It is that John 3:16 is a *public* text. It has a history of interpretation and a sociology of contemporary use in the church which almost frees it from the bounds of John's discourse. It is viewed something like the tablets of the law, written by the very finger of God and descended directly from the divine, or like Melchizedek, to be without contextual mother and father. Barbara Dancygier has argued that "Once the text becomes a shared cultural artefact it participates in the system of distributed cognition and is no longer treated as one speaker's communicative contribution."[2] I accept this as a statement of fact, but not that it represents prohibition against re-examination. One task of responsible scholarship is to continue to probe, to ask whether we might possibly have been wrong in our understanding, even on the most precious of texts. Whether we can change popular perception, or are fated to remain a voice at the margins, is another matter.

Relevance Theory and Biblical Exegesis

Relevance Theory (RT) was the real focus of interest at the New Orleans SBL session, and my application of it to support ecological readings of the Bible was merely by way of example. The tables are now turned and the focus of this present article is on the understanding of John 3:16 in multiple contexts. It may therefore be helpful to provide a short description of RT and its hermeneutical implications to highlight its particular usefulness.[3]

Relevance Theory is a pragmatic, cognitive explanation of human communication.[4] In communicating we do use grammatical and syntactical codes but, the results obtained when we decode a text are subjected to interpretation based on the extensive use of inference. Thus, the text of a message interacts with its context to prompt the audience towards the

2. Dancygier, *The Language of Stories*, 18.

3. The topic is treated in much more detail in Pattemore, *The People of God in the Apocalypse*; and Pattemore, *Souls under the Altar*.

4. The primary source is Sperber and Wilson, *Relevance: Communication and Cognition*, hereafter referred to as *Relevance*.

meaning communicated. This process of searching for meaning is driven by the desire to find the communication *relevant*. We are programmed, says RT, to understand messages by interpreting them in contexts that provide the best or most likely set of useful ideas. These contexts are sets of ideas that we already hold to be true or probably true. The sum of such ideas is our *cognitive environment*. An idea communicated is more *relevant* if it has lots of useful implications (called *cognitive* or *contextual effects*) for the listener, which may provide new information, or may strengthen, modify or negate information the listener already has. The communication is also more relevant if it requires less mental *processing effort* to understand. A communication is *optimally relevant* when it is worth the listener's effort to process it, and it is the most relevant text that could have been generated consistent with the speaker's abilities and preferences. When we receive an intentional message, we assume that there are good ideas that we can access for an acceptable amount of thinking.

These apparently common-sense ideas, carefully applied, prove helpful in understanding meanings communicated by ancient biblical texts. Relevance Theory is a cognitive theory: it focuses on what takes place in the minds of the communication partners. In particular, context—including co-text, intertext, and the context of situation—only influences communication to the extent that it influences the cognitive state of the communication partners. Communication aims to prompt the receiver to derive *cognitive effects* from the interaction of the text of the communication with his/her existing cognitive environment. So, RT is particularly sensitive to the context within which interpretation takes place. Relevance Theory has been accused by detractors of opposite persuasions of, on the one hand, supporting the post-modern destabilization of meaning, and on the other, of indulging the "intentional fallacy!" It does neither. It does not prescribe how we *ought* to understand texts, but explains how, in a given set of circumstances, an audience reaches a particular interpretation. Applied to biblical text, it has the potential to help us determine how the original audience would have understood a text, within their world, but also how a particular (historical or modern) reader will read it within the horizons of their own assumptions.

Treating texts as intention-laden communication is sometimes seen to conflict with a dominant assumption of contemporary literary criticism, namely that the author's context and intentions are inaccessible and unnecessary to interpretation.[5] However, the physical absence of a *contemporary*

5. See, for example, Ricoeur's "threefold semantic autonomy" of the text: Ricoeur, *Interpretation Theory*, 30; *Hermeneutics and the Human Sciences*, 145. See also Vanhoozer, *Biblical Narrative in the Philosophy of Paul Ricoeur*, 109n7.

author is clearly no barrier to the description of a mutual cognitive environment for author and audience. And neither is the absence of an *ancient* author an insuperable obstacle. As Fowler points out:

> True, old assumptions may be forgotten or unobvious. But while domains of assumption have changed in numerous ways, they have not changed beyond recognition. It is not in principle a hopeless task to learn enough to make sound inferences from the assumptions formerly taken to be optimally relevant.[6]

Gibbs notes that the attribution of intentions is a normal part of the human understanding process and goes on to argue that the same applies to the interpretation of texts and that there is no reason why the author's intentions should be either totally unrecoverable or irrelevant.[7].

But RT does not guarantee the recovery of the author's intended meaning. There is a double (cooperative) responsibility for meaning as the author must use clues that will stimulate the audience to deduce her intentions, but a given audience will choose their own assumptions to use.[8] The original audience of a biblical text will interpret the text using assumptions which are presumably close to those the author has guessed are available to them, in order to determine the author's informative intentions. However, when later audiences use *their* own cognitive environments, unconnected to the author, there is no guarantee that they will recover the author's intended meaning. The more you are removed in time, language and culture from the original context, the less confidence you can have that the immediately intuited meaning will reflect that read by the first audience. This will not diminish the importance of the search for relevance by the audience, but it will mean a progressive loss in confidence that the derived meaning in any way represents the author's intentions. Both naive and "interested" interpretations of the Bible say more about the readers' cognitive environment than about the author's meaning. Nevertheless, it is the task of scholars to sift contextual assumptions and try to establish both what was originally communicated and what different modern audiences read from the same text, a task guided both consciously and subconsciously by the search for relevance.

In the case of our focal text, John 3:16, RT will helpfully guide the search for the likely meaning in the original context, a meaning which I will argue includes the widest interpretation of the word *kosmos*, the object of

6. Fowler, "A New Theory of Communication," 17.

7. Gibbs, *Intentions in the Experience of Meaning*, 5, 15, 234–72.

8. Sperber and Wilson, *Relevance*, 43, 60.

God's love. But RT will also contribute towards an understanding of why some contemporary audiences do not hear it this way and what might be done about it.

Kosmos in John 3:16

And so, to John 3:16. Is it credible, in line with the author's narrative, to take this to refer to God's love for the entire universe, rather than just humankind? Commentators, on the whole, either ignore this issue, or assume without question that only humanity is intended, often on the basis of a lexicographic approach, in which they determine the sense of a word through a prior (though often non-explicit) *interpretation* of particular verses, and then use that sense to interpret the immediate verse![9] BAGD lists eight different senses of the word *kosmos*, beginning with "adornment," but including the universe, the earth, all of humanity, and humanity apart from God. The UBS Handbook on the Letters of John notes five different senses of *kosmos* covering much the same ground, including the typically Johannine negative meaning of that which is at enmity with God.[10] In a complex situation like this, the assumptions which the interpreter (commentator, dictionary maker) brings to the text will influence how they read the word in each context. Many of the passages assigned to "the world of humanity" in BAGD could readily bear the sense of *kosmos* as either physical location or as the object of God's light and love and salvation.[11] Even passages talking about the "sin of the world" (John 1:29; Matt 18:7; 1 John 2:2) could refer to sin within the created order, originating from a human source. Relevance Theory allows us to cut through some of this circular reasoning. The audience does not need to access a "different meaning" of the word *kosmos* but to extend or modify their existing default understanding of it, as they read or hear. An author's choice of a particular word is not so much a matter of

9. Westcott, *John*, 55: "loved all humanity considered apart from Himself"; Morris, *John*, 229: "God's love is wide enough to embrace all mankind"; Beasley-Murray, *John*, 51: "the love of God for a disobedient world"; Köstenberger, *John*, 35: "John uses the word κόσμος (*kosmos*, world) seventy-eight times in his Gospel. The expression can mean "physical universe" (1:9,10) or "a large number of people (12:19). Most characteristically, however, the term refers to sinful humanity (e.g. 3:16)." Keener, *John*, 329, probably most clearly illustrates a lexicographic approach, beginning, "The term κόσμος can refer to the universe, but this is not John's usage." See, however, Morris's helpful Additional Note, mentioned below, and Brown's Appendix I. 7, Brown, *John I–XII*, 508–9.

10. Haas et al., *A Translator's Handbook on the Letters of John*, 57.

11. The former might include 1 Cor 1:27; 4:14; Jas 2:5; 1 John 4:1,3; 2 Cor 1:12; 2 Pet 2:5;3:6. The latter, Matt 5:4; John 3:16,17; 4:42; 8:12; 9:5; 12:47; 17:6.

selecting from a number of possible senses, but using the lexical item to construct an ad-hoc concept which the audience is expected to interpret on-the-fly.[12]

Relevance Theory requires us to ask two distinct questions: What assumptions would the audience have brought to the text? And how does the text itself progressively work on and modify those assumptions? The first of these begs another question: Who is the intended audience?

I will shortcut a long discussion on the audience of John's gospel by quoting two writers over fifty years apart. C.H. Dodd held that:

> . . . the evangelist has in view a non-Christian public to which he wishes to appeal . . . the gospel could be read intelligently by a person who started with no knowledge of Christianity beyond the minimum that a reasonably well-informed member of the public interested in religion might be supposed to have by the close of the first century, and Christian ideas are instilled step by step . . . he is thinking . . . not so much of Christians who need a deeper theology, as of non-Christians who are concerned about eternal life.[13]

While more recently, Richard Bauckham has said,

> Read sequentially, the Gospel leads its readers and hearers progressively into a greater understanding of its themes by initiating them step by step into its symbolic world . . . I am also now inclined to think that its intended readership includes interested non-Christians . . . It is noteworthy that most of the Gospel's major symbolic images come from the common experience of all people of the time . . . It begins to look as though the Fourth Gospel envisages a wider readership than perhaps any other New Testament text does.[14]

I will assume, then, that the argument would have been understandable by an educated Greek speaker of the first century, without invoking specifically *Christian*, or even more specifically *Johannine* assumptions. What prior understandings of the concept *kosmos* would the author have presumed of such an audience? The evidence presented in lexicons suggests that rarely, and then only in later texts, is *kosmos* open to the narrower

12. See Green, "Lexical Pragmatics," 799–812.

13. Dodd, *Interpretation of the Fourth Gospel*, 8–9.

14. Bauckham, *The Testimony of the Beloved Disciple*, 120–23. There is general support for Bauckham's view in Trebilco, *Early Christians at Ephesus*, 237–40.

sense of "humanity."[15] The dominant understandings are the original "order, adornment" and thence "world order, universe." And the sense of *kosmos* as the world of humanity opposed to God, or "this present world regarded as the kingdom of evil" are in fact ad-hoc concepts in the Johannine writings, which become stabilized in those circles by repetition. It seems clear then that the most readily accessible assumptions connected with the word *kosmos* have to do with order and in particular the ordered universe.[16]

But what of the text of John's gospel itself? How might the reader's starting assumptions be used or modified as the reading/hearing proceeds? If the gospel is a single composition (and certainly for the early part of the gospel this is hardly controversial), the author likely uses *kosmos* in 3:16 assuming that its previous usage in chapter 1 forms part of the cognitive environment. John 1 from its opening phrase assumes Genesis 1 as a context for interpretation. This is reinforced when the author asserts the agency of the Word in the creation of "all things" (John 1:3) and speaks of light shining in the darkness (John 1:5; cf. Gen 1:3,4). The Word/light is then described as "coming into the *kosmos*" (John 1:9) and the following verse goes on to relate the Word/light to the *kosmos* in three further ways: he was *in* the *kosmos*, the *kosmos* came into being through him, the *kosmos* did not know or recognize him. In the cognitive environment created by the first few verses of the chapter, with the creation account of Genesis 1 prominent and accessible, the first three of these occurrences of *kosmos* default naturally and without undue processing to the readily available sense of the "ordered universe" or the "created order."[17] For the last of the four however, the processing effort for this equation is raised. How can the non-human part of the created order know or not know? This is not an insuperable barrier, but the fact that the subject of the verb "to know" is usually human may overlay the understanding of *kosmos* and create the ad-hoc concept of the world of humanity. The following verse may exercise some retrospective strengthening of this interpretation. "His own" clearly narrows the range of humanity yet further to the Jewish people. Yet, by the very nature of an ad-hoc concept, this does not eliminate the wider sense of *kosmos* in vv. 9,

15. BAGD lists a couple of obscure references in the pseudo-Sibyllines (date unknown but probably later than the NT), one from a fragment of Philo in Eusebius and two from Wisdom (2.24; 14.14; both of which could mean the earth rather than humanity). LSJ has only biblical references for "men in general, the world as estranged from God by sin . . . this present world regarded as the kingdom of evil."

16. See also the very helpful discussion in Morris's Additional Note B, "The World" (Morris, *John*, 126–28).

17. Genesis 1, LXX, does not use *kosmos*, but it is a natural equivalent of "the heavens and the earth".

10a, 10b. In fact, this movement from a "cosmic" to a human context, and then to a discrimination among humans, reflects the overall movement of the chapter. The Word is in the beginning, is God, is active in the creation of all things, comes into and is located within the created order—and then is either accepted and believed, or rejected by groups within humanity, with consequences following. The chapter concludes with the responses of very specific named people.

Chapter 3 evokes the cognitive environment of Chapter 1 in many ways. Nicodemus acknowledges that Jesus is "a teacher who has come from God" (3:2 cf. 1:6) and that his acts reveal the presence of God (3:2 cf. 1:1,14). Being born of flesh is contrasted with being born of the Spirit (3:6 cf. 1:12–13). The Son of Man has descended from heaven (3:13, cf. 1:18) Nicodemus and his company are among those who refuse to accept the verbal witness of Jesus (3:4, 12 cf. 1:11). And later, light and darkness form an important contrast (3:19–21 cf. 1:4,5,7–9). It is therefore a context where John 1, and behind that, Genesis 1, are readily accessible.

John 3:16 begins with the word οὕτως (*houtōs*), usually translated "so," which is often assumed to carry the implication that we are about to be told either in what way, or how much, God loved the *kosmos*. Gundry and Howell have argued, however, that *houtōs* "is best seen as functioning retrospectively . . . God loved the world by lifting Jesus on a cross as Moses lifted up the serpent in the wilderness (Num 21:4–9)."[18] It is one of Wong Loi Sing's substantive arguments that the effect of this retrospective reference on the progressive understanding of the significance of *kosmos* is that it blocks or suppresses access to the primeval created order as a referent. In verses 14–15

> . . . the strong signal of "world as created order" is now associated with a desert scene where snake-bitten people, humanity, is foregrounded. Snakes, part of the created order, and deserts do not benefit from God's or Moses' actions. The anaphoric reference to a world made up of bitten people reduces the activation of John 1, from a cosmic world to a world made up of snakes and deserts. God pitied that human condition.[19]

Let us assume that Gundry and Howell are right (though I suspect there may be arguments against). The immediately preceding passage may clearly influence interpretation whether or not οὕτως grammatically signals it. But does the objection therefore follow? I don't think so.

18. Gundry and Howell, "The Sense and Syntax of John 3:14–17," 24–39.

19. Wong Loi Sing, Response to Stephen Pattemore, private communication.

The "world of bitten people . . .of snakes and deserts" which is thus evoked is itself strongly intertextual with the primeval world which John 1 has made prominent to the audience. In the Genesis narrative, the world created by God has indeed undergone a change, described in Genesis 3. Not only humanity, but snakes and the earth itself are affected: enmity between snakes and people, and unproductiveness for the land. However we may want to qualify our understanding of Genesis 3 in the light of evolutionary history (and I certainly do) it is a coherent and important part of the development of the narrative which would have been assumed by any first -century person who was familiar with the Hebraic primeval story. What is more, the disquiet expressed by many in my evangelical church congregation to my friend's initial sermon stems from their belief that one of the fundamental tenets of *evangelical* theology is that all that is wrong with the universe is traceable to the interaction of the snake and the primeval couple. So, if anything, the reference to snakes and wilderness *strengthens* the sense that God's saving action is motivated by a love for the entire created order, both (primarily) for a first audience uninformed by the long history of evolutionary struggle and (incidentally) for an evangelical reader with a biblicist theology.

Therefore, when verse 16 opens "God so loved the *kosmos* that he gave his only Son . . ." there is plenty of reason why the sense of *kosmos*, as the created order, should be the most readily accessible interpretation, producing good cognitive effects. Genesis 1 repeatedly records God's assessment of the creation as "good" and finally "very good." And John 1 has affirmed the coming of the Word as light into the sphere of the created world. Even when John 3 goes on to talk about "those who believe" and "those who do not believe," this narrowing from a cosmic to a human focus precisely reflects the movement of thought in chapter 1. God and the Word have created and yet are present in the universe, bringing light. Yet it is the world of humanity that is faced with the challenge of a response to this movement of God—to believe or not to believe.

It may be argued that the object of the verb ἀγαπάω (*agapaō*, love) is usually either people or God. This is true, statistically, but there are plenty of examples in both the NT and the LXX where the object is something else. There is no prior use at all in John, but a few verses later (3:19) people are said to love darkness. There does not appear to be a rule which states that the object of *agapaō* must be personal.[20]

The developing context of the early chapters of John provides credible grounds for understanding the entire created order as the object of God's

20. Apart from many abstract concepts (righteousness, justice, evil, violence), the object is the house of the Lord in Ps 26:8, Mt. Zion in Ps 78:68, and Jerusalem in Ps 122:6.

love in 3:16. Wong Loi Sing, however, argued that prolepsis played an important role: that our text, indeed the whole gospel, may have been read many times, and that on recursive reading the restricted (anthropocentric) and decidedly negative senses of *kosmos* which are found later in the gospel would have led the audience to reject the broader sense here.[21] I readily accept the role of later parts of the text to influence the meaning derived in subsequent readings of the earlier part.[22] By the time readers or listeners get to the end of John's gospel, they will have multiple possibilities available to their cognitive processes regarding the word *kosmos*. But I would argue that these do not all push the interpreter in one direction. They continue to be varied throughout the book, with the sense of "ordered universe" remaining active right up to the last verse![23] So, readers who return to the early chapters may be more confused than when they first began, but they will not be locked into any one sense of the term. They will still have to make contextually based decisions in each case—in John 1 and again in John 3.

Given that the later environments are, by definition, less easily accessed cognitively than the more immediate ones, my analysis of John 1–3 allows that the first audience might well have discovered optimum relevance in the idea that God loved the entire created order. There appears, at least to me, no clear reason against such a reading. And yet, we have not shown that they would *necessarily* have understood it this way. It is possible that 1:10c might have been understood in a more restricted sense as humanity. The reference to the sin of the world in 1:29 might have reinforced this narrowing—though the singular *sin* is clearly open to this referring to the whole body of sin which exists in the created order. More would need to be known about the mutual cognitive environment of author and audience to come to a more definite conclusion.

Helpfully, RT also explains why different modern interpreters reach different conclusions. These conclusions will be based on the set of assumptions they bring to the text regarding God's interest in the non-human world, and the scope of salvation. An interpreter whose cognitive environment contains assumptions about the intrinsic value of the whole of creation, the current ecological crisis, and the contributions that some traditions of biblical interpretation have made to the abuse of the earth, the assertion of God's love for the entire universe here, together with the consequent challenge to a human response, will be productive of so many good cognitive effects as to

21. Wong Loi Sing, Response to Stephen Pattemore, private communication.

22. I assert as much in Pattemore, *The People of God in the Apocalypse*, 53–54.

23. John 21:25: "But there are also many other things that Jesus did; if every one of them were written down, I suppose that the world (*kosmos*) itself could not contain the books that would be written."

warrant the processing effort.[24] This is especially so if the context is widened to include the relationship between human and universal redemption found in Romans 8 and Colossians 1. If we are to be engaged as participants in an "interpretation for life" it will become an ethical choice.[25]

Would John's audience have understood it this way? I think the likelihood is that they would. The context, both immediate and more remote, leaves the wider interpretation readily available. God loved and continues to love the snake-infested, barren world with its sin-blighted human residents.

God's Love for the *kosmos:* A Ground of Hope

Why should it matter to establish a broad sense for *kosmos* in John 3:16? If the verse did not exist, or this broad meaning was not valid, are there not plenty more texts which encourage us to see God's relationship to the world as one of love and care and hopefulness? Certainly there are. But looking for "green" texts is in fact part of the problem. It was one of the dreams of A Rocha's founders, Peter and Miranda Harris, that the evangelical Christian community could become a powerful force for care of the earth.[26] In some places this has been realized.[27] But there remain vast tracts of the evangelical Christian world where the cause remains marginal at best, and excluded at worst.[28] It does not do any good to point these good people to Genesis 2, Colossians 1, Romans 8 or Revelation 21–22 as evidence of God's con-

24. Painter, "Earth Made Whole," argues that concern for the physical environment could not have been a pressing contemporary issue in John's day. Although he interprets John's treatment of Genesis in a way that has strong implications for the restoration of the earth, he is still limited by conventional lexicographic understandings of *kosmos*.

25. Most Bible translations retain the translation of *kosmos* as "world" in John 3.16, leaving the interpretational work to the reader. One exception is the CEV, which translates: "God loved the people of this world so much . . ." In the light of my analysis this is an unjustified restriction of the referential scope. For critique, using RT, of this tendency by some modern translations to skew meanings see Pattemore, "A Drift on a Sea of Implicature," 180–202. Elsewhere I have called for a review of translation decisions based on an earth-centred ethic: Pattemore, "Green Bibles, Justice and Translation," 217–26.

26. A Rocha's evangelical credentials are evident throughout the description of its distinctive features, http://www.arocha.org/en/distinctives/. Under the first heading "The conviction that Christ is Lord" it states: "A Rocha's work is a response to God's love for the whole creation, revealed in the Bible and personally in Jesus Christ." This could qualify as an evangelical reinterpretation of John 3:16.

27 See the article in *Christianity Today:* Lee, "Not Just Pope Francis."

28. In Aotearoa New Zealand my reading of the situation is that there may be a generational change taking place in these same circles. On the other hand, the *Christianity Today* article just quoted, says that skepticism regarding climate change is more prevalent amongst younger pastors in the USA!

cern for the non-human world, because they have a story of salvation that stretches from creation to second coming (perhaps via the rapture) which is focused solely on the plight of humanity. In the light of this overarching meta-narrative, any particular text is easily marginalized. It is in the nature of such a meta-narrative that, once established, all alternative narratives are rejected or squeezed to fit the main plot line. In RT terms, it is this constructed meta-narrative, rather than the primary context of communication, that forms the most relevant context of interpretation. John 3:16, functions in this scheme as a public text, frequently decontextualized, a summary of the story of salvation, and indeed the crowning piece of the whole story. To establish, then, that the divine motivation for God's salvific action in Jesus was his love for the whole created order is to attempt to modify the meta-narrative itself. This motivation is of course entirely in keeping with other texts, more frequently worked over in ecological hermeneutical circles, such as Colossians 1 and Romans 8, which talk of the outcome of God's action in Christ, and the connection between human and cosmic salvation.

I am under no illusion that modifying someone's meta-narrative of salvation is an easy task. I said earlier that this story has as yet no ending. I have not submitted this analysis to either my pastor or Professor Wong Loi Sing to see if it changes their view. But I have hope, at least partly because RT encourages us to investigate the original context of communication, the very place which is privileged above all others in evangelical hermeneutics, the locus of inspiration—that is, the story which John wrote for his first readers.

Nor do I make any pretense that my own position is somehow objective or disinterested. I believe that we live in critical times and that the context of the current environmental crisis sends us back to the text with questions we had previously not asked. I long for my evangelical friends to be seized with a passion for the care of "our common home." To interpret for the earth is an ethical imperative. And to use this public, evangelical text as a foundation of an earth-friendly interpretation is a pragmatic imperative, to help locate concern for the environment at the center of the understanding of God's program of salvation.

Bibliography

Arndt, William, et al. *A Greek-English Lexicon of the New Testament and Other Early Christian Literature*. Chicago: University of Chicago Press, 1979.

Bauckham, Richard. *The Testimony of the Beloved Disciple*. Grand Rapids: Baker, 2007.

Beasley-Murray, G. R. *John*. WBC 36. Dallas: Word, 2002.

Brown, Raymond. *The Gospel according to John I–XII*. Anchor Bible 29. New Haven: Yale University Press, 1969.

Dancygier, Barbara. *The Language of Stories*. Cambridge: Cambridge University Press, 2012.

Dodd, C. H. *Interpretation of The Fourth Gospel*. Cambridge: Cambridge University Press, 1953.

Fowler, Alastair. "A New Theory of Communication." *London Review of Books* 11 (1989) 16–17.

Gibbs, Raymond W. *Intentions in the Experience of Meaning*. Cambridge: Cambridge University Press, 1999.

Green, Gene. "Lexical Pragmatics and Biblical interpretation." *Journal of the Evangelical Theological Society* 50 (2007) 799–812.

Gundry, Robert H., and Russell W. Howell. "The Sense and Syntax of John 3:14–17 with Special Reference to the Use of 'οὕτως . . . ὥστε' in John 3:16." *Novum Testamentum* 41 (1999) 24–39.

Haas, C., et al. *A Translator's Handbook on the Letters of John*. London: United Bible Societies, 1972.

Keener, Craig S. *The Gospel of John: A Commentary*. Peabody, MA: Hendrickson, 2010.

Kostenburger, Andreas J. *John*. Grand Rapids: Baker, 2004.

Lee, Morgan. "Not Just Pope Francis: Evangelicals Praise Paris Climate Talks." *Christianity Today*, December 30, 2015. http://www.christianitytoday.com/gleanings/2015/december/evangelicals-paris-climate-talks.html.

Liddell, Henry George, et al. *A Greek-English Lexicon*. Oxford: Clarendon, 1996.

Morris, Leon. *The Gospel according to John*. Rev. ed. Grand Rapids: Eerdmans, 1995.

Painter, John. "Earth Made Whole: John's Rereading of Genesis." In *Word, Theology and Community in John*, edited by John Painter et al., 65–84. St. Louis: Chalice, 2002.

Pattemore, Stephen. "A Drift on a Sea of Implicature: Relevance Theory and the Pragmatics of Translation." *Journal of Biblical Text Research* 22 (2008) 180–202.

———. "Green Bibles, Justice and Translation." *Bible Translator* 61 (2010) 217–26.

———. *The People of God in the Apocalypse: Discourse, Structure, and Exegesis*. SNTSMS 128. Cambridge: Cambridge University Press, 2004.

———. *Souls under the Altar: Relevance Theory and the Discourse Structure of Revelation*. UBS Monograph 9. New York: UBS, 2003.

Ricoeur, Paul. *Interpretation Theory: Discourse and the Surplus of Meaning*. Fort Worth: Texas Christian University Press, 1976.

———. *Hermeneutics and the Human Sciences*. Cambridge: Cambridge University Press, 1981.

Sperber, Dan, and Deirdre Wilson. *Relevance: Communication and Cognition*. 2nd ed. Oxford: Blackwell, 1995.

Trebilco, Paul. *The Early Christians in Ephesus from Paul to Ignatius*. WUNT 2, 166. Tubingen: Mohr/Siebeck, 2004.

Vanhoozer, Kevin. *Biblical Narrative in the Philosophy of Paul Ricoeur*. Cambridge: Cambridge University Press, 1990.

Westcott, B. F. *The Gospel according to St. John: Authorised Version with Introduction and Notes*. London: Murray, 1882.

Wong Loi Sing, Julius. Response to Stephen Pattemore (SBL 2009), private communication, 2015.

9

"What are Human Beings that You are Mindful of them" (Heb 2:5)

An Anthropological/Ecological Reading of Hebrews 2:5–9

Philip Church,
A Rocha Aotearoa New Zealand

Introduction

In his Anchor Bible Commentary on Hebrews, Craig Koester argues that the quotation and interpretation of Ps 8:4–6 in Heb 2:5–9 identifies the principal issue being addressed in the book: that is, the ultimate destiny of humanity.[1] This Psalm is a musical rendition of Gen 1:26–30 where God gives humans dominion over the non-human creation, a text that Lynn White Jr. judged to make Christianity "the most anthropocentric religion the world has seen." White continues, that Christianity ". . . not only established a dualism of man and nature but also insisted that it is God's will that man exploit nature for his proper ends."[2] While White's views have been the subject of intense scrutiny and critique over the past fifty

1. Koester, *Hebrews*, 84–85. Forty years earlier, Caird proposed that the quotation of Psalm 8 in Heb 2:5–8 "controls the argument of the preceding chapter, for from the first mention of angels at 1:5 [sic; angels appear in 1:4] throughout the formidable catena of texts in ch. 1 the author's one aim is to illustrate the theme of the psalm that man has been destined by God to a glory excelling that of angels and that this destiny has been achieved by Christ" (Caird, "Exegetical Method," 49). As Caird shows, Heb 2:5 continues the discussion of human salvation extending from 1:1–2:4, and that this discussion continues to the end of Heb 2 as the reference to angels in 2:16 indicates. See also Schenck, "Celebration," 469–85; Moffitt, *Atonement*, 58–59.

2. White, "Historical Roots," 1205.

years,[3] not everybody has disagreed with him, and indeed, some contributors to the Earth Bible Project have argued in a similar vein. In particular, Norman Habel consistently refers to the "dominion" of Gen 1:26, 28 as "domination,"[4] and refers to the Genesis text as the "mandate to dominate all other living creatures."[5]

In what follows I start with the Genesis text, move to Psalm 8, and then to Heb 2:5–9.[6] I will argue that Heb 2:5–9 refers to the subjection of the world to come to humans (rather than to Jesus as some maintain). I will also argue, over against White and others, that the author of Hebrews sees this as a good thing, and the ultimate outcome of God's intention for the creation.[7] Thus eschatology corresponds to protology, with humans "ruling" over the new creation as in the garden at the beginning.

Genesis 1:26–30

Genesis 1:1–2:3 is a carefully structured narrative, with a seven day schema as its most obvious structural feature. Everything happens around these "days," with the seventh day as the climax. A Torah-observant Jew in the second Temple period reading this narrative would be drawn towards the seventh day, wondering, as each day progressed, what God would do on the Sabbath. Thus, God's rest is the climax of the narrative,[8] rather than the creation of humanity as some maintain.[9]

3. An early critique was Barr, "Man and Nature," 9–32. Rogerson, "Creation Stories," 21–23, details some other responses to White's article. It is difficult to know where to start and where stop in any list of works responding to White's essay. Routinely, discussion of human dominion begins with a mention of White. See, e.g., Berry, ed., *The Care of Creation*, which begins by reprinting White's article (31–42); Berry, "Introduction: Stewardship: A Default Position," 4; Harrison, "Genesis and the Mastery of Nature," 17–19; and more recently Marlow, "What Am I," 36.

4. See Habel, *An Inconvenient Text*, 1–10, an essay on Gen 1:26–28 that he entitles "The Mandate to Dominate."

5. Ibid., 5. On the frontispiece, he adds the adjective "notorious." See also Carley, "Psalm 8: An Apology for Domination," 111–24. For other critiques of the notion of human dominion, see Bauckham, *Bible and Ecology*, 2–12.

6. Other texts that reflect the idea of human dominion over nature include Ps 115:16; Wis 9:2–3; Sir 16:26—17:14; 2 En 58:1–5; Philo, *Opif.* 83–88; 2 Bar 14:18; 4 Ezra 6:53–54; Apoc. Mos. 10–11.

7. Calvin, *Commentary on the Book of Psalms*, 105–6, sees human dominion as a gracious gift of God.

8. Wallace, "Rest for the Earth?," 50, 53–54; Bauckham, *God and the Crisis of Freedom*, 173; *Bible and Ecology*, 15; Deane-Drummond, "Living from the Sabbath," 6.

9. Wenham, *Genesis 1–15*, 26; Habel, "Geophany," 34. Ibid., 35, Habel argues

Another noteworthy structural feature is the inclusio in 1:1 and 2:1–3:

> In the beginning God created the heavens and the earth . . . (1:1)
>
> And the heavens and the earth and all their host were completed . . . (2:1).

These lines act as a heading and the beginning of a conclusion,[10] and this, along with the absence of any creative word from God in 1:2, indicate that the narrative concerns God's careful transformation of the "uninhabited and uninhabitable" (תהו ובהו) cosmos into what God could describe as "very good" (תוב מאוד).

On the sixth day God created domesticated and undomesticated animals, small creatures and the human creature. While the human is an animal like the other animals, and eats from the same table as the animals (Gen 1:29–30), it is undeniable that humans are differentiated.[11] Unlike the other animals, which the earth "brings forth," God "creates" (ברא) the human. God addresses the heavenly council when about to do this,[12] resolves to make them in God's image and likeness, and gives them "dominion" (רדה) over the animals. God then performs the corresponding creative act, and commands them to "subdue" (כבש) the earth and to "have dominion" (רדה) over the other creatures. The problematic words here are the commands to "have dominion" over nonhuman creatures and to "subdue" the earth.

Habel argues that there have been three main readings of God's mandate that humans are to have dominion over the animals and to subdue the earth. Some see it as a hierarchal mandate that implies "domination and oppression" that "unjustly reduces Earth and Earth community to an inferior status"; some emphasize the royal aspects of the commands to rule, and claim that the mandate gives to humans the right to be "responsible 'royal' stewards who should govern . . . with knowledge and justice";[13] and others "soften the import" of the words, arguing that they mean something akin to "care for" and "show kindness."[14] I make the following points.

against the view that God's rest is the climax of the narrative, suggesting that the creation of humans represents "a sharp conflict of plot and perspective."

10. Habel, "Geophany," 35–36; Waltke and Fredricks, *Genesis*, 55. This view is not without its detractors as the NRSV translation of Gen 1:1–2 witnesses with the two verses comprising a single sentence. Brett, "Earthing the Human," 74, sees Gen 1:1 as God's first creative act, and claims that there is insufficient evidence to decide between these two options.

11. Brett, "Earthing the Human," 76–77.

12. Waltke and Fredricks, *Genesis*, 64.

13. See e.g. Dyrness, "Stewardship of the Earth," 52–55.

14. Habel and Trudinger, "Is the Wild Ox Willing to Serve You?," 180; Habel,

The verb "to have dominion" (רדה) appears twenty-three times in the OT, including Gen 1:26, 28,[15] and Habel argues that it implies oppression and violent domination.[16] I note that in Lev 25:43, 46, 53, where the people of Israel are not permitted to deal violently with slaves, the word "dominion" is qualified with the word פרך ("violence"). Isaiah 14:6 is similar. It describes the harshness of Babylon's rule over the exiles. Here "dominion" is qualified with "anger" (אף) and "unrelenting persecution" (מרדף בלי חשך). If force and oppression were intrinsic to the word these qualifiers would not be needed.

Dominion is also expressed positively. The word describes Solomon's rule in 1 Kings 2:24 (MT 5:4), resulting in universal peace. Psalm 72 describes the rule of the king, with רדה appearing in v. 8. Carley overstates his case when he says it cannot be used to describe the positive conditions described in vv. 1–7.[17] While it does head up a new section, expressing "the wish for worldwide acknowledgment of the king,"[18] and even for the king's "forceful leadership in the world as a whole,"[19] the conclusion to the section in vv. 12–14 explain why the king's dominion is so beneficial,

> . . . he delivers the needy when they call,
>
> the poor and those who have no helper.
>
> He has pity on the weak and the needy,
>
> and saves the lives of the needy.
>
> From oppression and violence he redeems their life . . .

"Design, Diversity and Dominion," 62. For an example of such a reading, see Murray, *Cosmic Covenant*, 98–99.

15. Gen 1:26, 28; Lev 25:43, 46, 53; 26:17; Num 24:19; 1 Kgs 5:4, 30; 9:23; Neh 9:28; 2 Chr 8:10; Ps 49:15; 68:28; 72:8; 110:2; Isa 14:2, 6; 41:2; Lam 1:13; Ezek 29:15; 34:4; Joel 4:13. The word has a quite different sense in Lam 1:13. It is unwise to draw conclusions from Isa 41:2, which describes the rule of Cyrus. Here the NRSV has "tramples kings under foot," although the form of the verb is unattested elsewhere, with an uncertain sense. 1QIsa[a] has a different word, which may be behind the NIV "he subdues kings before him." In Joel 4:13 the word refers to treading (grapes), and here too it may be a different word (ירד, "to go down" [into a vat], rather than רדה, since the sense "tread" is not found elsewhere), See HALOT 1190. There is another strange form in Ps 68:27 (MT 28), where Benjamin, the smallest tribe "leads" the procession of God's people.

16. E.g., Habel and Trudinger, "Wild Ox," 180–84; Habel, "Design, Diversity and Dominion," 61–64; Habel and Wurst, "Introducing Ecological Hermeneutics," 6.

17. Carley, "Psalm 8," 119.

18. Goldingay, *Psalms 42–89*, 387.

19. Ibid.

Finally, I refer to Ezek 34:1–10 where the rulers of God's people are castigated for not ruling properly:

> You have not strengthened the weak, you have not healed the sick, you have not bound up the injured, you have not brought back the strayed, you have not sought the lost, but with force (חזקה) and harshness (פרך) you have ruled (רדה) them (v. 4).[20]

Given the complete lack of any indication of enmity between animals and humans in Gen 1, these ideas can be extended to that text, and rather than "domination," the word describes the proper care of the animals by the human.[21] The issue, therefore, is not with dominion, but with poor exercise of dominion. That some humans dominate is true, and that some express proud optimism at the power that humans can potentially wield is also true, but this does not compel us to read the text in this way.[22]

The other word, כבש ("to subdue") is more difficult. It appears fourteen times in the Hebrew Scriptures, including Gen 1:28, and in a variety of contexts. Its objects are varied, but particularly pertinent are those cases where the "land" (ארץ) is subdued (Num 32:22, 29; Josh 18:1; 1 Chron 22:18). The Numbers and Joshua texts concern the context of the conquest of Canaan, where the word probably has the sense "take possession,"[23] and the Chronicles text describes Solomon's peaceful reign. Canaan was a gracious gift from God to his people, which they were to possess, always remembering that it was God's land, and that they were to care for it and live righteously in it, following the Torah, lest they too be expelled. A variety of regulations governed how they were to care for that land, including the weekly Sabbath and the Sabbath year when the fields were to lie fallow allowing undomesticated animals to eat its produce.[24]

Genesis 1 describes how God transformed an uninhabited and uninhabitable world so that it could support plant and animal life. Taking the context of these other texts where ארץ is described as subdued, it is apparent

20. For a discussion of the application of Ezek 34:4 and Ps 72 to Ps 8, see Limburg, "Who Cares for the Earth?" 50.

21. Cf. Rogerson, "Creation Stories," 26: "[I]n Genesis 1 . . . [*radah* and *kabash*] occur in the context of a non-violent world."

22. Marlow, "What Am I," 38, critiques the methodology of the Earth Bible Project for its "focus on the standpoint of the interpreter . . . [and neglect of] the world of the text itself."

23. Bauckham, *Bible and Ecology*, 16. It would be a diversion to discuss the problematic hermeneutical, theological, and ethical issues related to the conquest of Canaan.

24. Cf. Rogerson, "Creation Stories," 28–31.

that there was work for humans to do once God had finished his creating.[25] Humans are co-creators with God, continuing the work of creation, ordering the world to support plant and animal life as it fruitfully multiplies.[26] It is this aspect that Gen 2:15 adds to the word כבש. There the human God had formed was to "serve" (עבד) and "preserve" (שמר) the garden that God had placed him in.[27] And while Habel critiques the practice of harmonizing Gen 1:28 and Gen 2:15,[28] it seems valid to let each text illuminate the other. Pope Francis summarizes this well:

> The earth was here before us and it has been given to us. This allows us to respond to the charge that . . . the Genesis account which grants man "dominion" over the earth (cf. Gen 1:28), has encouraged the unbridled exploitation of nature by painting him as domineering and destructive . . . This is not a correct interpretation . . . Although it is true that we Christians have at times incorrectly interpreted the Scriptures, nowadays we must forcefully reject the notion that our being created in God's image and given dominion over the earth justifies absolute domination over other creatures. The biblical texts are to be read in their context, with an appropriate hermeneutic, recognizing that they tell us to "till and keep" the garden of the world (cf. Gen 2:15).[29]

On the seventh day, God, having placed God's image in the cosmic temple, entered his rest.[30] Humanity, in God's image, was to represent God and continue God's creative work. This is God's place where God's people live under God's rule and foster the conditions for all creatures, human and non-human alike, to live and flourish under God.[31]

25. Wallace, "Rest for the Earth?," 59, notes that there is still work for the human to do: "striving for the wholeness of creation involves an ongoing struggle against chaos."

26. Bauckham, *Bible and Ecology*, 16–18, reads "subdue" in terms of agriculture.

27. The glosses "serve" and "preserve" are from Bookless, "The Bible and Diversity," 3.

28. Habel and Wurst, *An Inconvenient Text*, 54. In "Wild Ox," 182–84, Habel and Trudinger argue that the Genesis 2 story undermines the Genesis 1 story at this point.

29. Pope Francis, *Laudato si'*, para. 67.

30. For "rest" connected with the temple see Ps 95:11; 132:8; 2 Chr 6:41–42.

31. Cf. Fretheim, who writes: "[P]ositively the human being is needed to bring at least the earthly orders to their fullest possible potential and that would entail their fullest possible potential for praise. There remains work to be done in nature by human beings in order for this to be realized." "Nature's praise of God," 28. Cf. also Hos 4:3 where, as a result of human rebellion, "the land mourns, and all who live in it languish; together with the wild animals and the birds of the air, even the fish of the sea are perishing." Over against this is Hos 2:18 (MT 2:20) where God looks to the eschatological future, "I will make for you a covenant on that day with the wild animals, the birds of the air, and the creeping things of the ground; and I will abolish the bow, the sword, and

Psalm 8:3–6

Psalm 8 is a communal song of praise to YHWH the creator on account of his majestic name (vv. 1–2, 9). It also contains an individual reflection (vv. 3–8).[32] In vv. 3–4 the psalmist wonders why YHWH should lavish such care on humans who are so small when compared with the cosmos, and vv. 5–6 explain that, though seemingly insignificant, they have great dignity being only "slightly inferior to God" (מעט מאלהים).[33] The Psalm claims that humans are crowned with glory and honor and assigned the responsibility to "rule" (משל) the works of God's hands, listed in vv. 7–8 as small and large domesticated animals, wild animals, birds, fish and sea monsters. All these have been placed "under the feet" (תחת רגלים) of the human. Verse 9 repeats the opening words, forming an inclusio and providing the context in which the readers are to understand the reflection on the insignificance, yet dignity of humanity.[34]

Rather than רדה ("exercise dominion"), Ps 8:6 uses the word משל, the normal word for "rule over."[35] The parallel expression is "you have put all things under their feet" (כל שתה תחת רגליו). If משל corresponds to רדה, then these words correspond to כבש. While Carley writes that the expression "clearly indicates vigorous conquest by a superior force," this is not the whole story. This rare expression refers to the beneficial results of Solomon's reign in 1 Kings 5:3 (MT 4:17) enabling a temple to be built. It also appears in Ps 47:3 where the people "subdued" (כבש) under the feet of the people of Israel are summoned to clap their hands and shout to God with loud songs of praise (v. 1). These are the people who, at the end of the Psalm become the people of the God of Abraham. It was good to be subdued by the people of Abraham's God and to become the people of that God. Consequently, Psalm 8 need not be read as expressing violent domination and oppression, but rather the diligent exercise of rule that benefits all life.

---

war from the land; and I will make you lie down in safety." On these texts, see DeRoche, "The Reversal of Creation in Hosea," 400–409; Dyrness, "Stewardship" 57–63; Marlow, *Biblical Prophets and Contemporary Environmental Ethics*, 177–79; 191–94.

32. I use English versification. Both the Hebrew text and the LXX count the superscription as v. 1, with 10 verses rather than 9.

33. Murray, *Cosmic Covenant*, 196n3, suggests that in vv. 4–5 of Ps 8 "the status of the human being as 'little less than *ĕlohim* . . . comes close in meaning to the 'image' formula."

34. Limburg, "Who Cares for the Earth?," 47.

35. Ibid., 49. Humans are therefore seen as royalty in this Psalm. This verb is used in Gen 1:14–18 for the "rule" of the sun and moon over day and night.

Psalm 8:4–6 in Hebrews

Psalm 8:4–6 (LXX 5–7) appears in Heb 2:5–8a, apart from one line of v. 6.[36] The text as quoted agrees with the LXX, which renders the words "you have made them a little less than God" with "you have made them a little lower than the angels" (ἠλάττωσας αὐτὸν βραχύ τι παρ' ἀγγέλους) words that probably attracted the attention of the writer of Hebrews to the Psalm as he reflected on the relationship of Jesus, humans and angels. The Hebrew words for humanity (אנוש, "man" and בן אדם, "son of man") in v. 4, rendered with ἄνθρωπος and υἱὸς ἀνθρώπου ("man" and "son of man"), have led some readers of Hebrews to see a reference to Jesus, the one made a little lower than the angels, now crowned with glory and honor.[37] I argue that this reading is suspect, and that the reference is to humanity ruling the world to come. I adduce the following reasons.[38]

The Flow of the Discourse

Hebrews 1–2 concerns Jesus, angels and human salvation. Hebrews 1 starts with the exaltation of Jesus above the angels (1:1–4) and concludes with the claim that angels are sent to serve those who will inherit salvation (1:14). Hebrews 2:1–4 encourages the readers not to neglect this salvation. The NRSV obscures the transition between 2:4 and 2:5 with its translation of the particle γάρ ("for") with "now." When the "for" is restored it becomes clear that vv. 5–9 are also about salvation.[39] Hebrews 2:10 describes this salvation as God bringing many heirs to glory through Jesus, the pioneer, and v. 16 rounds off the discussion of angels with the claim that Jesus did not become human for the sake of angels but for the sake of the descendants of Abraham—God's people. A discussion of the rule of Jesus over the world to come would be an intrusion into this discourse about salvation, while a discussion of the role of humans in the world to come is appropriate.

36. Ps 8:7a (MT) reads "you have caused them [him] to rule over the works of your hands" (Heb תמשילהו במעשי ידיך, LXX καὶ κατέστησας αὐτὸν ἐπὶ τὰ ἔργα τῶν χειρῶν σου). The LXX can be translated "you have appointed them [him] over the works of your hands." The evidence for the inclusion or exclusion of this line is evenly matched, but it seems that it may have been added in some MSS to conform the text to the LXX.

37. E.g., Peterson, *Hebrews and Perfection*, 51–55; Attridge, *Hebrews*, 69–77; Mackie, *Eschatology and Exhortation*, 43–44. Moffitt, *Atonement*, 120–29, argues that in v. 6 the referent of ἄνθρωπος is humanity in general and that the referent of υἱὸς ἀνθρόπου is Christ the pioneer or representative human.

38. An earlier version of the material that follows appears in Church, *Hebrews and the Temple*, 298–303.

39. Moffitt, *Atonement*, 59–61.

The Grammar of Hebrews 2:8b–9

Hebrews 2:8b begins a new paragraph, again starting with the causal particle γάρ ("for"), explaining the Psalm quotation. The words ὑποτάσσω / ἀνυπότακτος ("to subject"/ "not subject") appear three times, indicating that the writer is dealing with the last line of the Psalm quotation ("he has subjected all things under their feet").[40] The subjection of all things "to him" (αὐτῷ) is comprehensive.[41] Nothing is omitted, although this is not yet evident. Those who read the Psalm with reference to Jesus read v. 8b as a discussion of the submission of all things to the Son. But the grammatical construction in v. 9, beginning as it does with τὸν δέ ("but"), and ending with Ἰησοῦς ("Jesus") in the final, emphatic position (τὸν δέ . . . βλέπομεν Ἰησοῦν, "but . . . we see Jesus") implies a contrast where Ἰησοῦς is set over against the "him" (αὐτόν) of v. 8. The sense of Heb 2:8 is that the subjection of all things to "humanity" is comprehensive, but presently unclear (νῦν δὲ οὔπω ὁρῶμεν). Verse 9 claims, by way of contrast, that the exaltation of Jesus is evident for his people to see (τὸν δὲ . . . βλέπομεν Ἰησοῦν).

The Tense Change between the Verbs Quoted in the Psalm and their Interpretation

Two expressions taken from the Psalm (βραχύ τι παρ' ἀγγέλους ἠλαττωμένον), "made a little lower than the angels," and δόξῃ καὶ τιμῇ ἐστεφανωμένον, "crowned with glory and honour") qualify the reference to Jesus. While the verbs in the quotation itself are aorist indicatives (ἠλάττωσας, "you made lower"; ἐστεφάνωσας, "you crowned"), in the author's exegetical comments they are perfect passive participles (ἠλαττωμένον, "made lower"; ἐστεφανωμένον, "crowned"). While, in the Psalm, these expressions describe the dignity of humanity as made in God's image, they are sometimes read as describing a sequence in Hebrews: Jesus was made lower than the angels (in his incarnation), and has now been exalted above the

40. "Their" in this line translates αὐτοῦ the masculine singular genitive pronoun. The antecedent of this pronoun is ἄνθροπος, υἱὸς ἀνθρώπου ("man," "son of man") in v. 6, which, I am arguing, is to be read generically, referring to humanity.

41. The word αὐτῷ ("to him") appears twice in this verse, and possibly a third time, always referring to the one to whom the world to come is subjected. The editors of NA28 include the first occurrence in square brackets (ἐν τῷ γὰρ ὑποτάξαι [αὐτῷ] τὰ πάντα . . . "for in the subjecting of all things [to him] . . . because several witnesses to the text omit it." See the discussion in Metzger, *Textual Commentary*, 594.

angels.[42] However, the change from aorist indicative verbs to perfect passive participles suggests that this is not the most natural reading.

Perfect passive participles act as verbal adjectives,[43] and they describe Jesus as we see him now, not with respect to some sequence of events in the past. We see one who is a true human (a member of the class of those "made a little lower than the angels," βραχύ τι παῤ ἀγγέλους ἠλαττωμένον),[44] "crowned with glory and honor" (δόξῃ καὶ τιμῇ ἐστεφανωμένον). What is true of humanity, but presently unclear, is both true and evident in the case of Jesus. What we see in Jesus anticipates the future of humanity as vv. 10–13 show.

Hebrews 2:10–13

Hebrews 2:10–13, also beginning with the causal particle γάρ, explains the purpose clause of Heb 2:9, with the claim that God is "bringing many heirs to glory" (πολλοὺς υἱοὺς εἰς δόξαν ἀγαγόντα),[45] and the claim that it was proper that, in doing this, God should make perfect "the author of their salvation" (ἀρχηγός τῆς σωτηρίας αὐτῶν) through suffering.

The claim that God is leading many sons (and daughters) to glory reflects the language of the Exodus, where God leads his people through the wilderness to the promised land.[46] But in Hebrews, God does not simply lead them to the promised land. God leads them to "glory" (δόξα). This is the "glory and honor" (δόξα κὰι τιμή) of Ps 8:6, which in Heb 2:7 describes the not-yet-apparent dominion of humanity over all things, and in 2:9, the present visible exaltation of Jesus. The glory to which God is leading humanity in Heb 2:10 is the restoration of humanity's rule over the cosmos, granted in Genesis 1, celebrated in Psalm 8, and worked out in Hebrews 2.

42. Peterson, *Hebrews and Perfection*, 214–25; Lane, *Hebrews 1–8*, 47–48; Thompson, *Hebrews*, 62; Moffitt, *Atonement*, 55.

43. Campbell, *Basics of Verbal Aspect*, 111; *Verbal Aspect in Non-Indicative Verbs*, 26. There are twenty-nine perfect passive participles in Hebrews. Two of these are in periphrastic constructions (4:2; 10:10), and five are substantives (9:13, 15; 12:11, 27; 13:3). The remainder are adjectival (2:8, 9; 4:2, 13, 15; 5:14; 7:3, 26, 28; 9:4, 6, 13; 10:2, 22; 11:12; 12:12, 18, 23; 13:23). The "present state of a past action" is evident only in 4:15; 5:14; 13:23.

44. The Greek expression βραχύ τι, like the corresponding Hebrew word מעט, can have either a spatial or a temporal sense ("a little" or "a little while"). I argue that the perfect participle requires a spatial sense.

45. NRSV reads πολλοί υἱοί as "many children," but this misses the dignity of the sonship expressed in this verse.

46. Lane, *Hebrews 1–8*, 56; O'Brien, *Hebrews*, 104; Moffitt, *Atonement*, 129. In Exod 3:8 God leads his people "out" (ἐξάγω) of Egypt and "into" (εἰσάγω) the promised land.

The LXX of Num 13–14, a text echoed several times in Heb 3–4,[47] is probably behind the use of ἀρχηγός ("author," "pioneer") in this verse.[48] Here "pioneers" (ἀρχηγοί) are selected to enter in advance and spy out the land, and the rebels look to select a "leader" (ἀρχηγός) to take them back to Egypt. The choice of the word ἀρχηγός to describe Jesus here echoes these texts. Jesus the "pioneer" has achieved the goal, being crowned with glory and honor, and through him, God is leading many heirs to the same goal.[49]

Psalm 8:6 is quoted twice in the NT (1 Cor 15:25–27; Heb 2:6–8) and scholars have detected several allusions.[50] Both quotations and all the allusions apply Ps 8:6 to Jesus, and read it with an eschatological orientation. Moreover, both Eph 1:20–22; 1 Pet 3:22 combine Ps 8 with Ps 110, as in Heb 2. The authors of these texts share a tradition with the author of Hebrews that combines these two Psalms and applies them to Jesus. However, the application to Jesus in Heb 2:5–9 is more subtle than elsewhere, for, in Hebrews, Jesus is exalted as the representative human, the pioneer who anticipates the exaltation of humanity and humanity's dominion over the new creation. "The world to come" (ἡ οἰκυμένη ἡ μέλλουσα) has been made subject to humanity, but while, as v. 9 points out, this is not presently evident, it is clear that Jesus, a real human being, is now crowned with glory and honor. Through him, God is bringing many heirs to glory, that is, restoring to humanity the dignity given to them at the creation. This is the great salvation of Heb 2:3—God's plan that humanity live out their calling/

47. Psalm 95 (LXX 96), quoted in Heb 3, mentions the rebellion at Massah and Meribah, suggesting a background in either Exod 17:1–7 and/or Num 20:1–3, although Num 14:1–35 has more points of contact with the Psalm. Hofius, *Katapausis*, 117–53, argues that this is its true background, followed by Laansma, *"I Will Give You Rest,"* 262–64.

48. The precise sense of ἀρχηγός needs to be determined by the literary and cultural context. For the semantic range, see Johnston, "Christ as Archegos," 381–85 (who surveys the English translations offered in a variety of sources, and opts for "prince," equivalent to the Hebrew word נשיא, and Müller, "ἀρχηγός, οῦ, ὁ," 163–64. Käsemann, *Wandering People of God*, 128–33, argued for the derivation of the term from its use in incipient Gnosticism, for which there is no evidence at the time Hebrews was written. Others have made connections with the Hellenistic cult of the hero (e.g., Delling, "ἄρχω, κ.τ.λ.," 56–57. Guthrie, *Hebrews*, 107–8, translates the word with "champion"). A more appropriate background is the use of the word in the LXX, although there it has several senses (Müller, "ἀρχηγός, οῦ, ὁ," 163). The word appears four times in the NT (Acts 3:15; 5:31; Heb 2:10; 12:2), always as a christological title, and always related to the death and subsequent exaltation of Jesus. I use "pioneer" (following NRSV), conveying the notion of a leader, who is first in a series, and "providing the impetus for further developments" (BDAG 138, s.v., ἀρχηγός, 2). See Moffitt, *Atonement*, 129–30.

49. Bruce, *Hebrews*, 80; Ellingworth, *Hebrews*, 160–61; O'Brien, *Hebrews*, 106–7.

50. Eph 1:20–22; Phil 3:21; 1 Pet 3:22 seem to be clear allusions. Rom 3:23; 8:20; Phil 2:6–11 are also possible allusions, although not so clear.

commission given in Eden and thus serve and preserve the new creation that God has inaugurated in Christ.

Conclusion

I began by noting that some are critical of the idea of human dominion in Genesis 1, reading it as "domination." I have sought to demonstrate that such dominion is God's intention for humanity, but that this dominion is not domination but rather diligent care for all God's creation. I have also argued that Hebrews 2 sees human dominion from an eschatological perspective. Jesus is now exalted to the right hand of God in the world to come as a "pioneer" through whom God is leading many sons and daughters to glory. In the eschaton, the fullness of creation—giving glory and praise to its Creator—will be manifest and humanity will exercise dominion. Thus, God's purposes will be fulfilled, with humans made in God's image serving and preserving the new creation as God's trustees.

The Old Testament prophets envisage this age to come in utopian terms of enduring peace, abundance, long and healthy lives and the overcoming of death, including the end of predation.[51] How all this happens in practice is difficult to imagine. Nevertheless, as Towner argues, such "sketches in biblical eschatology . . . are neither science nor history written in advance . . . they are truth claims about . . . God's intention for the created order."[52] Such claims, he suggests, come to us "not as metaphysical claims but as moral ones," that need to "shape our behavior now toward each other and . . . [the non-human creation]."[53]

In Rom 13:11–14 the imminence of the dawn of the new age had implications for the way the readers lived. While the apostle was not talking about the care of creation, the principle still applies. "Let us live," he says, "as though the day was already here." As James Dunn writes, "those who look for the coming of the kingdom . . . must live as citizens of that kingdom."[54] This means we are called to care for and maintain the creation

51. See, e.g., Isa 2:2–4; 11:6–9; 65:25; Ezek 34:25–31; Amos 9:13; Hos 2:18 (MT 2:20); 14:4–8; Mic 4:3–4. Bauckham, "Jesus and the Wild Animals," 15, points out that in Isa 11:6–9 "there is no mention of peace between the predatory wild animals and the *wild* animals . . . which they usually hunt and kill, but only of peace between the predatory wild animals and the domestic animals which they sometimes attack." Nevertheless, he finds the end of predation implied in the lion and the bear becoming vegetarian.

52. Towner, "The Future of Nature," 30.

53. Ibid., 30–31.

54. Dunn, *Romans 9–16*, 789.

now in our present age, in the same way as we will in the age to come. As Towner suggests

> If abundance of life, taken now to mean both quality of life and biodiversity, is manifested in the Eden ahead . . . then we can do nothing better now than attend to the rain forests . . . [and] cut back on our over consumption . . . [55]

The issue we face in our contemporary age is not human dominion, but human rebellion, human greed, and human anthropocentrism. Hebrews 2 presents hope for the future. The "great salvation" (Heb 2:3) involves redeemed humans caring for the new creation as God intended.

Bibliography

Attridge, Harold W. *The Epistle to the Hebrews*. Hermeneia. Minneapolis: Fortress, 1989.

Barr, James. "Man and Nature: the Ecological Controversy and the Old Testament." *BJRL* 55 (1972) 9–32.

Bauckham, Richard. *Bible and Ecology: Recovering the Community of Creation*. Sarum Theological Lectures. London: Darton Longman & Todd, 2010.

———. *God and the Crisis of Freedom: Biblical and Contemporary Perspectives*. Louisville: Westminster John Knox, 2002.

———. "Jesus and the Wild Animals (Mark 1:13): A Christological Image for an Ecological Age." In *Jesus of Nazareth Lord and Christ: Essays on the Historical Jesus and New Testament Christology*, edited by Joel B. Green and Max Turner, 3–21. Grand Rapids: Eerdmans, 1994.

Berry, R. J., ed. *The Care of Creation: Focusing Concern and Action*. Downers Grove, IL: InterVarsity, 2000.

———. "Introduction: Stewardship: A Default Position." In *Environmental Stewardship: Critical Perspectives—Past and Present*, edited by R. J. Berry, 1–13. London: T. & T. Clark, 2006.

Bookless, David. "'Let Everything That Has Breath Praise the Lord': The Bible and Diversity." *Cambridge Papers* 23, no. 3 (2014) 1–6.

Brett, Mark G. "Earthing the Human in Genesis 1–3." In *The Earth Story in Genesis*, edited by Norman C. Habel and Shirley Wurst, 73–86. Earth Bible 2. Sheffield: Sheffield Academic, 2000.

Bruce, F. F. *The Epistle to the Hebrews*. NICNT. Rev. ed. Grand Rapids: Eerdmans, 1990.

Caird, G. B. "The Exegetical Method of the Epistle to the Hebrews." *CJT* 5 (1959) 44–51.

Calvin, John. *Commentary on the Book of Psalms*. Grand Rapids: Eerdmans, 1949.

55. Towner, "The Future of Nature," 33. Towner adds "and limit the growth of the human population." Over against this I cite Pope Francs again, "To blame population growth instead of extreme and selective consumerism on the part of some, is one way of refusing to face the issues. It is an attempt to legitimize the present model of distribution, where a minority believes that it has the right to consume in a way which can never be universalized, since the planet could not even contain the waste products of such consumption" (Pope Francis, *Laudato si'*, para. 50).

Campbell, Constantine R. *Basics of Verbal Aspect in Biblical Greek*. Grand Rapids: Zondervan, 2008.

———. *Verbal Aspect in Non-Indicative Verbs: Further Soundings in the Greek New Testament*. Studies in Biblical Greek 15. New York: Lang, 2008.

Carley, Keith. "Psalm 8: An Apology for Domination." In *Readings from the Perspective of Earth*, edited by Norman C. Habel, 110–24. Sheffield: Sheffield Academic, 2000.

Church, Philip. *Hebrews and the Temple: Attitudes to the Temple in Second Temple Judaism and in Hebrews*. NovTSup 171. Leiden: Brill, 2017.

Deane-Drummond, Celia. "Living from the Sabbath." In *Biodiversity and Ecology: An Interdisciplinary Challenge*, edited by Denis Edwards and Mark Worthing, 1–13. Adelaide: ATF, 2004.

Delling, G. "ἄρχω, κ.τ.λ." In *TDNT*, edited by Gerhard Kittell, 1: 478–89. Grand Rapids: Eerdmans, 1964.

DeRoche, Michael. "The Reversal of Creation in Hosea." *VT* 31 (1981) 400–409.

Dunn, J. D. G. *Romans 9–16*. WBC 38b. Dallas: Word, 1988.

Dyrness, William. "Stewardship of the Earth in the Old Testament." In *Tending the Garden: Essays on the Gospel and the Earth*, edited by Wesley Granberg-Michaelson, 50–65. Grand Rapids: Eerdmans, 1987.

Ellingworth, Paul. *The Epistle to the Hebrews*. NIGTC. Grand Rapids: Eerdmans, 1993.

Pope Francis. *Encyclical Letter Laudato si' of the Holy Father Francis on Care for Our Common Home*. Rome: Libreria Editrice Vaticana, 2015.

Fretheim, Terence E. "Nature's Praise of God in the Psalms." *Ex Auditu* 3 (1987) 16–30.

Goldingay, John. *Psalms*, Vol. 2, *Psalms 42–89*. BCOTWP. Grand Rapids: Baker Academic, 2007.

Guthrie, George H. *Hebrews*. NIVAC. Grand Rapids: Zondervan, 1998.

Habel, Norman C. "Design, Diversity and Dominion: Biodiversity and Job 39." In *Biodiversity and Ecology: An Interdisciplinary Challenge*, edited by Denis Edwards and Mark Worthing, 55–64. Adelaide: ATF, 2004.

———. "Geophany: The Earth Story in Genesis 1." In *The Earth Story in Genesis*, edited by Norman C. Habel and Shirley Wurst, 34–48. Earth Bible 2. Sheffield: Sheffield Academic, 2000.

———. *An Inconvenient Text: Is a Green Reading of the Bible Possible?* Adelaide: ATF, 2009.

———. "Introducing Ecological Hermeneutics." In *Exploring Ecological Hermeneutics*, edited by Norman C. Habel and Peter Trudinger, 1–8. SBL Symposium 46. Atlanta: SBL, 2008.

———. "'Is the Wild Ox Willing to Serve you?' Challenging the Mandate to Dominate." In *The Earth Story in Wisdom Traditions*, edited by Norman C. Habel and Shirley Wurst, 179–89. Cleveland: Pilgrim, 1994.

Harrison, Peter. "Genesis and the Mastery of Nature." In *Environmental Stewardship: Critical Perspectives—Past and Present*, edited by R. J. Berry, 17–31. London: T. & T. Clark, 2006.

Hofius, Otfried. *Katapausis: Die Vorstellung vom endzeitl. Ruheort im Hebräerbrief*. WUNT 11. Tübingen: Mohr/Siebeck, 1970.

Johnston, George. "Christ as Archegos." *NTS* 27 (1981) 381–85.

Käsemann, Ernst. *The Wandering People of God: An Investigation of the Letter to the Hebrews*. Translated by Roy A. Harrisville and Irving L. Sandberg. Minneapolis: Augsburg, 1984.

Koester, Craig R. *Hebrews: A New Translation with Introduction and Commentary*. AB 36. New York: Doubleday, 2001.

Laansma, Jon C. *"I Will Give You Rest": The Rest Motif in the New Testament with Special Reference to Mt 11 and Heb 3–4*. WUNT 2/98. Tubingen: Mohr/Siebeck, 1997.

Lane, William L. *Hebrews 1–8*. WBC 47A. Dallas: Word, 1991.

Limburg, James. "Who Cares for the Earth? Psalm Eight and the Environment." In *All Things New: Essays in Honor of Roy A. Harrisville*, edited by Arland J. Hultgren et al., 43–52. WW Supplement 1. St. Paul, MN: Luther Northwestern Theological Seminary, 1992.

Mackie, Scott D. *Eschatology and Exhortation in the Epistle to the Hebrews*. WUNT 2/223. Tübingen: Mohr/Siebeck, 2007.

Marlow, Hilary. *Biblical Prophets and Contemporary Environmenal Ethics: Re-Reading Amos, Hosea and First Isaiah*. Oxford: Oxford University Press, 2009.

———. "'What Am I in a Boundless Creation?' An Ecological Reading of Sirach 16 & 17." *BibInt* 22 (2014) 34–50.

Metzger, Bruce M. *A Textual Commentary on the Greek New Testament: A Companion Volume to the United Bible Societies' Greek New Testament (Fourth Revised Edition)*. 2nd ed. Stuttgart: Deutsche Bibelgesellschaft, 1994.

Moffitt, David M. *Atonement and the Logic of Resurrection in the Epistle to the Hebrews*. NovTSup 141. Leiden: Brill, 2011.

Müller, P.G. "ἀρχηγός, οῦ, ὁ." In *EDNT*, edited by Horst Balz and Gerhard Schneider, 1: 163–64. Grand Rapids: Eerdmans, 1990.

Murray, Robert. *The Cosmic Covenant: Biblical Themes of Justice, Peace and the Integrity of Creation*. Heythrop Monographs 7. London: Sheed and Ward, 1992.

O'Brien, Peter T. *The Letter to the Hebrews*. PNTC. Grand Rapids: Eerdmans, 2010.

Peterson, David G. *Hebrews and Perfection: An Examination of the Concept of Perfection in "The Epistle to the Hebrews."* SNTSMS 47. Cambridge: Cambridge University Press, 1982.

Rogerson, John W. "The Creation Stories: Their Ecological Potential and Problems." In *Ecological Hermeneutics: Biblical, Historical and Theological Perspectives*, edited by David G. Horell et al., 21–31. London: T. & T. Clark, 2010.

Schenck, Kenneth L. "A Celebration of the Enthroned Son: The Catena of Hebrews 1." *JBL* 120 (2001) 469–85.

Thompson, James W. *Hebrews*. Paideia Commentaries on the New Testament. Grand Rapids: Baker Academic, 2008.

Towner, W. Sibley. "The Future of Nature." *Int* 50, no. 1 (1996) 27–35.

Wallace, Howard N. "Rest for the Earth? Another Look at Genesis 2.1–3." In *The Earth Story in Genesis*, edited by Norman C. Habel and Shirley Wurst, 49–59. Earth Bible 2. Sheffield: Sheffield Academic, 2000.

Waltke, Bruce K., and Cathi J. Fredricks. *Genesis: A Commentary*. Grand Rapids: Zondervan, 2001.

Wenham, Gordon J. *Genesis 1–15*. WBC 1. Waco, TX: Word, 1987.

White, Lynn, Jr. "The Historical Roots of Our Ecological Crisis." *Science* N.S. 155, no. 3767 (1967) 1203–7.

Theology

10

Jesus, the Sabbath and the Hope of Creation

Selwyn Yeoman,
Presbyterian Church of Aotearoa
New Zealand

Introduction

The boy stripped off his clothes and laid them at the feet of his watching older sister. Like Saul of Tarsus, she knew she was about to witness a death. The hot February sun reflected from a patina of perspiration as he plunged into the sparkling sea. While their parents stayed at home to rest, now was the children's moment of revolution. Happy to connive at this Sabbath breaking but not yet quite ready to take the plunge herself the sister watched as he began to wash away their forbears's suffocating Sunday afternoons.[1]

THE OBSERVANCE OF SUNDAY as a strict Sabbath has been a controversial element in New Zealand's history.[2] The Sabbatarian impulse has origins in two quite disparate movements which have often operated as uneasy allies—the Scots' Puritan and evangelical desire to establish a godly society and the

1. As witnessed near the Auckland Harbour bridge in February 1974 by this writer, who would soon marry the older sister.

2. Clayworth, "Story: Weekend" has said: "A 1950 handbook for European immigrants warned that 'to the Continental European our Sundays usually appear to be very dull, because no entertainment of any kind is available on that day and normally every week-day activity closes down. Not all New Zealanders agree with this state of affairs, but most of us feel that the old tradition of keeping one day in the week for religious worship and quiet family reunion, is preferable to any other. You must make the best of these things and try not to pass judgment until you understand why they are so.'"

desire of working people to establish an order liberated from the crushing demands of industrialized nineteenth-century Britain. The sad irony is that while heated debates have raged around what is proper to allow on Sunday there has been virtually no reflection on the Sabbath vision for the establishment of a just or regenerative social and environmental order. The Dunedin City fathers who attempted to prohibit Sunday access to the city's Botanical Gardens (the first such gardens in the country) were the same people held to account in Rev Rutherford Waddell's momentous sermon "On the Sin of Cheapness,"[3] or even more critically remembered in John A. Lee's novel "Children of the Poor."[4] In twenty-first-century New Zealand, however, Sabbath observance is in full retreat. Even the once sacrosanct ANZAC,[5] Christmas and Easter days are under assault from the forces of unrestrained consumer capitalism.

Sabbath in the Hebrew Scriptures and Inter-Testamental writings:

It is widely recognized that the creation account in Genesis 1:1—2:4 is part of a project by writers with priestly interests to provide disheartened Jewish exiles in Babylon with renewed faith and secure identity in the face of the national disaster of 587BCE. Such Documentary Hypotheses propose that the whole Pentateuch is a theologically motivated collection of material drawn from a number of different sources usually identified as J, E, D and P, with Genesis 1 being among P (Priestly) material.[6] For these exiles, Sabbath offered a liberating alternative to the endless labor for the gods which characterized the role of human beings in the Babylonian creation myths, in which cultural environment they now found themselves. David Pleins describes the whole Priestly enterprise as "a bold and visionary program of social reform,"[7] directed towards a renewed post-exilic national life.

3. See Breward, "Waddell, Rutherford." In the ensuing church discussion Waddell made it quite clear that business people were themselves pressured by consumers and all people, of any class, were complicit through their quest for cut-price bargains.

4. Lee, *Children of the Poor.*

5. ANZAC. Acronym for Australia New Zealand Army Corps whose landings at Gallipoli, Turkey, on 25th April 1915 are now commemorated on that date each year, along with all other military conflicts that have engaged the nation.

6. Lohfink, *Theology of the Pentateuch*, 136–39, and 136n3. See also Knight, *A Christian Theology of the Old Testament*, 23n1; Schottroff, "The Creation Narrative," 24–38, 25; and Jonsson, *The Image of God*, 15–24.

7. Pleins, *Social Visions*, 69.

Claus Westermann argues that this first creation account must be read, even experienced, as confessional in character and as shaped by liturgical considerations. "Creation myths are not firstly intellectual reflection on beginnings but liturgical enactments elucidating our place in the world and ensuring its stability."[8] Jon Levenson notes that, "in the Jewish liturgy this passage serves as an introduction to the Kiddush, the prayer over the wine to sanctify the Sabbath . . . the type of repetition suggests it might have served as a liturgy already in antiquity."[9] The liturgical cast of the passage is also suggested in the establishment of the great lights, the sun and moon in Gen. 1:14, to rule over night and day and to mark the times for seasons and festivals. Heather McKay demonstrates that New Moon festivals are almost always linked to Sabbaths and are referenced more frequently than any other in instructions regarding worship.[10] New Moon was an integral part of the calendar of Jewish worship. Not only the historical events of liberating salvation but also the cycles of creation served to order, inspire, and focus worship. At the heart of their life with God these people were subject to creation and guided by its cycles. Furthermore, they lived on Earth alongside other creatures for whom God had also made specific provision (Gen.1:22 and 30), and were not free to subject creation to their every whim.[11]

Indeed, the creation of human beings is not the end of this creation account and nor are they the end and goal of Yahweh's activity of creation. The passage is not anthropocentric but theocentric. Richard Bauckham speaks for many in observing that the climax of it all is the Sabbath.[12] It is on the seventh day, and not the sixth, that we are told, "God finished the work that he had done and he rested on the seventh day from all the work that he had done (Gen 2:2)." Thus the finishing and the resting are an integral part of the whole creation account. Then follows a blessing of the seventh day (Gen 2:3), which reflects the blessings pronounced earlier upon the creatures of

8. Westermann, *Genesis 1–11*, 21–22. See also Anderson, *From Creation to New Creation*; Berry, *Critical Perspectives*, 32–50. On the formative role of liturgy in establishing identity, see Neville and Westerhoff III, *Learning Through Liturgy*; and Smith, *Desiring the Kingdom*.

9. Levenson, "Introduction to Genesis," 9–10.

10. McKay, *Sabbath and Synagogue*, 25–42. McKay demonstrates that formal activities of prayer or worship were not part of Sabbath practice probably until Qumram. I do not believe this undermines the position that the P material, including Genesis 1, has liturgical intentions.

11. For a more comprehensive coverage of references to God's provision for animals equally with humans, see Bauckham, *Living with Other Creatures*, 87–91.

12. Bauckham, "Modern Domination of Nature," 46. See also, including a critique of the impact of the much later chapter division between Genesis 1 and 2, Lowery, *Sabbath and Jubilee*, 87 and 50–53.

sea and air on the fifth day (Gen 1:22), and upon the humans, and all other land dwelling creatures with them, on the sixth day (Gen 1:28). Howard Wallace argues that

> in Gen.2:1 humans are subsumed within "all that was within" the sky and earth . . . they are not afforded a special place . . . all creation is held under the sovereignty of God . . . thus Gen. 2:1–3 stands as a check against any interpretation of the role of humans in Gen.1:28 that ignores the harmony and wholeness of all the work God has done in creation.[13]

Sabbath therefore is to be received as a blessing not a burden; a gift not a demand. To take Sabbath rest is to show trust in the abundant provision of God through creation, and be reminded that we inhabit an Earth which is fruitful far beyond mere necessity. We identify ourselves as creatures, sharing this utterly dependent identity along with all God's other creatures. In this resting we may contemplatively enjoy creation, as God also does.

Sabbath is not dismissive of human work but it does relativize it. Work too is part of this order of Creation and necessary for human life to flourish. By it the Earth can be blessed. In contrast to Babylon or Egypt however, this work is not to be servile and it is not to be endless. It functions within limits, it can trust in "enough," because creation has been blessed to thrive. Thus, Sabbath is both a perpetual encouragement to trust and a restraint upon the avarice that fails to trust.

Richard Lowery demonstrates the relation between the "resting" of Genesis 2:1–4 and biblical examples of *shalom* and concludes, "Sabbath rest is a celebration of God's enthronement as universal sovereign."[14] Howard Wallace likewise recognizes the connection between God's rest and God's sovereignty and suggests this

> introduces the note of redemption to the story. That not only has implications for moral or religious reforms . . . but for ecological reforms as well. In particular . . . from any misappropriation of the notice in Gen. 1:26.28 that humans are given dominion over the earth and other creatures.[15]

Nevertheless, there are, he suggests, always forces in the world that act against the movement towards God's rest and we human-beings are

13. Wallace, "Rest for the Earth?" 53.
14. Lowery, *Sabbath and Jubilee*, 89.
15. Wallace, "Rest for the Earth?" 54.

involved in this struggle.[16] All this will have implications for Jesus' proclamation of the Kingdom of God.

Sanctuary, Jubilee and Liturgy

Furthermore, and consistent with the liturgical interests of the passage, we note connections between the creation story in Gen 1 and the establishment of the sanctuary as recorded in the Exodus narrative. In P material "there are more than 200 references to the tabernacle . . . while the tabernacle is mentioned only three times in E and never in J and D."[17] According to Norbert Lohfink, "building the sanctuary is paralleled with the divine building of the world, and the encounter with God in the sanctuary is paralleled with the divine rest on the seventh day."[18] Even the pattern of 6 days and 1 is repeated (Exod 24:16). The sanctuary is a model of the whole Creation. Douglas Knight writes,

> the temple is a complex sign system and working model of creation that relies on the logic of the microcosm. The temple represents the land and provides a matrix of analogies with which complex theological statements about God's relationship to his people and the world he gives them may be made . . . The building and maintenance of the temple form an analogy for and microcosm of the cultivation and rule of the world . . . the now ordered waters of chaos appear as the spring that waters the world . . . The Sabbath is here, and all things in the completed creation are very good.[19]

We should note here firstly a sense of joyousness about the Sabbath as a celebration of God's goodness in creation which has been notoriously, indeed destructively absent from much Sabbatarianism; secondly, the degree to which the Sabbath vision is inextricable from the land and life in the land; and thirdly that this connection between Sabbath and Sanctuary will prove vital in exploring the implications of Jesus' Sabbath practice.

16. Ibid., 58.

17. Miller and Huber, *The Bible*, 34.

18. Lohfink, *Theology*, 131. See also Westerman, *Genesis*, 170, who explores parallels in his notes on Gen 2:2a.

19. Knight, *The Eschatological Economy*, 149–50. Wallace however suggests that God's sovereignty is not expressed in temple building (the conditions of exile were not conducive to grand claims for the temple), but in the control of desolation and darkness by word and act bringing into being and maintaining interrelatedness and harmony. Wallace, "Rest for the Earth?" 54.

The creation account in Genesis 1 and 2 provides the introduction for the more comprehensive accounts of Sabbath found in Exodus, Leviticus and Deuteronomy. The Lord's resting in Creation provides the reason for Sabbath rest in Exod 20:11 and 31:17, which is to be a permanent sign of their covenant identity as God's chosen people. Their liberation from slavery in Egypt is the reason for rest in Deut 5:15 and 15:15.

In these passages from Exodus, Sabbath relates not only to the weekly rest (which includes rest for all animals as well as foreign workers) but also to Sabbath cycles of seven years culminating in the great Jubilee to be celebrated every fiftieth year. Here are the regulations concerning release for slaves, from debts, rest for the land itself and in the Jubilee, restoration of alienated lands to their original tribal occupants. Lowery recognizes Exodus, Leviticus and Deuteronomy as three different and sometimes conflicting Sabbath traditions—a reminder there is a range of understandings of Sabbath. Leviticus, especially in relation to Sabbath years for the land, he regards as a "utopian vision of the world . . . that would be utterly impractical for Israel . . . If it were fully implemented, it would lead to mass starvation."[20] Nevertheless, the real point is

> public affirmation of the land's freedom under Yahweh's sovereign rule . . . Sabbath year is the land's rest from work for Israel. Sabbath year, like the creation-Sabbath narrative in Genesis 1, rejects an overly anthropocentric view of the world . . . God established the value of creation long before human beings enter the picture . . . the land is worthwhile in its own right, apart from its usefulness to human beings. The land has its own justice, enforced by Yahweh, that cannot be overridden by human needs and wants . . . Owned by Yahweh (Lev. 25:23), the land is liberated from human bondage. The earth has its own vocation to obey and worship God and its own worth apart from its usefulness to human beings. The land exists in relationship with human society as a partner, not as an objectified commodity to be exploited without limit.[21]

So important is this partnership that the writers of both Leviticus (Lev 26:34–35) and Chronicles (2 Chr 36:21) assert that the seventy years of exile in Babylon is to allow the land recovery of the Sabbaths which it has been denied. Unrestrained human priority is also rejected by Sabbath protection

20. Lowery, *Sabbath and Jubilee*, 59. On p. 54 he explores the possibility that in Exod 23 the seventh year law is not required for every field at once but envisions some kind of rotation.

21. Ibid., 61–62.

for the interests of wild animals (Exod 23:11). Reflecting the idea of partnership with the rest of Creation, Margaret Barker suggests that

> the command to eat only what grows of itself in the field (Lev. 25:12) and the older injunction to share this equally with the poor and the animals (Exod 23:11), indicates that the Sabbath year was a time when the land and people returned to . . . the original state of creation.[22]

Furthermore, this proclamation being made on the Day of Atonement (Lev 25:9), was a sign that "jubilee was a practical application of the atonement."[23] Atonement is thus not only an experience of personal, inner cleansing and reconciliation, but a participation in a restoration of the land and Creation itself.

Pleins cites an observation by Lohfink that due to short life expectancy "most Israelite victims of poverty would never see a year of Jubilee."[24] They would, however, experience some of the anticipatory Sabbath years and in this light one can imagine how Jubilee would take on a powerful eschatological character. Knight suggests that "Israel's liturgical task is the labor of imagining, modeling, and preparing for the new creation, and so participating in its arrival."[25] Sabbath thus takes on an eschatological and messianic orientation. Moltmann similarly recognizes,

> The Sabbath . . . divides up human time. It brings interruption, interval and rhythm into human temporal experience. But of course, all the other "festal" divisions of time do this too. What is special about the Sabbath commandment is, on the one hand, the remembrance of God's eternal Sabbath of creation, from which the command to sanctify the Sabbath springs; and on the other, the promise of the eternal Sabbath of the messianic era.[26]

Long before priestly pastors compiled the Pentateuch as we now have it, the complaint of the prophet Amos was not that his people did not rest on the Sabbath, even if resentfully, but that the work they were eager to return to was the antithesis of all that the Sabbath was meant to mean (Amos 8:4–6). Lowery suggests this concern is also mirrored in Isa 58:13, Neh 10:31 and 13:15–22, and Jer 17:21–27 (one could also add Isa 1:13–15).[27] In

22. Barker, "The Time Is Fulfilled," 23.

23. Ibid., 24.

24. Pleins, *Social Visions,* 89n68.

25. Knight, *Eschatological Economy,* 96.

26. Moltmann, *God in Creation,* 286.

27. Lowery, *Sabbath and Jubilee,* 112–14.

this conception, Sabbath not only provides a rhythm and structure to time but also an indication of what is appropriate work and what is not on days outside the Sabbath. Animals and human labor were the only sources of energy to drive economic activity in the ancient world. That Sabbath includes animals, indentured laborers and—every seventh year, the land also, is a clear indication the intention was not merely rest from work but a reminder there are limits within which all economic activity should take place.

That the anticipation of Sabbath should shape the living of daily life is a developing theme in post-exilic practice, eventually forming the context in which Jesus exercised his ministry. Heather Mckay having surveyed the inter-testamental literature observes that although there is a wide range of attitudes towards the Sabbath it is generally held in increasingly high regard as a holy day—not simply a rest day.[28] Judith's Sabbath, for example, is not a fast but a blessing and its joys are not confined to that day only, but are anticipated in the preceding days (Jdt 8:6). Sabbath possesses intrinsic qualities which impact on normal time and there is a sense of the future breaking into the present.[29] In 1 Maccabees 2, a decision is made that profaning the Sabbath by fighting is appropriate in order to secure a better future for the Sabbath. Apart from such an exception however, Sabbath observance becomes the subject of increasingly detailed prescription. Ritual washings are introduced—for which there is no scriptural warrant.[30] In the book of Tobit on the other hand, "the Sabbath is never referred to at all . . . evidence of how varied the attitudes to the sabbath were."[31] The Dead Sea Scrolls indicate a community highly conscious of the need to keep a tightly regulated Sabbath, in which restrictions on work are also extended to restrictions upon thought. The book of *Jubilees* builds on all this, even to applying the death penalty for breaches of the Sabbath. Following VanderKam, McKay suggests that in *Jubilees* keeping proper Sabbath "has the power to influence the cosmic harmony on behalf of Israel, and perhaps . . . has influence over God himself."[32] Here again, the nature and power of Sabbath impacts upon ordinary time. Nevertheless, despite the many prohibitions, what they must do on the Sabbath is, "eat, drink, bless the Creator and be satisfied, rest and refrain from all work."[33] All these sources increasingly view Sabbath as a

28. McKay, *Sabbath and Synagogue*, 43–60.

29. Ibid., 47.

30. Ibid., 49.

31. Ibid., 50.

32. Ibid., 57.

33. Ibid., 58.

sign of Jewish identity, its faithful observance necessary for their national well-being, and for some at least, "a privilege not open to Gentiles."[34]

Alongside this increased honoring of the Sabbath lay the actual challenge of practicing it, especially those aspects relating to land and property, when increasingly the land was subject to foreign rulers and property in the hands of absentee estate owners. In this situation it is easy to imagine how the vision of Jubilee would take on eschatological and even revolutionary meanings. Nick Spencer and Robert White recognize this central eschatological dynamic when describing

> chapters 40–66 of Isaiah as truly visionary. They are poems of hope, joy and celebration. They imagine the deliverance and restoration of God's people, the vindication of God's rule, and the inauguration of a renewed order that reflects God's plans for creation.[35]

These are the chapters that by the time of Jesus had taken on the character of a rousing political manifesto, deeply shaping the whole national consciousness and central to Jewish messianic hopes and political discourse. W. D. Davies writes of "the boiling cauldron of eschatological anticipation of first-century Judaism,"[36]and Margaret Barker analyses this heating-up by demonstrating how post-exilic time was being measured in Jubilees.[37]

The historical and theological significance of Sabbath I have traced thus far provides the background for the ministry of Jesus.

Sabbath In and After the Ministry of Jesus

Luke introduces Jesus' public ministry by describing events in the synagogue at Nazareth during which Jesus reads from the prophet Isaiah (chapter 61) and then announces that the long anticipated day of the Lord has arrived in his reading of the passage (Luke 4:16–21).

Michael Hardin notes that this was "a lectionary passage for the Year of Jubilee."[38] We can surely assume a degree of deliberation on Jesus' part about timing his moment. As Margaret Barker argues,

> Tenth Jubilee fervour and expectation were the context for the ministry of Jesus . . . if Jesus was born in 7/6 BCE and was

34. Ibid., 59n48.
35. Spencer and White. *Christianity, Climate Change and Sustainable Living*, 101.
36. Davies, *The Gospel and The Land*, 255.
37. Barker, "The Time Is Fulfilled," 25–26.
38. Hardin, *The Jesus Driven Life*, 60–61.

> baptized when he was about 30 years old (Luke 3:33), he began his ministry during the crucial first "week" of the tenth Jubilee . . . Luke's account . . . shows that he claimed to have inaugurated the final Jubilee; no other interpretation can be put on the claim to have fulfilled that day.[39]

Jubilee, as we have seen, was the Sabbath of Sabbaths and, beyond the requirements of weekly Sabbath, involved the whole land and provided for the needs of all living creatures. Therefore, in identifying his mission with a Jubilee Jesus was identifying care of the land and healing for Creation as an integral element of his ministry. As he traversed the land proclaiming the imminence of the Kingdom of God he was effectively announcing Jubilee and reclaiming the Earth for its healing.[40]

Moltmann suggests that Protestant theologies and dogmatics have generally read Jesus's Sabbath teaching in terms of opposition to Jewish law, whereas his use of the Sabbath proclamation in Luke 4 "is the proclamation of the imminent kingdom of God, whose unparalleled closeness he authenticates through the signs of the messianic age."[41] Read in this light, all Jesus's Sabbath encounters may be regarded as applications of Jubilee, even when Jubilee is not mentioned.

Mark's account of Jesus's ministry begins with him in the desert with the wild animals. Bauckham considers that Mark is here making a deliberate connection to Isaiah 11 with the wild animals being neither dominated nor co-opted, but simply befriended.[42] "Jesus in the wilderness enacts . . . the peace between the human world and wild nature that is the Bible's hope for the messianic future."[43] Thus despite the absence of the Jubilee declaration found in Luke 4, we can with some confidence suggest that Mark also envisages the inauguration of the peaceable kingdom of the Jubilee. His introduction provides the framework within which the rest of Jesus' ministry may be assessed.

Neither Mark nor Matthew place the Nazareth proclamation at the beginning of the ministry, nor do they make reference to the Isaiah passage. But they both have Jesus coming into Galilee, newly empowered by the Spirit and proclaiming the arrival of the Kingdom of God. We have previously

39. Barker, "The Time Is Fulfilled," 27–28. Kraybill also identifies the Nazareth sermon as a proclamation of Jubilee, with numerous sources in support while acknowledging a minority of dissenting voices, in *The Upside-Down Kingdom*, 97 and 313n2.

40. On Jesus' travels, see further, Freyne, *Jesus, a Jewish Galilean*, 40, 57 and 76.

41. Moltmann, *God in Creation*, 291.

42. Baukham, *Living with Other Creatures* 75.

43. Ibid., 76.

noted that Sabbath in Genesis is a declaration of divine sovereignty and here we find the themes of Jubilee and the reign of God being linked in Jesus's ministry. Both Gospels are pregnant with messianic implications in speaking of "the good news of God," and the time of "fulfillment" (Matt 4:13–17; Mark 1:14–15). Thus, they gather to Jesus all the eschatological significance that had become attached to the Sabbath.

From the outset this Jubilee proclamation proved controversial, rejecting as it did divine vengeance,[44] racial and nationalistic exclusivism,[45] and recourse to violence,[46] but advocating "a new and creative interpretation of the kingdom of God."[47] At the heart of the controversy is the nature of Jesus's authority, and Mark 2 and 3 introduce three contentious issues. First, they concern the authority to forgive sins (Mark 2:1–12), to extend the circle of God's welcome to outsiders (vv. 13–17), and, significantly, to reinterpret the laws regarding the Sabbath (2:23–3:6). Jesus clearly states that "The Sabbath was made for humankind, and not humankind for the Sabbath." Second, "The Son of Man is Lord even of the Sabbath" (Mark 2:27–28). Richard Lowery argues that by running the two observations together Jesus is actually identifying the Lordship of the Son of Man with the Lordship of all humanity.[48] James Dunn also suggests, thirdly, "in response to criticism of his disciples, Jesus was remembered as defending their action as appropriate to the lordship which God had given to humankind (or Israel) over all his creation."[49]

While Jesus promotes a generous, life-giving understanding of the Sabbath in contrast to one that he considered to be characterized by "hardness of heart" (Mark 3:5), it is nonetheless a Sabbath under his Lordship and only upon this basis will human beings be able to properly exercise their lordship.

Other Sabbath incidents are also models of Jubilee. Lowery, for example, suggests the Pharisees interpret the grain-plucking incident (Matt 12:1–8; Mark 2:23–28; Luke 6:1–5) through the lens of the Exodus 34 prohibition on work. However, for Jesus,

44. Hardin, *Jesus Driven Life*, 62.

45. Ibid., 62; see also Lowery, *Sabbath and Jubilee*, 138–39; and Brueggemann, *The Land*, 162–63.

46. Barker. "The Time Is Fulfilled," 32.

47. Freyne, *Jesus, a Jewish Galilean*, 140. See also Wright, *Jesus and the Victory of God*, 389; and Davies, *The Gospel and The Land*, 352–53.

48. Lowery, *Sabbath and Jubilee*, 125.

49. Dunn, *Jesus Remembered*, 741.

> the more fitting association, is the gleaning tradition (Lev. 19:9; 23:22; Deut. 24:19–21; Ruth 2), and the Sabbath and Sabbath-year laws in Exodus 23:9–12, which ground seventh day and seventh year in economic support for the resident alien . . . Jesus' disciples pluck grain, not as householders who own the crop and have the right to sell it, but as the economically vulnerable who have a God-given right to take what they need to survive.[50]

In this light, the example of David in the sanctuary may also be read within the gleaning and Sabbath-year traditions. Similarly, in writing of the Sabbath release for the woman burdened by years of disability (Luke 13), Tom Wright argues

> Jesus was claiming that Israel's longing—for a great Sabbath day when all her enemies would be put to shame, and she herself would rejoice at God's release—was being fulfilled in him . . .the Sabbath day was the most appropriate day (for her healing), because that day celebrated release from captivity, from bondage, as well as from work.[51]

A fourth contentious issue is implied within some disputes regarding the Sabbath: the particular illustration Jesus uses, of David taking and sharing the sacred bread from the sanctuary (Mark 2:25–26; Matt 12:1–14 and Luke 6:1–11), suggests that while staking his claim to authority over the Sabbath he is also making a claim to authority in the Sanctuary. Matthew adds the reminders that "priests in the temple break the Sabbath" (12:5), and that God "desires mercy rather than sacrifice" (12:7), the example of rescuing a sheep in trouble (12:11–12), and the observation that "something greater than the temple is here" (12:6). The connection between Sabbath and sanctuary, with all its implications for the land, is one we have previously explored in relation to Genesis 1 and 2 and any doubt about the link must be dispelled by Jesus own apparent readiness to use a sanctuary example to support a Sabbath practice.

Jesus' Sabbath vision clearly extends to include appropriate Lordship over and healing for the land, issues around work and economic justice, while also incorporating the reconciliation and worship offered through the sanctuary.

In his account of Jesus' relationship with the Sabbath Ben Witherington writes,

50. Lowery, *Sabbath and Jubilee*, 128.

51. Wright, *Jesus and The Victory of God*, 394. See also Lowery, *Sabbath and Jubilee*, 134–35.

> Jesus' point of view seems to be that human beings do not exist for the sake of the law, but rather the converse. The function of the Sabbath is to restore and renew creation to its full capacity, just as leaving the land fallow for a sabbatical year might do . . . this meant that at least some of the old rules no longer applied, for a new situation was dawning, a divine dominion was breaking in through the ministry of Jesus.[52]

Jesus seems clearly to have intended that his proclamation of the reign of God in a year of Jubilee had implications for the Earth itself. But how was this expressed in his ministry? All our examples have involved people. However, conscious of the inter-dependence of human and non-human creation outlined in Hebrew thought, it is safe to suggest that healing for a human is also healing for the wider creation, and conversely, restoration for some aspect of non-human creation will also entail blessing for human beings.[53]

Jesus' teaching on the Kingdom does include wild nature when reflecting on the Sabbath vision. "What will we eat?" is a question raised by Sabbath year requirements that the land must be given rest (Lev 25:18–22 cf. Matt 6:31–34). Jesus' answer is not to ignore the needs of the land but to trust that your heavenly Father knows what you need. That the well-being of his people is inextricably tied up with that of other creatures is affirmed in the reminders that their heavenly Father cares for the birds, clothes the wild flowers and knows the fate even of sparrows (Matt 6:25–34; Luke 12:22–31). Just as we are part of the wider community of life, this care is also experienced communally—hence the admonition to cast anxiety aside by "seeking first the Kingdom of God" (Matt 6:33–34; Luke 12:31–34). Tithing, gleaning and alms-giving are all aspects of Kingdom living and "hard work and community sharing are the channels by which the Creator's provision supplies the needs of all."[54] Nevertheless, while God does thus preserve the life of each of his creatures, humans remain one with all other life in that God will also allow that life to end in its time. Death is also within the orbit of God's sovereign care.

Jesus's interest in nature is noteworthy. Bauckham[55] and Freyne[56] both explore Jesus's extensive use of examples from nature in his teaching, and the significance of his nature miracles. Nature for Jesus is not simply a source of analogies but a place where God is at work and through which we

52. Witherington III, *The Christology of Jesus*, 68–69.
53. See Yeoman, *Is Anyone in Charge Here?* 41
54. Ibid., 144. See also Freyne, *A Jewish Galilean*, 47–48.
55. Bauckham. *Living with Other Creatures*, 64–75.
56. Freyne, *A Jewish Galilean*.

may learn more of God's ways. In comparison, "the rabbinic parables . . . are much less connected with the everyday world (natural and occupational) of ordinary people."[57]

Jesus's ministry was a proclamation of Jubilee. The Kingdom of God was breaking in—but not in quite the way many of his contemporaries had envisaged. The end of this disappointment, or offense, was of course Jesus's crucifixion, an outcome which overturned all his claims. W. D. Davies in the concluding paragraph of *The Gospel and the Land* writes

> a Jew, Jesus of Nazareth proclaimed the acceptable year of the Lord only to die accursed on a cross and so to pollute the land, and by that act and its consequences to shatter the geographic dimension of the religion of his fathers.[58]

Only resurrection could serve to vindicate him. Resurrection is the sign that, "God himself has confirmed the pre-Easter activity of Jesus."[59] The dynamic of vindication is a recurring feature of the preaching recorded in Acts where we frequently read, "you killed him . . . but God raised him from death." It is resurrection that declares Jesus to be "Lord and Messiah" and clarifies a cosmic significance to his ministry of proclaiming Jubilee.[60]

Subsequently, the writer of Hebrews 4 appropriated the image of Sabbath rest to describe the salvation achieved by Christ. Paul reminded the Colossians (Col 2:16–18) that disputes about New Moon festivals or Sabbaths served only to detract from the reality to which they pointed, which was Christ. While the motif of the Kingdom of God is more common in the New Testament writings—perhaps being a more culturally transportable idea—it is crucial to note that theologically and for Jesus the Kingdom and the Jubilee are inextricable.[61]

Similarly, while the motif of Kingdom grows, that of Sabbath does not disappear from the tradition of theological and pastoral reflection but remains a recurring theme among the patristic writers. Sabbath provided the integrating theme for Augustine's vision. The soaring finales of both *The Confessions* and *The City of God* are celebrations of Sabbath. Sabbath, not humanity, is the goal of God's creative work whereby the whole Creation will be drawn to ultimate rest in its Creator. This is the eschatological vision that infuses all Augustine's work. This is pre-figured for Creation

57. Bauckham, *Living with Other Creatures*, 69.

58. Davies, *The Gospel and the Land*, 375.

59. Pannenberg, *Jesus: God and Man*, 67–68.

60. See further, Yeoman, *Anyone in Charge?* 259–60, and notes.

61. See Appendix, "Kingdom of God in Early Christian Literature," in Wright, *Jesus and The Victory Of God*, 663–70.

in Jesus's death, resting in the tomb and resurrection and we can begin to experience it now by faith, through the contemplative life in the monastic community, in the practicalities of daily life, even in the encounter with nature through gardening.[62]

Benedict ordered monastic life around the Sabbath, both in the daily hours of prayer and by his structuring of the week. The hymns for Saturday—the day of Sabbath rest and the gathering of the whole Creation in praise—are also the hymns for Sunday, the first day of creation and the day of the Lord's resurrection, the beginning of the new Creation. Thus the rhythm of life in the monastic community revolves around sharing in the praise of all Creation, and that praise anticipates the renewal of Creation signified in the Sabbath.[63]

The sanctification of time is a central theme in the monastic engagement with Creation. The need to understand and predict the seasons was vital to a properly ordered life and so two centuries after Benedict, Bede carefully calculated *The Reckoning of Time*.[64] Bede's goal is to discern and fit into what God has established within nature, and at the heart of this is the relation between Sabbath and Easter.[65] He finds parallels between the week of Creation and six other kinds of week in Scripture, "all of which, if I am not mistaken, point to a single end: that is they urge us to hope for endless peace in the grace of the Holy Spirit when all good works are accomplished,"[66] and this is the age of the Sabbath.

Following the Cistercian reforms, three centuries later, Sabbath remained central, for "on Sundays and some fifty other days during the year no manual work was done by the choir monks."[67]

The significance of this cursory examination is that in the light of Jesus's resurrection, Sabbath as Jubilee was seen even more clearly than previously to have Christological and cosmic dimensions. Christ's resurrection is God's guarantee, within the materiality of the world, that Creation will be healed. The resurrection gift of the Holy Spirit is the foretaste enabling something of that future to be lived out now. Sabbath as Jubilee provides a model for such hopeful living.

62. Harrison, "Augustine and the Art of Gardening"; also Yeoman, *Anyone in charge?* 120–28.

63. Yeoman, *Anyone in charge?* 165–67.

64. Bede, *The Reckoning of Time.*

65. Bede, *On Genesis*, 96, and notes 122 and 123; Bede, *On Time*, 274; and see further, Yeoman, *Anyone in Charge?* 167–69.

66. Bede, *On Time*, 32.

67. Knowles, *The Monastic Order in England*, 212.

Jubilee and Ecological Hope

We too are called, as were our ancient forebears, to Sabbath rest and restoration in the presence of God. Simply to stop for the duration of a day, is a radical relativization of the culture of work that has become despotic in contemporary society. Sabbath keeping is arguably the most radical, yet accessible, counter-cultural act of witness in which members of the Christian community could engage. Jonathan Sacks notes that the Sabbath was largely unintelligible, even suspect, to non-Jews in the ancient world, but at its heart, then and now, was

> the idea that there are important truths about the human condition that cannot be accounted for in terms of work or economics. The Sabbath is the day on which . . . we stop making a living and learn instead simply how to live.[68]

Lynne Baab writes personally,

> Sabbath has been a great gift to me by slowing me down and inviting me to share God's rest—not just analyze it . . . Sabbath has also enabled me to learn from Jesus, to take his yoke on my shoulders rather than live in response to the world's demands and my own unhealthy desires. Keeping a Sabbath has taught me the deep truths of God's love.[69]

Such resting has public policy implications in the face of scientific/technological/commercial interests "which are training us to be transcendent-vision-blind"[70] consuming the Earth and severely limiting our understanding of what it means to be human.

We rest in Christ, free from the burden of having to prove ourselves by works. Even in a secularized culture supposedly characterized by religious indifference, this is in fact a critical issue. Baab suggests that the contemporary culture of busyness and pride in productivity is actually a form of idolatry. She quotes Dorothy Bass: "To act as if the world cannot get along without our work for one day in seven is a startling display of pride that denies the sufficiency of our generous Maker."[71] But most of us don't want

68. For a more comprehensive survey of Sabbath, see Sacks, "Morals and Markets," 45–46.

69. Baab, *Sabbath Keeping*, 10.

70. Gregorios, *The Human Presence*, 95.

71. Baab, *Sabbath Keeping*, 96.

to stop "interfering" in the world. We really don't want to acknowledge that the world belongs to God.[72]

Resting in the risen Christ represents a vital antidote to the message of secular salvation through the endless pursuit of things, from which there is never any rest. "Many of society's richest people now think it's cool to be overstretched . . . 'Busyness, and not leisure, is now the badge of honour.'"[73] Leaders in politics and business are frequently lauded for their 16–20 hour days. New Zealanders who have employment are now working twenty percent more hours than they did in the 1960s, despite the remarkable increase in labor-saving devices.[74] Yet such increases in hours of work are not matched by similar increases in personal well-being—indeed the opposite is often the case.

> Not only have measures of wellbeing and happiness ceased to rise with economic growth but, as affluent societies have grown richer, there have been long-term rises in rates of anxiety, depression and numerous other social problems.[75]

Augustine would probably assess the situation in terms of his famous "restless heart."

Sabbath Practice: Eating and Contemplation

This culture of busyness—of Sabbath breaking—is also the one that allows no restraint upon our consumption of the Earth. Indeed, the modern economy is predicated upon the illusion of an indefinite supply of resources. But Sabbath declares that there are rhythms and constraints. Like much modern science it reminds us that life upon Earth is lived within delicately established parameters. In *A Fine Tuned Universe,* Alister McGrath explores the significance of "anthropic phenomena."

> the emergence of human life in the aftermath of the big bang is governed by a mere six numbers, each of which is so precisely determined that a miniscule variation in any one would have made both our universe and human life, as we know them,

72. Ibid., 96.

73. Naish, *Enough,* 114.

74. Ibid. quotes similar figures for the United Kingdom.

75. Wilkinson and Pickett, *The Spirit Level*, 6; and see Fig. 1.2, 9. Also see Lowery, *Sabbath and Jubilee*, 1–5.

> impossible. Roger Penrose also speaks of an "extraordinary degree of precision (or 'fine-tuning')" required for life.[76]

These numbers are the constants of the universe and impervious to human interference. But levels of CO_2 and other Greenhouse gases are rising steadily to dangerous levels, almost entirely due to the prodigious burning of fossil fuels to meet the energy demands of the world's wealthiest economies, and secondarily to the loss of vast tropical forests which have hitherto served to soak up large quantities of carbon.[77] Of course, while it lies within human power to alter levels of CO_2 within the Earth's atmosphere, we are powerless to alter the inexorability of the physics. Refusal to acknowledge the truth of our createdness, that life is lived within limits despite our human creativity, is leading to a global environmental crisis in which other Sabbath concerns such as well-being for animals and economic justice are becoming more pressing than ever. Sabbath reminds us that alongside inviolable physical limits we also live out our humanity within the constraints of ecological, economic and social relationships. Jubilee living recognizes the necessity of living within the constraints of Creation—and this is modeled for us in the incarnation.

Below, I will outline two brief examples of Sabbath observance. First, to live attentive to the rhythms and limits of creation, will shape our diet. Modern patterns of trade and technology now enable food to be delivered to our tables out of season and ostensibly fresh at any time of the year. The effect is to insulate us from the passage of the seasons and, ironically, make life less rather than more interesting. Life becomes bland because we no longer live in anticipation (an aspect of the eschatological hope in Sabbath), and with almost every kind of food always available nothing is ever new. To eat seasonally reconnects us with the rhythms of the natural world, the challenges of food production and the experiences of anticipation, fulfillment and joy. It also has the potential to make us much more attuned to the particular realities of our own locale. Similarly, the practice of grace before meals reflects aspects of Sabbath. There is deliberate stopping, reflection upon what has been provided—both through and quite independently of our own work, there is deliberate thanksgiving and ideally and easily this can become a creative ritual.

However, enjoyment of the Creator's good gifts can easily (especially in a consumerist culture) become a religiously legitimized form of

76. McGrath, *The Re-Enchantment of Nature*, 85. On the six numbers themselves, see Rees, *Just Six Numbers*.

77. Flannery, *The Weather Makers*; Lee, "Christian Conversations"; McKibben, "Remember This."

consumerism. Therefore, the resting and enjoyment of Sabbath cannot be pursued apart from being located within the spiritual disciplines of the *contemplative life*. Creation is an experience of rich provision—a provision that extends beyond humanity to all living beings. Contemplative attentiveness to the world will issue both in joy and wonder and in a renewed hunger for justice in the Creation that still groans, awaiting its final redemption. Thus Richard Foster urges that in the face of "abysmal ignorance,"[78] there must be a renewal of classic spiritual disciplines if the enjoyment of Sabbath is not to become mere indulgence, and the resting of Sabbath not crushing boredom. Consumers must become contemplatives. In an age dangerously disconnected from the processes of the Earth of which we are still inescapably a part, to be such a contemplative requires deep attentiveness to "the lilies of the field . . . and the birds of the air (Matt 6:24–30)." Sunlight fragmented into a thousand rainbows through morning dew-drops offers us diamonds beyond the wealth of Solomon, in a gift equally to our neighbors as to ourselves. Such attentive immersion will find joy in the invigorating sting of cold water or the caressing bubbles of warm waves, swimming with gratitude on a Sunday afternoon.

Bibliography

Anderson, Bernhard. *From Creation to New Creation: Old Testament Perspectives*. Minneapolis: Fortress, 1994.

Baab, Lynne. *Sabbath keeping. Finding Freedom in the Rhythms of Rest*. Downers Grove, IL: InterVarsity, 2005.

Barker, Margaret. "The Time Is Fulfilled: Jesus and the Jubilee." *Scottish Journal of Theology* 53 (2000) 22–32.

Baukham, Richard. *Living with Other Creatures: Green Exegesis and Theology*. Milton Keynes: Paternoster, 2012.

Baukham, Richard. "Modern Domination of Nature—Historical Origins and Biblical Critique." In *Environmental Stewardship: Critical Perspectives, Past and Present*, edited by R. J. Berry, 32–50. London: T. & T. Clark, 2006.

Bede. *On Genesis*. Translated, introduced and notes by Calvin B. Kendall. Liverpool: Liverpool University Press, 2008.

———. *The Reckoning of Time*. Translated and introduced by Faith Wallis. Liverpool: Liverpool University Press, 1999.

Berry, R. J., ed. *Critical Perspectives, Past and Present*. London: T. & T. Clark, 2006.

Breward, Ian. "Waddell, Rutherford." In *Dictionary of New Zealand Biography*, 1993. Te Ara—The Encyclopedia of New Zealand, http://www.TeAra.govt.nz/en/biographies/2w1/waddell-rutherford. Accessed 2 February 2017.

78. Foster, *Celebration of Discipline*, 3, 29–30.

Clayworth, Peter. "Story: Weekends." 5 September 2013. Te Ara—The Encyclopedia of New Zealand. http://www.TeAra.govt.nz/en/weekends/page-3. Accessed January 12, 2018.

Davies, W. D. *The Gospel and The Land: Early Christianity and Jewish Territorial Doctrine.* Berkeley: University of California Press, 1974.

Brueggemann, Walter. *The Land: Place as Gift, Promise, and Challenge in Biblical Faith.* Minneapolis: Fortress, 2002.

Dunn, James D. G. *Jesus Remembered.* Grand Rapids: Eerdmans, 2003.

Flannery, Tim. *The Weather Makers.* Melbourne: Text, 2005.

Foster, Richard. *Celebration of Discipline: The Path to Spiritual Growth*, 3rd ed. San Francisco: HarperCollins, 1998.

Freyne, Sean. *Jesus, a Jewish Galilean.* London: T. & T. Clark, 2004.

Gregorios, Paulos. *The Human Presence: An Orthodox view of Nature.* Geneva: World Council of Churches, 1978.

Hardin, Michael. *The Jesus Driven Life. Reconnecting Humanity with Jesus.* Lancaster PA: JDL, 2010.

Harrison, Carol. "Augustine and the Art of Gardening." In *Studies in Church History,* edited by R. N. Swanson, 37. Woodbridge, UK: Ecclesiastical History Society, 2002.

Jonsson, Gunnlauger A. *The Image of God: Genesis 1:26–28 in a Century of Old Testament Research.* Lund: Almqvist and Wiksell, 1988.

Knight, Douglas. *The Eschatological Economy: Time and the Hospitality of God.* Grand Rapids: Eerdmans, 2006.

Knight, George A. F. *A Christian Theology of the Old Testament.* London: SCM, 1959.

Knowles, David. *The Monastic Order in England,* 2nd ed. Cambridge: Cambridge University Press, 1966.

Kraybill, Donald. *The Upside-Down Kingdom.* Scottdale, PA: Herald, 1978.

Lee, Bill. "Christian Conversations about Climate Change and Conservation." Paper presented at the South Island Ministry Conference, East Taieri Presbyterian Church, Dunedin, New Zealand, 10 May 2011.

Lee, John A. *Children of the Poor.* Wellington: Whitcoulls, 1973.

Levenson, Jon D. "Introduction to and annotations of "Genesis."" In *The Jewish Study Bible,* edited by A. Berlin et al., 8–101. Oxford: Oxford University Press, 2004.

Lohfink, Norbert. *Theology of the Pentateuch.* Edinburgh: T. & T. Clark, 1994.

Lowery, Richard H. *Sabbath and Jubilee.* St. Louis: Chalice, 2000.

McKibben, Bill. "Remember This: 350 Parts Per Million." *Washington Post,* December 28, 2007. http://www.washingtonpost.com/wpdyn/content/article/2007/12/27/AR2007122701942.html.

McGrath, Alister. *The Re-Enchantment of Nature: Science, Religion and the Human Sense of Wonder.* London: Hodder and Stoughton, 2002.

McKay, Heather A. *Sabbath and Synagogue: The Question of Sabbath Worship in Ancient Judaism* Leiden: Brill, 1994.

Miller, Stephen M., and Robert D. Huber. *The Bible: A History.* Oxford: Hudson, 2004.

Moltmann, Jürgen. *God in Creation: A New Theology of Creation and the Spirit of God.* Minneapolis: Fortress, 1993.

Naish, John. *Enough: Breaking Free from the World of More.* London: Hodder and Stoughton, 2008.

Neville, Gwen Kennedy, and John H. Westerhoff III. *Learning Through Liturgy.* New York: Seabury, 1978.

Pannenberg, Wolfhart. *Jesus: God and Man.* Translated by Lewis L. Wilkins and Duane A. Priebe. London: SCM, 1968.

Pleins, J. David. *The Social Visions of the Hebrew Bible.* Louisville: Westminster John Knox, 2001.

Rees, Martin. *Just Six Numbers: The Deep Forces that Shape the Universe.* London: Weidenfeld & Nicolson, 1999.

Sacks, Jonathan. "Morals and Markets." *Cutting Edge* 56 (2002) 41–47.

Schottroff, Luise. "The Creation Narrative: Genesis 1:1—2:4a." In *A Feminist Companion to Genesis,* edited by Athalya Brenner, 24–38. Sheffield: Sheffield Academic, 1993.

Smith, James K. A. *Desiring the Kingdom: Worship, Worldview, and Cultural Formation.* Grand Rapids: Baker Academic, 2009.

Spencer, Nick, and Robert White. *Christianity, Climate Change and Sustainable Living.* London: SPCK, 2007.

Wallace, Howard. "Rest for the Earth? Another Look at Genesis 2:1–3." In *The Earth Story in Genesis,* edited by Norman C. Habel, and Shirley Wurst, Sheffield: Sheffield Academic, 2000.

Westermann, Claus. *Genesis 1–11.* Minneapolis: Augsburg, 1984.

Wilkinson, Richard, and Kate Pickett. *The Spirit Level: Why More Equal Societies Almost Always Do Better.* London: Lane, 2009.

Witherington III, Ben. *The Christology of Jesus.* Minneapolis: Augsburg Fortress, 1990.

Wright, N. T. *Jesus and the Victory of God.* Minneapolis: Fortress, 1996.

Yeoman, Selwyn C. "Is Anyone in Charge Here? A Christological Examination of the Idea of Human Dominion over Creation." PhD diss., University of Otago, 2012.

11

Creative, Apophatic Hopes

Temporality, Resonance Machines, and Entangled Misty Futures

Scott Kirkland,
Australian Catholic University

Frederic Jameson once said that "it has become easier to imagine the end of the world than the end of capitalism."[1] Mark Fisher identifies this as "capitalist realism." That is, "the widespread sense that not only is capitalism the only viable political and economic system, but also that it is now impossible even to *imagine* a coherent alternative to it."[2] Hope invokes the future as the site of an improved, alternate order, and yet in the present, as Henry Giroux and Brad Evans argue, our political imaginings seems to have been quelled, limited by dystopian visions of mere survival.[3] This is evidenced, for Fisher, Giroux and Evans, in the multiple sites in popular culture where the demands of an uncertain future seem to be continually collapsed into the present. For instance, in the 2006 film, *Children of Men*, contrary to emphases in P. D. James's novel where a Warden, who has taken executive powers to himself, suspends democratic order, the film makes little of this:

1. Jameson, "Future City," 73.

2. Fisher, *Capitalist Realism*, 2. Whether capitalist realism is a more helpful indicator of our current situation than postmodernism, or late-modernity, or liquid modernity, is contestable. However, Fisher's highlighting of the ways in which what is real is what is available to be commodified is helpful insofar as it allows us to diagnose something endemic to present ecological concerns.

3. Evans and Giroux, *Disposable Futures*, 1–44.

> For all we know the authoritarian measures that have been put in place could have been implemented by a system that remains, notionally, democratic. The War on Terror has prepared us for such a development: the normalization of crisis produces a situation in which the repealing of measures to deal with an emergency becomes unimaginable (when will the war be over?).[4]

This inability to imagine a future is pressed upon us on at least two fronts: the world without capitalism, and the world free from impending ecological doom, both of which become entangled as capitalism finds ways to make hope for the future the disciplining of consumptive desire.

Kathryn Tanner has argued convincingly in her recent Gifford Lectures, *Christianity and the New Spirit of Capitalism*, that finance dominated capitalism shrinks temporal horizons themselves into a series of disconnected presents, where the financially impoverished lurch from crisis to crisis.[5] Capitalism offers no room for hope beyond making it to the next rent payment, by whatever means possible, irrespective of whether those means will make the payment beyond even more improbable.[6] Temporality is fractured such that the concerns of ecological responsibility become something for the increasingly endangered middle classes. Ecologically responsible action is subsumed within bourgeois consumption. So it is that capitalism is morphing, as it continually does, under the pressure of the environmental crisis. As western liberal governments look to adapt to the new environmental realities, the continual supposed trade-off is that of established economic relations and environmental collapse. Critical to this rhetoric is the assumption that our existing economic patterns of relation needn't be disrupted by environmental catastrophe, rather we simply need to find more sophisticated ways of performing the balancing act of exploitation of the environment and economic growth in order to maintain the same patterns of consumption. The alienation of consumption from an unruly "nature" is clear in this political climate—creation itself is reacting to exploitative pat-

4. Fisher, *Capitalist Realism*, 1. Evans and Giroux make much of the reemergence of the zombie genre, and the lurch from crisis to crisis that breeds a certain kind of emergency political order within the broken political communities that remain, *Disposable Futures*, 17–20. See also Giroux, *Zombie Politics*.

5. This is made particularly clear in Tanner, "Nothing But the Present," 2016 Gifford Lectures, lecture four.

6. One thinks of the manifestly unjust high interest rates on payday loans and the ways in which these companies prey upon the uncertainties of the present, furthering the instability of the future. Yet, because the demands of the present dominate the imagination, the future falls from consideration, and becomes an impossibility. Hopeful action becomes impossible. Again, one simply wants to survive. For further discussion, see Lazarrato, *Governing by Debt*; Lazarrato, *The Making of Indebted Man*.

terns of consumption in industrialized western democracies. So, one reads on the COP15 website about several of the summit's corporate "partners," each of whom claims to be performing a kind of ecological responsibility that allows the consumer (be they individual, corporate or government) to continue in their same patterns of consumption while performing the good. This is what Žižek has called the "Starbucks effect"—that is, corporations will now cloak their activity in ethical responsibility in such a way that the act of consumption is itself seen as an act of environmental responsibility.[7] So, for instance, Coca-Cola, a COP15 partner, feigns a kind of localism,

> Coca-Cola sells in France 11 brands and sixty references, half of which is sugar-free or reduced sugar content. For 90 years, Coca-Cola has been an integral part of the lives of the French. 95% of drinks sold in France are manufactured in six plants located in French territory.[8]

Market hegemony is taken for a good, for Coca-Cola forms an integral part of "the lives of the French." If one were to visit the Grand Palais where various corporations have trade displays showcasing their efforts to fight climate change, you will "discover and learn" about the life cycle of a Coca-Cola bottle, you will be able to "dialogue and share" via various social media tools what you have learned of Coca-Cola's ecological efforts, etc. So, we can see that ethical responsibility has been turned to economic advantage. And yet our patterns of consumption remain unquestioned; we remain *homo economicus*. We are given shape by our consumptive desires; we simply have to make them ecologically sustainable. The nihilism of perpetually unsatisfied consumptive desire requires, then, a world on which it can continue to feed.

It is critical to note the way capitalism is functioning to discipline and to mediate desire such that ecological consciousness is itself commodified. It is precisely this that I wish to contest here. For it is capitalism's capacity to commodify our relation with the world that is disruptive of proper relation, mediated by a common desire for the end of all things, God. That is, capitalism is here functioning as a kind of faux transcendence, with disastrous ecological consequences. The domination of temporal horizons with the concerns of "mere survival," and the destruction of the possibility of thereby thinking an alternate order of things, becomes amplified in the church

7. In Fiennes, *The Pervert's Guide to Ideology*, New York: Zeitgeist films, 2012.

8. Some may object that I am reading this cynically. However, my point is that the patterns of excess consumption that have in part caused the ecological crisis we now face, remain unquestioned at the point at which we simply clean up the product itself. The ethical intent of Coca-Cola in this instance, then, is irrelevant.

in what William E. Connolly names the "evangelical capitalist resonance machine."[9] Connolly argues that certain forms of evangelicalism have created an echo chamber of media, culture, preaching, and forms of life, which all deny the reality of climate change. One reads a newspaper where one is told climate science is a hoax, one then listens to the news and is told again, one follows politicians who assure you of the same, and, finally, then, one lives as if the end were not nigh. "Spiritual sensibilities, economic presumptions, and state priorities slide and blend into one another, though each also retains a modicum of independence from the others."[10] There is no simple causal relation between these spheres of influence, rather a "system of dependence between separate factors, morphs into energized complexities of mutual imbrication and interinvolvement, in which heretofore unconnected or loosely associated elements *fold, bend, blend, emulsify, and resolve incompletely into each other,* forging a qualitative assemblage resistant to classical modes of explanation."[11] So it is that these complex relations are constitutive of this chaosmos, out of which arises the phenomenon of the climate change denying evangelical right. There is no one single diagnosis adequate to these phenomena, fuelled by corporate interests and complex historical relations between capitalism and Protestantism. What is in evidence, however, is the disciplining of desire by a set of interests alien to a credibly orthodox theological vision.

Further driving this resonance machine is, as Catherine Keller argues, the way climate change denial operates by preying upon the evangelical public's inability to deal with scientific *uncertainty*.[12] That is, while we can now say that there is a consensus among 97 percent of scientists that anthropogenic climate change is real, consensus is not equivalent to certainty—and never should be. The earth is "a complex system, fraught with known and unknown unpredictabilities." Yet this uncertainty is used to the advantage of climate change denial. Keller's insight is that "an apophatically canny ecotheology may . . . invite us to embrace, even to *feel*, the adaptive resilience of the planetary web of a living interconnectivity."[13] That is to say, the oscillation between complexity, uncertainty, entanglement and the

9. Connolly, *Christianity and Capitalism*, 39–67.

10. Ibid.,

11. Ibid.,

12. Keller, *Cloud of the Impossible*, 275. Uncertainty is, of course, basic to the scientific task. Yet, publicly, scientists are so often turned into the merchants of "truth," "fact," and certainty. See, for instance, the recent discussion between public physicist Brian Cox and the skeptical Australian politician Malcolm Roberts: Slezak, "QandA Smackdown".

13. Keller, *Cloud of the Impossible*, 275–6.

divine is precisely what theology offers resources for thinking *through* without evasion. Rather than being a cause for despair, perhaps the manifold of uncertain (though not anarchic) possibility in created being is cause for hope, and I would add, to Keller, that is the case insofar as hope is grounded in transcendent actuality. Though I differ from Keller in a number of key ways, this fundamental insight is helpful. Certainty is perhaps not any more a theological than a scientific virtue, for, as we have shall see in Meister Eckhart, it is the *ekstatic* nature of desire, the contingency of all things, that is their ground, and it is the ground of *all things*, for *all* share in the contingency and complexity of relation. Complexity is, then, potentially, a source of resistance to what Bruno Latour names popular 'factishism'.[14]

What are we to make of this strange, and complex, set of relations between the future, capitalism, Christianity, and ecology? In this paper, I propose to rethink human desire as directed by, and formed by, hopeful performance—desire directed otherwise. For the Christian, the end of things is not contingent upon any catastrophe within created being as such. The ultimate hope of the Christian is in the return of Christ, the one who is the *eschatos* himself. That does not mean, however, that we are unable to hope for the good of our fellow creatures preemptively revealing the ultimate healing activity to come. If we have hope, it is not grounded in sheer immanent possibility, but rather in that God who brings all things into being *ex nihilo*, and who sustains them, guiding them to their promised end. To hope is to *perform* the future in the present, it is to be formed by the promise of God in which our faith is anchored. We may want to enlist Karl Barth here: the Christian, "does not believe because he [*sic*] hopes, for he has no ground for hope apart from believing. But as and because he believes, putting *active* trust in the Word spoken to him as God's Word, he also hopes."[15] Hope, grounded in the divine promise, is *active*, hope orders us to the *telos* of God's life as we venture forth into the future. The future remains "an absolutely open and wholly unwritten page, or even an impenetrable sea of mist."[16] Yet, it is faith, the motor of hope, allowing us to venture forth into the misty space of the future—the space of possibility. Hope, then, "takes place in the act of taking the next step."[17] The church must be able to offer a hopeful political imagination in the face of, indeed in spite of, a *possibly* unspeakably bleak future. Yet it is precisely because hope is ambivalent to

14. Latour, *On the Modern Cult*. On "complexity as a source of resistance," see Williams, "Trinity and Ontology," 71–92.

15. Barth, *Church Dogmatics*, *CD* IV/3.2:913.

16. Ibid., *CD* IV/3.2:905.

17. Ibid., *CD* IV/3.2:939.

these possibilities (for it is anchored in God) that it is such a vital tool in the church's repertoire of creative resistance. For, if hope were contingent upon the flux of likelihoods of possible futures, the collapse into either despairing cynicism or facile optimism would never be far from the moment. Hope, when predicated upon sheer immanent possibility, is subject to constant change as contingent possibilities unfold. Hope becomes anarchic as we are beholden to historical movement as such, or to a darkly transcendent *deus ex machina* to intervene on our behalf. Hope, that is, must remain grounded in the transcendent, the transcendent generative of the possibilities of the immanent, *posse ipsum*.[18] We must learn, then, to enter into this darkness of pregnant possibility—of relation borne not by capital, but funded by the infinite relation that is the divine life.

An Origami Cosmos: Meister Eckhart's Unfolding of the Logic of Desire

Enfolded and Unfolded

First of all, then, I want to explore Meister Eckhart's logic of creation and desire. This will allow us to see how for Eckhart, *all* creaturely being is directed to the singular eschatological end that is the divine being.[19] Yet this end is infinite, and so the realm of creaturely possibility opens up before us as a space of movement into the infinite. This will further allow us to begin to interrogate the ways in which creaturely desire is being disordered by the mediation of relations with capital in contemporary capitalism.

Eckhart begins an exposition of Sirach 24:29 "They that eat me, shall yet hunger," with an exposition of this pervasive metaphysical and eschatologically ordered logic of desire. For Eckhart, a finite thing's finite hunger, or end, can be temporarily satisfied. However, it is "the opposite in things whose goal is infinite, for such things always hunger and thirst, and hunger more ardently and avidly the more they eat."[20] In order to think the

18. As Keller notes, this is one of Nicholas of Cusa's favorite "nicknames" for God. How we construe Cusanus's insertion of possibility into the divine being, however, will differ. Keller elegantly argues that Cusanus seems to insert possibility at a late stage in his career. I suspect the evidence she cites for this is perhaps more slight than she seems to suggest, and in need of contextualization. Keller, *Cloud of the Impossible*, 2, 87–123. For an alternate reading, see Hoff, *The Analogical Turn*.

19. Divine being, however, remains darkly "without a why." See Schürmann, *Wandering Joy*, 206–9.

20. Eckhart, *Teacher and Preacher*, 174. We come across similar language later in Kierkegaard's communion discourses: "Father in heaven, longing is your gift; no one

singular directness of desire in created being Eckhart employs the logic of Aristotelian prime matter—indicating that all creaturely agents are on the same ontological plain—yet radicalizes it in a neo-platonic direction. Prime matter is "infinite in relation to the number of forms that can be generated."[21] However, it never appears without determinate form, it appears as all particular existing things. Thus the hunger for infinite form is never satisfied in any particular form in the world as no created thing is the true *telos* of its desire. The point of Eckhart's illustrative use of prime matter becomes clearer as we see that he is using it as a way of speaking of the infinite end of created being as such. For, because there is no unformed prime matter, but it is always instantiated in particularity, all the diversity of forms in the world strive after the one goal that is the infinite in which one can perpetually eat but only ever have one's desire amplified.

As Eckhart continues his use of the language of prime matter is displaced by his use of the language of existence. For, both in nature and in art, existence is "what everything thirsts and hungers for, seeks and desires."[22] No-thing in the world can be the ground of its own existence, for then it would be the "root and principle of itself".[23] This means that existence is not some-thing that the world has in and of itself, but God gives it. Uniting the desire for existence and this radical contingency, then, Eckhart states, "every being and everything that belongs to the number of beings does not possess the existence it thirsts for, hungers for, and desires from itself, but from some superior."[24] Existence, then, is not even something that is then granted to created being as such, but is something far more intimate, for God is the very ground of the continued existence of things. Like Nicholas of Cusa, rather than construing the relation between creator and creation as one primarily analogous to efficient causality, Ekhart sees God as the formal cause of things. God's perpetual gift of himself (that is, Existence) to each creature is constitutive of its continued being. Hence, because the creature's ground is the Infinite's desire for the Infinite that is the divine life, the end of the creature is also this constitutive perpetual desire. "This is why it always thirsts for its superior's presence, and it is better and more proper to say

can give it to himself; if it is not given, no one can purchase it, even if he were to sell everything—but when you give it, he can still sell everything in order to purchase it. We pray that those who are gathered here today may come to the Lord's table with heartfelt longing, and that when they leave it they may go with intensified longing for him, our Savior and Redeemer." Kierkegaard, *Christian Discourses*, 251.

21. Eckhart, *Teacher and Preacher*, 174.

22. Ibid.

23. Ibid., 175.

24. Ibid.

that it continually receives its existence than that it has existence in itself in a fixed or even initial way."[25] The thirst for existence is the thirst for God. As Eckhart himself puts it, this is the true meaning of the text—"They shall eat me, and yet hunger"—for the fact that they eat and continue to hunger is because they "are empty in themselves and in potency to existence. This potency is a desire and a thirst for existence itself."[26] Hence, Eckhart is simply radicalizing the claims of *creatio ex nihilo*: created being does not exist in and of itself, it is called into being out of nothing, and so its continued suspension in existence is not an autonomous quality of finite being as such, but is a product of divine gift.

On this account, created being is fundamentally receptive. For it receives existence only through thirsting, "and this is why it hungers and thirsts, because through hunger it receives the existence by which it is and which it devours."[27] Desire is, then, both constitutive of, and the possibility of, existence. It is precisely because of this receptivity that creaturely being is analogous with—not univocally identical with—divine being.[28] As Eckhart states, a consequence of the analogical relation between creator and creature is that "goodness and justice and the like [i.e., perfections] have their goodness totally from something outside to which they are analogically *ordered,* namely, God."[29] That is to say, analogates do not have the form of that to which they are analogically ordered in themselves, yet "every created being is analogically ordered to God in existence, truth and goodness."[30] Every created being is therefore entirely and radically contingent upon God, and precisely as such radically "possesses existence, life and wisdom from and in God" not from its creaturely being as such. The creature therefore always eats as something created, but hungers because it is "always from another and not from itself."[31] Negatively the analogical negation, because it is between the infinite and the finite, is a negation in which any similarity between creator and creature is always shadowed by an ever-greater dissimilarity. However, it is also the site of creaturely becoming, the space in which the complex set of creaturely entanglements and relations can be thought.

25. Ibid.

26. Ibid.

27. Ibid., 176.

28. On Eckhart's vision of analogy and its difference from Aristotle, see Schürmann, *Wandering Joy,* 173–77.

29. Eckhart, *Teacher and Preacher,* 178.

30. Ibid.

31. Ibid., 179.

Creaturely Plurality

In order to see this logic play out more fully we need to see how it functions within Eckhart's construction of a Trinitarian grammar. In a sermon on justice Eckhart argues "all the virtue of the just, and every work that is wrought by the virtue of the just is nothing but this, that the Son is begotten of the Father." For there to be an act of justice, there must be an idea of justice. And, vice versa, for there to be any idea of justice, justice must be performed, for it only exists as enactment. Here emerges his Trinitarian logic, for "if the Father and the Son, justice and the just man, are one and the same in nature, it follows . . . that the just man is equal to, not less than, justice, and similarly with the Son in relation to the Father."[32] So, the concrete enactment of justice is just as important to justice as is the idea of justice which it enacts. In order to recognize justice we must see it enacted in a particular circumstance (the concrete universal), and yet we must also be able to recognize its universality by virtue of its repeatability. Hence, as Milbank notes, "in the unique and even exceptional circumstance we really do glimpse the ineffable universal pattern of justice. Inversely, this universal pattern *is* only its ceaseless expression in particular acts of justice".[33] That is to say, it is precisely the infinite potential for repetition that is the ground of the particular act of justice. So, to further extend the Trinitarian ground of justice, it is not that justice is exhausted in its particular enactment in Christ, but rather that "the idea of justice is all the more affirmed as 'source' in its open and mysterious horizon, even though we now see that all this idea consists in is the 'generation' of actual deeds of justice."[34]

One can see this further as an extension of Eckhart's doctrine of creation and analogy. As I have already indicated, the analogy between creator and creature is always framed in terms of an infinite exceeding of the creature on the part of the creator. However, it is precisely in that infinite interval that we are able to think the performance of the creature as participation in God. For if, following the radicalized Thomist logic of substantive relations in Eckhart, the Father simply *is* exhausted in the filial image which he expresses, it is equally true that the filial image is an *image* of what it expresses. Crucially, then, Eckhart continually relates the procession of the Son from the Father with the creative act. Not that the two are identical, but that it is one and the same motion of expression and return that is at work in the creaturely world, as it reflects the infinite multiplicity of the Father, expressed in the Son, by the Spirit. The Spirit, then, emerges as the agent who refuses to allow the relation both of the Father to the Son and of the world to the Father

32. Ibid., 228.

33. Žižek and Milbank, *Monstrosity of Christ*, 187.

34. Ibid.

and the Son to be exhausted in any straightforward identity. Again Milbank is helpful, "the 'third,' which is the Spirit is not a synthesis, neither one that favors the univocal source, nor one that favors the equivocal difference of the effect . . . Rather it is the confirmation . . . that the ecstatic passage between Father and Son is indeed a love between two."[35] Hence the Spirit re-opens the Paternal *arche* [source], refusing the exhaustion of creative possibilities/meaning. The Spirit maintains the analogical interval, the space of becoming in which creaturely being is perpetually re-inspired.

It may be helpful to draw in an enigmatic distinction of Kierkegaard's at this point, between Socratic "recollection" and modern "repetition." Kierkegaard hints in his difficult text *Repetition,* that the difference between Socratic thought and Christianity is that the true knowledge of things for Socrates is a matter of recollecting the ideal, that is, stripping away the layers of accidental appearances and accessing the world of essences behind things, as it were. So, the idea of the thing precedes any particular thing, and the purest knowledge of the thing lies in recollecting the idea of the thing, disentangled from the vaguely reflective mirroring surface of time and space. The Christian, on the other hand, believes in "repetition," that is, the Christian isn't trying to access the idea of the thing, for there is no such *unmediated* idea, but each and every particular instantiation of the thing is a boiling over of the intentional creative resource of the infinite.[36] In a sense, one could read this as a way of explicating *creatio ex nihilo*—all things are the product of the superabundant gift of God, and their continued existence is a product of the continuity of the surprise of this gift. God is not absent from the immanent development of creation, creation is not the product of a demiurge, corrupting what is pure and immaterial; rather creation is *good,* and is continually renewed as such each and every moment. So *creatio ex nihilo* is not simply about origins, but is about the continued suspension of created being in existence by the spilling over of the divine Logos in the Spirit. As Eckhart argues in a sermon, God's creative activity is a "boiling over" [*ebullitio*] of God's very life, the life that is the relation between Father and Son in the Spirit. Indeed, to speak of the creature's *being* is to speak of the constitutive relation between the Father and the Son, as it is within this dynamic motion of "boiling" [*bullitio*] that the Father begets the Son (so the creation realizes temporally what God is already actually). As Rowan Williams notes in speaking of Hans Urs von Balthasar, "God is not *a* subject, nor even a plurality of subjects in intimate connection. God is intrinsically that life which exists only and necessarily in the act of bestowal, in a self-alienation that makes possible the freedom and love of an other that is at the same time itself *in* otherness." Hence, God is no static identity, for "the

35. Ibid., 185. See also Milbank, "The Second Difference," 213–34.

36. Kierkegaard, *Fear and Trembling/Repetition*, 131–76.

only identity in question is precisely the total and eternal self-bestowal that constitutes the other."[37]

A Hopeful Apophatic Ecotheology

At the beginning of this chapter I reflected on the nature of the entanglement of ecological concern and capitalism to the end that ecological action itself has been commodified. Why is this concerning? It is not necessarily theologically concerning because capitalism as such is no more problematic an economic model than any other option. It is theologically concerning because of the way in which capitalism constructs a complex web of relations through which it mediates our relation to the environment, and therefore, in our current predicament, our relation to the future. Further, this extends into the church to the extent that climate change denial is lubricated by the "evangelical capitalist resonance machine." To the extent that we accept the modelling of climate scientists, we are being asked to put our faith in the promise of innovative technologies driven by the pressing demands of climate change, and in the market adjusting to new conditions. We are being asked to have faith that capitalism will mediate our relation to the future, because, in many cases, it already is. The uncertain future is being managed by the mediation of capital and financial interests. Christians should protest this, not necessarily because they might object to capitalism as such (though they might), but because they should object to any idolatry disciplining our hopes and desires this way.[38]

What if we were to say that the uncertainty of the future were a gift, the opening of the "misty" space of creaturely possibility grounded in divine being? Or, to return to Keller: what if an apophatic rendering of ecological problematics allows us a vision of being itself as embedded within an infinite relation of creative self-gift? Perhaps this kind of being could also be the source of hope—the source of imagination for a world otherwise, and that which might fund a community living otherwise. For, while our futures may all indeed seem terrifying and uncertain, and while we may seem powerless in the face of the forces of capitalism, it is only as we come to understand that God is the source and ground of all inextricably complex relations that we can see the future as the site of hope, and thereby enliven an honest ecologically attuned theopolitical imaginary beyond dystopia. That is, an apophatic eco-theology can provide resources for thinking uncertainty as

37. Williams, "Making Differences," 176.

38. This is the argument of Bell in *The Economy of Desire*. Long, in another similar vein, shows the ways in which, for certain proponents of capitalism, theology has been subordinated to economics. Long eventually identifies capitalism as a form of heresy. Long, *Divine Economy*, 358–60.

the space for hopeful action empowered by the movement of divine self-giving. Even as hope is the act of taking the next step (Barth), it remains a step into the unknown; into new entanglements, new productive relations, new forms of being creatures together.[39]

What Eckhart's ontology allows us to think, then, is the common *goal* of human and non-human creatures, that is desire for God in whom all relations are comprehended, who is the *coincidentia oppositorum*. By refusing any form of transcendence that would abandon the world to itself, we refuse to make any thing an end in itself, but always as related to another mediated by a common desire. All our relations, therefore, mediate the fundamental relation of creator to creature. By construing creaturely being as ordered to God as infinitely complex and mysterious source, we are able to think the relations between creatures as reparative of this fundamental ontological relation to the extent that we venture further and further into this mysterious complexity—indeed that we continue to non-identically "repeat" the source of our being. If we believe in *creatio ex nihilo* we must protest any logic that would play financial gain off against ecological responsibility, for it is only as we recognize that we are nothing in ourselves that we can recognize that what we are is gift, and that our being as gift cannot be possessed, but must continually reflect divine self-giving. Our relation with other creatures is entirely mutually constitutive, and only when we begin working to construct a world, a home, *oikos*, as such will we be able to think being otherwise than as caught in this alienation.

Perhaps the indeterminacy of our futures is the site of potential for renewed relation, the rhapsodic site of gift exchange in which we can overcome the alienation between ourselves and the world not with any false mediator but through the mediation of God, who stands in the between of all our relations, thus continually re-establishing a beautiful complexity.

Bibliography

Agamben, Giorgio. *The Highest Poverty: Monastic Rules and Form of Life*. Translated by Adam Kotsko. Stanford: Stanford University Press, 2013.

Barth, Karl. *Church Dogmatics*. 14 vols. Edited by G. W. Bromiley and T. F. Torrance. Translated by G. T. Thomson et al. London: T. & T. Clark, 2009.

Bell, Daniel M. *The Economy of Desire: Christianity and Capitalism in a Postmodern World*. Grand Rapids: Baker Academic, 2012.

39. For instance, we might look to forms of ancient and medieval monasticism and their constructions of common use (*usus*) of property in relation to vows of poverty. If we consider ourselves not as those who *possess* any-thing, but rather as those who are given use of some-thing in the context of a common form of life, our relation to things is significantly altered. For the beginnings of an exploration of this dynamic in relation to the question of a genealogy of law, see Agamben, *The Highest Poverty*.

Connolly, William E. *Christianity and Capitalism, American Style*. Durham, NC: Duke University Press, 2008.

Eckhart, Meister. *Meister Eckhart: Teacher and Preacher*. Translated and introduction by Bernard McGinn. Mahwah, NJ: Paulist, 1986.

Evans, Brad, and Henry Giroux. *Disposable Futures: The Seduction of Violence in the Age of Spectacle*. San Francisco: City Lights, 2015.

Fiennes, Sophie, director. *The Pervert's Guide to Ideology*. New York: Zeitgeist Films, 2012.

Fisher, Mark. *Capitalist Realism: Is There No Alternative?* Winchester: Zero, 2009.

Giroux, Henry A. *Zombie Politics and Culture in the Age of Casino Capitalism*. New York: Lang, 2011.

Hoff, Johannes. *The Analogical Turn: Rethinking Modernity with Nicholas of Cusa*. Grand Rapids: Eerdmans, 2013.

Jameson, Frederic. "Future City." *New Left Review* 21 (2003) 65–79.

Keller, Catherine. *Cloud of the Impossible: Negative Theology and Planetary Entanglement*. New York: Colombia University Press, 2015.

Kierkegaard, Søren. *Christian Discourses/The Crisis and a Crisis in the Life of an Actress*. Translated by Howard and Edna Hong. Princeton: Princeton University Press, 1997.

———. *Fear and Trembling/Repetition*. Translated by Howard and Edna Hong. Princeton: Princeton University Press, 1983.

Latour, Bruno. *On the Modern Cult of the Factish Gods*. Durham, NC: Duke University Press, 2010.

Lazarrato, Maurizio. *Governing by Debt*. Cambridge, MA: MIT Press, 2013.

———. *The Making of Indebted Man*. Cambridge, MA: MIT Press, 2012.

Long, D. Stephen. *Divine Economy: Theology and the Market*. Radical Orthodoxy. London: Routledge, 2002.

Milbank, John. "The Second Difference: For a Trinitarianism without Reserve." *Modern Theology* 2, no. 3 (1986) 213–34.

Schürmann, Reiner. *Wandering Joy: Meister Eckhart's Mystical Philosophy*. Great Barrington: Lindsfarne, 1997.

Slezak, Michael. "QandA Smackdown: Brian Cox Brings Graphs to Grapple with Malcolm Roberts." *The Guardian*, 15 August 2016. https://www.theguardian.com/australia-news/2016/aug/16/qa-brian-cox-brings-graphs-malcolm-roberts. Accessed 27 August, 2016.

Tanner, Kathryn. "Nothing But the Present." Lecture 4, 2016 Gifford Lectures. http://www.giffordlectures.org/lectures/christianity-and-new-spirit-capitalism. Accessed 31 August, 2016.

Williams, Rowan. "Trinity and Ontology." In *Christ Ethics and Tragedy: Essays in Honour of Donald M. MacKinnon*, edited by Kenneth Surin, 71–92. Cambridge: Cambridge University Press, 1989.

Williams, Rowan. "Afterword: Making Differences." In *Balthasar at the End of Modernity*, edited by Lucy Gardner et al., 173–80. Edinburgh: T. & T. Clark, 1999.

Žižek, Slavoj, and John Milbank. *The Monstrosity of Christ*. Edited by Creston Davis. Short Circuits. Cambridge, MA: MIT Press, 2009.

12

On Finishing Well

The Deification of Nature

Myk Habets,
Carey Baptist College, Auckland

THAT THE WORLD CURRENTLY faces an ecological crisis is nothing new. In countless scientific reports, government and NGO sponsored studies, earth-watchdog essays, and popular magazines, the warning bells have been ringing for some time now about how the human population is using more of the earth's resources than it has to give. The world is being destroyed and we must do something about it. Solutions to our ecological crisis almost always coalesce around scientific solutions. In a technocratic age where ultimate faith is placed in human science, that is not surprising. Or is it? It is estimated that more than 80 percent of the world's population is religious, and a third of those are Christian.[1] Given such figures, it is astonishing that spiritual solutions to our ecological crisis have not been more prominent. The following essay is a re-evaluation of creation from a theocentric perspective, and offers a vision of how the notion of the deification of nature offers the Christian a way to live well in the world.

Is Christianity to Blame?

While there are many documented reasons for the ecological crisis,[2] Christianity has come into specific critique. The "ecological complaint" is the

1. The Pew Forum, "The Global Religious Landscape."

2. See Northcott, "Ecology and Christian Ethics," 210–13. Contributing factors to the ecological crisis include rapid population growth over the last four centuries,

charge that the Christian faith is the culprit in the crisis.[3] Christianity is said to be the primary, or at least a significant cause, of ecological degradation. It is so human-centered that it is inherently, or at least has been historically, indifferent or hostile toward nature and, therefore, anti-ecological, or so the story goes. The ecological complaint accuses Christianity of advocating human domination and/or damnation of the biospherical world for the sake of material exploitation or spiritual elevation. Consequently, claim the complainants, Christianity should be superseded or abandoned, in favor of a new religion, or at least exchanged for a radically altered Christianity.

Often the ecological complaint against Christianity has been called "the Lynn White thesis." White was not the first to conceive the thesis but has been the most influential—popularizing the idea with a vengeance.[4] White argued that the distinctive Western tradition of modern technology and science is "deeply conditioned," historically and presently, by Christian beliefs.[5] Primarily, but not exclusively in its Western forms (Roman Catholic and Protestant), Christianity is "the most anthropocentric religion the world has seen," since it operates on the assumption that "God planned all of this explicitly for man's benefit and rule: no item in the physical creation had any purpose save to serve man's purposes." Modern science and technology, which operate on assumptions about the mastery and exploitation of nature, emerged out of Christian attitudes that are almost universally held by Christians. Christianity bears "a huge burden of guilt" for our crisis until we reject the Christian axiom that nature has no reason for existence save to serve humanity. White concludes by calling for an ecological egalitarianism, "the democracy of all God's creatures." White's original thesis has been repeated often and by many, sometimes far more harshly and unambiguously than White himself expressed it.[6]

---

aspects of the industrial economy of the west, and technological enhancement of the human capacity to adapt the physical environment for human purposes,.

3. See the very good overview in Bouma-Prediger, *For the Beauty of the Earth,* 67–86.

4. White, "The Historical Roots of Our Ecological Crisis," 203–7. See also his "Continuing the Conversation," 55–64.

5. O'Riordan in his 1976 book *Environmentalism*, suggests that western ideas about the environment can be divided into one of two basic categories: "technocentrism" and "ecocentrism." These are broadly related to the distinction between "exploitative" and "non-exploitative" society and nature relations. Technocentrism encourages and attempts to justify the social exploitation of nature. Ecocentrism, on the other hand, argues for the establishment of "non-exploitative" relations with nature. Furthermore, technocentrism is anthropocentric. See Phillips and Mighall, *Society and Exploitation Through Nature*, 13–25.

6. See Sheldon, "Twenty-one Years," 156.

While White's thesis was tremendously influential, it has perhaps had its day. Nevertheless, the ecological complaint against Christianity persists, and responses to new versions are necessary if contemporary Christians are to interpret their faith soundly and to have credibility in environmentalist circles.[7] Indeed, White himself did not propose the abandonment of the Christian religion. He believed, on the contrary, that only religion has the motive power to change the direction of modern civilization, and points to St Francis as a paradigm to follow.[8]

The collapse of the myth of progress in the wake of historical factors such as the threat of nuclear holocaust and the ecological crisis led to a crisis of hope in the late 1960s. As Thomas Berry points out, modern theology (from Descartes onward) failed to understand the enchantment of nature—the fact that the earth is a "numinous" community. Our failure, it is argued, to recognize this, is the reason for the current ecological disaster.[9] Sally McFague speaks of the Christian influence in terms of a monarchical metaphor for God that " . . . attends only to the human dimension of the world; and it supports attitudes of either domination of the world or passivity toward it."[10] Since the 60s two trends have converged. On the one hand, the trinitarian renaissance in which God is conceived as a Trinity of loving relationships in Godself, and for creation, and on the other hand, the realization of the interconnectedness of all things, not only God-humanity or human-human, but the interconnectedness in ecological relationships as well.[11] In this sense, to be faithful to the Christian tradition requires us to be ecological.

On the basis of the accounts briefly narrated, dogmatic theology might appear to be struggling to come to an understanding of God that takes into account the full implications of the ecological crisis.[12] If we find absolute moral value in ecological systems we are letting ecology take the place that was traditionally occupied by theology. Once we give nature absolute moral value or goodness it becomes difficult to distinguish between con-

7. See the very good response to these issues in Nash, *Loving Nature*, 72–92.

8. St Francis of Assisi has become something of the patron saint of Christian environmentalism.

9. Berry, *The Dream of the Earth*, chaps. 1–2.

10. McFague, *Models of God*, 69.

11. Finger, *Self, Earth and Society*, brings these two themes together in his ecological theology.

12. See Innes, *Caring for the Earth*, 66. Northcott, *The Environment and Christian Ethics*, presents a comprehensive overview of the range of Christian attempts at eco-theology. He uses the simple categorical distinction: 1) Humanocentric Approaches, 2) Theocentric Approaches, and 3) Ecocentric Approaches.

flicting interests. This assessment, however, would not be accurate. There is an emerging consensus amongst theologians that the way to address our ecological crisis is to retrieve the theology of the early church in which the proper starting point for considering ethical action starts with the triune God, moves to creation *ex nihilo*, and only then addresses humanity. This triadic relation is essential and offers a unitary point of view for the current global ecological crisis. Anestis Keselopoulos expresses this relation well when he writes:

> When communication between humans and God is removed, relations between them are disrupted, and the consequence is misuse of creation and violation of the environment. Only when man has a relationship with God and creation which is in accordance with nature can we speak of true communion and the attainment of salvation . . . [13]

Everything is Spiritual

The church today has to reclaim the idea that "everything is spiritual," as Rob Bell has called it.[14] The old dichotomy between sacred and profane, spiritual and material, has to be bridged with a unitary way of thinking. Here we can learn from Patristic and Eastern Orthodox theology. Central to such a theology is the intrinsic communion between the triune God and creation, including humanity. A thoroughly theocentric view of the world does not necessarily lead to an oppressive and tyrannical control of the environment, and an anthropocentric view, subordinate to that of a theocentric one, does not automatically lead to the exploitation and misuse of our social and natural environments. Rather, understanding the triune God *in se* and only then moving to God's works *ab extra* will provide a vision of the world that is centered in Jesus Christ and his worldly body the church. From such a vantage point it will be evident that the world is bound up with the salvation of humanity such that we can speak of the deification of the world as part and parcel of the deification of human beings.

Reflecting a unified view of creation and humanity under the triune creator God, Alexander Schmemann writes:

> In the Bible the food that man eats, the world of which he must partake in order to live, is given to him by God, and it is given as *communion with God*. The world as man's food is not something

13. Keselopoulos, *Man and the Environment*, 3.

14. Bell, *Everything Is Spiritual*.

> "material" and limited to material functions, thus different from, and opposed to, the specifically "spiritual" functions by which man is related to God. All that exists is God's gift to man, and it all exists to make God known to man, to make man's life communion with God.[15]

In addition to eating—clearly a metaphorical use of the term—humanity is given the task of naming the animals, something which Schmemann further comments on:

To name a thing is to manifest the meaning and value God gave it, to know it as coming from God and to know its place and function within the cosmos created by God.

> To name a thing, in other words, is to bless God for it and in it. And in the Bible to bless God is not a "religious" or a "cultic" act, but the very *way of life*. God blessed the world . . . and this means that He filled all that exists with His love and goodness . . . So the only *natural* (and not "supernatural") reaction of man, to whom God gave this blessed and sanctified world, is to bless God in return, to thank Him, *to see the world as God sees it* and—in this act of gratitude and adoration—to know, name and possess the world.[16]

To see the world as God sees it. That is the vision for everyday life we require today. In order to see the world as God sees it, we must be Godlike; and that means not only giving but also receiving. Such a gift is possible only as we are in communion with God. The Gift cannot be abstracted from the Giver. All of this, the Orthodox, and many Western thinkers, subsume under the grand idea that humans are the God-ordained "priests of creation."[17] The Spirit of God woos and entices us into this priestly vocation. Again, Schmemann writes:

> The first, the basic definition of man is that he is *the priest.* He stands in the center of the world and unifies it in acts of blessing God, of both receiving the world from God and offering it to God—and by filing the world with his Eucharist, he transforms his life, the one that he receives from the world, into life in God, into communion with Him.[18]

15. Schmemann, *For the Life of the World*, 14–15.

16. Ibid., 15.

17. The concept of "priest of creation" is well known in Orthodox theology and has been adopted by a number of western thinkers as well, notably Linzey, *Animal Theology*, 52–56; and Torrance (see below).

18. Schmemann, *For the Life of the World*, 15.

It is human sin and fallenness which prevents us from fulfilling this vocation and instead sends us into slavery.[19]

If we continue with Schmemann and the idea of food, then we can see that the fruit off the tree of the knowledge of good and evil was forbidden because it was not offered as a *gift* to humanity in Genesis 1–3. He says:

> Not given, not blessed by God, it was food whose eating was condemned to be communion with itself alone, and not with God. It is the image of the world's love for itself, and eating it is the image of life understood as an end in itself . . . The world is a fallen world because it has fallen away from the awareness that God is all in all . . . The natural dependence of man upon the world was intended to be transformed constantly into communion with God in whom is all life. Man was to be the priest of a Eucharist, offering the world to God, and in this offering he was to receive priestly power to do this. His dependence on the world becomes a closed circuit, and his love is deviated from its true direction. He still loves, he is still hungry. He knows he is dependent on that which is beyond him. But his love and his dependence refer only to the world in itself . . . For "the wages of sin is death." The life man chose was only the appearance of life. God showed him that he himself had decided to eat bread in a way that would simply return him to the ground from which both he and the bread had been taken . . . Man lost the Eucharistic life, he lost the life of life itself, the power to transform it into Life. He ceased to be the priest of the world and became its slave.[20]

Such is the story of humanity living east of Eden! And such is the story of life lived in the twenty-first century. We can affirm with Keselopoulos, "The ecological crisis is an expression and a generalization of the social problem."[21] While there is no simple *solution* to the ecological crisis, indeed there may be no human solution available at all, there is, arguably, a suitable response, and it is a deeply Christian one. In short, when creation is correctly understood both archaeologically and teleologically, we see the possibility of nature "being sanctified through the churching of the world—its grafting into the deified human Body of Christ, which is the Church,

19. Throughout this essay I am using "fall" and "fallen" to refer to the literary fact that the scriptural narrative refers to a good creation fallen through the actions of humanity. In light of evolutionary theory, a literal fall is being questioned or radically reconceived. For the purposes of this essay, I am following the biblical narrative and not making comment on the literal mechanism of creation's disorder in relation to evolution; I leave that to others.

20. Schmemann, *For the Life of the World*, 16–17.

21. Keselopoulos, *Man and the Environment*, 8.

and the raising of matter to participation in life through the mystery of the Divine Eucharist."[22] What follows is an outline of what this may mean.

The Two Hands of God in the World

The early church father, Irenaeus, was fond of speaking of God's involvement in the world as the Father who works with two hands—the Son and the Spirit.[23] This is a delightful image and one with plenty of rhetorical punch. God works in the world! But the God who works is the triune God, the Father of the Lord Jesus Christ revealed by the Holy Spirit. Thus, the first thing we have to say—and keep saying—is that God is triune and there is no other God conceivable in Christian discourse. The identity of the triune God, in nature and tripersonality, is what gives coherence to creation—God's external works, including humanity. Once we know and affirm the freedom and aseity of God, *creatio ex nihilo* makes sense, and with it, we can comprehend the place of humanity in creation.

The early church summarized the work of God in the world with the maxim that all things generally operate in the world *from* the Father, *through* the Son, and *in* the Holy Spirit. It was Basil the Great who said so clearly that the Father is the "original cause," the Son is the "operative cause," and the Spirit is the "perfecting cause" of all things.[24] One God working in the world in a tri-personal way. Such is the beginning and end of Christian theology. There is no suggestion here that the three persons of the Godhead have different jobs, nor that one person does one job exclusively (a denial of divine simplicity). Rather, the one God is the creator but it is appropriate to ascribe a certain action to one person as opposed to the other. All of this is summarized by John Webster:

> The task of the Christian doctrine of creation is rational contemplation of the Holy Trinity in the outward work of love by which God established and ordered creaturely reality, a work issuing from the infinite uncreated and wholly realized movement of God's life in himself. The matter of the doctrine arranges itself as three topics: the identity of the creator; the character of his act of creation; the several natures and ends of creatures.[25]

22. Ibid., 10–11.
23. Irenaeus, *Against Heresies*, 1059.
24. Basil of Caesarea, *On the Holy Spirit*, 16, 38, 71.
25. Webster, "Trinity and Creation," 4.

Given the fact that all things generally operate in the world *from* the Father, *through* the Son, and *in* the Holy Spirit, we can affirm several corollaries. First, the work of the Spirit co-indwells that of the Son. Second, the work of the Son is understood to be that of the *incarnate* Christ, thus the vicarious humanity of Christ comes to the fore. Third, the work of the Spirit is to sustain the relationship between the triune God and contingent creation. Fourth, the incarnation is a union not only with all human creatures but with *all* creation—the entire ecology of life, and it is so through the vicarious humanity of Christ. The Spirit unites us to *this* human (Christ), and unites all creation to *this* humanity (Christ's). Through this union the future of the created order is both revealed and secured and the goal and basis of human cultural activity is established. Thus we are to focus on Christ and the work of the Spirit with Christ if we are to work towards the great *telos* of creation, and not our own *teloi.*

The Ordering of Creation

If we are to think of God working in the world and human creatures participating in God's work, then we have to have a *Christian* concept of creation. A useful way to do this is to use the category of *order* and extrapolate from that the state of creation and our place within it. By way of summary we may say that creation has four great movements: 1) Created Order—creation narrative; 2) Disorder—fallenness; 3) Re-order—Redemption; and 4) Trans-order—Renewal. Briefly unpacking each movement will be helpful as we proceed.

In terms of the Created Order we read, "In the beginning God created the heavens and the earth . . ." (Gen 1:1). Creation is just that—it comes from nothing other than the spoken and creative Word of God and the sending of his Spirit. Creation thus has an order, a rationality, and a purpose given to it by God. At the end of each "day" of the creation process God steps back and says, "it is good," culminating in God's approval of the creation as "very good." But it is here that the reader is meant to stop and say: "Humanity is good for what . . . exactly?" Good to garden in a place called Eden? Good to rule over animals and fish? Good to name and look after the other creatures? Good to relate to God? Yes, to all of the above, but none of those answers yet address the central message of Scripture. As Colin Gunton once remarked, "Creation is a project. As created, it is perfect, because it is God's project: what God purposes for that which is not God but creation, and therefore intrinsically finite and temporal. But it is not perfect in the sense that it is complete. It has somewhere to go . . ."[26] Indeed it does—creation itself has a *telos*.

In the fullness of time the eternal Son was born of a virgin, Mary, as the Holy Spirit settled upon her, and he is, we are repeatedly told, the image of God (Phil 2:7–8), the visible form of the invisible God (Col 1:15), the Word of God (John 1:1), and Immanuel—God with us (Matt 1:23). Jesus is, exclusively, the image of God on earth, the archetype of all humanity. And Jesus, throughout his life of obedience to God the Father, full of the Holy Spirit, died for us, rose again on the third day, and ascended into heaven to the right hand of God the Father from where he will return, in time, to consummate the Kingdom of God on earth. Jesus does this as a human being, resurrected and glorious. In this mode of resurrected existence, Christ is still our image, still our archetype, and still our goal. He gives us his Spirit, in part, so that we have a spiritual birth and we become new creations; he gives us the Spirit to bring to mind his words and to do his works, and at the great resurrection he gives us what Paul calls "spiritual bodies" (1 Cor 15:44). That is, physical bodies which are more real, more substantial, more glorious, and more Christ-like than they are now, or have ever been in the history of creation, because now they are fully capable of having the Holy Spirit settle upon them. And along with new bodies we are given a new home; new heavens and a new earth, a renewed environment in which to live and play. Many Christians in the east fittingly call this great eschatological future the eighth day of creation.

Human creatures, however, are fallen in the sense of using our freedom to usurp God's purposes. We have already heard from Schmemann about humans taking that which was not offered and thus distorting the Gift and exchanging life for the appearance of life. In short, human cultural activity is now a mix of wheat and tares, of order and disorder. The effect upon the natural environment is obvious to all who care to look.

But we worship a God of order and not of chaos, a God of law and not anarchy, and a God of freedom and not slavery. Thus in Christ all things are made new and reconciled to God's will and ways. This is affirmed in many texts but perhaps most clearly in Col 1:13–20:

> For He rescued us from the domain of darkness, and transferred us to the kingdom of His beloved Son, in whom we have redemption, the forgiveness of sins. He is the image of the invisible God, the firstborn of all creation. For by Him all things were created, both in the heavens and on earth, visible and invisible, whether thrones or dominions or rulers or authorities—all

26. Gunton, *The Triune Creator*, 202.

> things have been created through Him and for Him. He is before all things, and in Him all things hold together. He is also head of the body, the church; and He is the beginning, the firstborn from the dead, so that He Himself will come to have first place in everything. For it was the Father's good pleasure for all the fullness to dwell in Him, and through Him to reconcile all things to Himself, having made peace through the blood of His cross; through Him, I say, whether things on earth or things in heaven.

In this regard we would do well to be reminded again of N. T. Wright's lament that:

> The theological equivalent of supposing that the earth goes round the sun is the belief that the whole of Christian truth is all about me and my salvation. I have read dozens of books and articles . . . on the topic of justification. Again and again the writers, from a variety of backgrounds, have assumed, taken it for granted, that the central question of all is, "What must I do to be saved?" or (Luther's way of putting it), "How can I find a gracious God?" or, "How can I enter a right relationship with God?" . . . But we are not the center of the universe. God is not circling around us. We are circling around him. It may look, from our point of view, as though "me and my salvation" are the be-all and end-all of Christianity . . . God made humans for a purpose: not simply for themselves, not simply so that they could be in relationship with him, but so that through them, as his image-bearers, he could bring his wise, glad, fruitful order to the world.[27]

One unforeseen fruit of the ecological crisis has been the turn to a robust ecotheology amongst Christian theologians. Whilst muted in many places, the message is catching on. As Wright says, Christ re-orders creation; human, animate, and inanimate. *And Christ is central*—let us never forget this. Thomas Torrance once noted in this regard:

> The continuing existence of the universe is ontologically bound to the crucified and risen Jesus and destined to partake in the consummation of God's eternal purpose in him . . . [for through the Son and in the Spirit] God irreversibly binds the created universe to his own Existence and his own Existence to the universe.[28]

27. Wright, *Justification*, 7.

28. Torrance, *The Christian Doctrine of God*, 217.

Finally, there is the eschatological trans-order to come; the great *telos* of creation which will one day be realized. Creation has an inbuilt *telos* as revealed and secured *from* the Father, *through* Christ, and *by* the Spirit. Once again, as Schmemann alerted us to earlier: Humans—become the *"mediators of order,"* the "priests of creation"—those tasked with representing creation, and facilitating its transformation into a glorious *hymn of praise* to its Creator. This task cannot be fulfilled without the empowerment of the Spirit.

Because we currently exist in the tension between dis-order and re-order, and the yet to be consummated trans-order, human creatures, and the earth in general, finds itself pulled in two directions—down into disorder and forward into the eschatological trans-order to come. In his work *Creation Regained,* Al Wolters speaks of the concept of "direction" as follows:

> Direction . . . designates the order of sin and redemption, the distortion or perversion of creation through the fall on the one hand the redemption and restoration of creation in Christ on the other. Anything in creation can be directed either toward or away from God—that is, directed either in obedience or disobedience to his law [*telos*]. This double direction applies not only to individual human beings, but also to such cultural phenomena as technology, art, and scholarship, such social institutions as labor unions, schools, and corporations, and to such human functions as emotionality, sexuality and rationalities. To the degree that these realities fail to live up to God's creational design [*telos*] for them, they are misdirected, abnormal, distorted. To the degree that they still conform to God's design [*telos*], they are in the grip of a countervailing force that curbs or counteracts the distortion. Direction therefore always involves two tendencies moving either for or against God.[29]

It is the Holy Spirit that directs creation to its *telos*. However, the Spirit is not a *force majeure*; rather, the Spirit works in gentle and personal ways. God does not crush what is personal, but heals and establishes it, and part of that work is the healing and establishing of the social relations and cultural products that make personal life possible, for personal life is life in relation, life in community—human to human, human to God, and human to creation.

29. Wolters, *Creation Regained*, 49.

Priests of Creation

Picking up the concept of the re-ordering of creation and of the role human creatures play in this grand design of God we may surmise arguably, as Torrance insists, that, "Nature itself is mute, but human being is the one constituent of the created universe through whom its rational structure and astonishing beauty may be brought to word in praise of the Creator."[30] As such humanity is the *mediator of order* and the *priest of creation*, a creation freely brought into being by the will of God and graciously entrusted to a creature crafted after the image of God.

The Orthodox theologian, Dumitru Staniloae, prefers to describe men and women as creation's "masters" (*archōn*), its created "co-creators," "co-workers" or "continuators."[31] Staniloae considers the world as God's gift to humanity in order that humanity may gift it back to God. In this way, argues Staniloae, the sacrifice offered to God by men and women is a Eucharist, making every person a priest of God for the world.[32] The language of Eucharist reminds us of priestly duty, specifically the priestly duty of humanity to represent the world to God. We see this in the original creation story of the Garden of Eden. We must ask ourselves, is Eden merely a Mesopotamian farm and Adam and Eve its first gardeners? If so, does Genesis 1–2 then provide human creatures with a work ethic—to till the ground, multiply, and steward? Quite simply, No.

Human responsibility is not so much farming as priestly. The Garden of Eden functions as the earthly archetypal temple and Adam and Eve are its first priest.[33] The details need not detain us here, given they are articulated at length by others, but if we look for it we see the following evidence for viewing Eden as a temple. 1) It is located in the "east"—a position of blessing in the OT (Ezek 11:1, 23; 43:1–4 etc.). 2) It is on a mountain top, the place where God resides (Gen 2:10–14; Ezek 28:14–16; Exod 3:1; 18:5; 24:13; Ps 48:1–2). 3) The river of life flows out of Eden to water the garden (Gen 2:20; Ps 46:4; Ezek 47:1, 8). 4) The trees of life and knowledge in the Garden find counterparts in subsequent temple imagery (Gen 2:9; 3:6; Ps 19:8–9; Rev 22:2, 14). 5) The precious stones and metals also find their counterparts in subsequent temple imagery (Gen 2:10–14; 16:2; Ezek 28:13; Rev 21:10). 6) In

30. Torrance, *Christian Doctrine of God*, 213.

31. Staniloae, *The Experience of God*, 21–112.

32. Staniloae, "The World as Gift," 662–73.

33. For what follows, see Fesko, *Last Things First*, 57–75. I acknowledge here also the extensive work of Linzey on the priestly function of human beings in the creation. See for instance, *Animal Theology*. This essay has been written using Torrance's works alone.

Genesis 3 we read that two cherubim stand guard outside the east entrance of the garden (Gen 3:24)—throughout Scripture the cherubim are the guardians of God's temples (1 Kings 6:23–28; Exod 25:18–22; 26:31; 1 Kings 6:29). 7) God metaphorically "walks" in the garden (Gen 3:8; Lev 26:11–12; Deut 23:14; 2 Sam 7:6). Indeed, 2 Sam 7:6 says that God does not live in a house but has been moving/walking in a tent as a dwelling. And 8) God created the garden in the same way he created subsequent temples—note the 7 days of creation and the 7 speeches of God to Moses in the construction of the desert tabernacle (Exod 25:1–9). The combined evidence suggests that the Genesis narrative identifies the Garden as the holy of holies, in which human creatures had access to the presence of God.

And so we ask what was the "work" for which Adam and Eve, and all their sons and daughters, were created? God placed humans in the garden "to work it and keep it" (Gen 2:15). Many simply read this as "cultivation"—thus "farming." God meant for us all to be farmers! But that is not what the text is saying at all. The exact same vocabulary—"*avad*" and "*shamar*" is used to describe the priestly responsibilities in the tabernacle: "They shall keep guard over him . . . before the tent of meeting as they minister/work at the tabernacle" (Num 3:7–8; 8:26; 18:5–6 cf 4:23–24, 26). This is the only other time in the Pentateuch these words are used together—something the Rabbis noticed in their midrash. Thus, we are on safe ground to assert that Adam and Eve's responsibilities in the garden are primarily priestly rather than agricultural! As John Fesko has stated:

> Adam was an archetypal priest, not a farmer. Scanning the horizon of redemptive history, we find further confirmation of the garden-temple thesis. At the end of redemptive history it is not a massive city-farm that descends out of the heavens, but a city-temple. If the end of redemptive history represents God's intentions from the beginning, then he planted a temple in Eden, not a farm.[34]

It is from this relationship of Creator to creature that human beings derives their significance and responsibility in the formation of the world towards its final consummation. *This* creature is constituted and uniquely called to improvise with God as, "scientist," "midwife," "priest," "poet," "instrument," and "artist," to name but a few metaphors, in order to draw the created order toward its *telos*.

Telling the story of God's work in the world involves the embodiment and expression of God's purposes for it. This story cannot be told apart from the formation of specific communities and their concrete action *in*

34. Fesko, *Last Things First*, 75.

the world. When human persons act in the world they function, implicitly or explicitly, as "mediators of order." They cannot escape the fact that their actions have a purpose and that purposeful action is rooted in an overarching and comprehensive conception of order. Everything is spiritual after all. Consequently, the way in which human communities order their social and physical environments becomes a form of embodied worship, a living and concrete witness to their most comprehensive ideas of order, value, and purpose formed in conversation with a real and objective world. Our relationships with others, the created order, and God, form the fundamental basis upon which this activity takes place. The quality of these relationships will also determine whether the result of that activity will sustain or subvert the very relations upon which it is built. Those relations, and the cultural environments they produce and sustain, can only be morally legitimated as they enable the embodiment of God's purposes for the created order and by so doing sustain the personhood and integrity of human agents created in God's image.

In other words—when men and women function in their God-given roles as *priests of creation* and *mediators of order*, they initiate the great shalom of God, they embody worship (Rom 12:1), and they represent the world to God in their representation of God to the world. As such we work towards creating the "order that ought to be"—the nudging of creation towards its intended *telos*. Eric Flett correctly argues that:

> If that relation is construed properly, that identity and mission will thrust [the church] into the world as a royal priesthood, whose activity in the world of culture will not only bear witness to the God she worships, but will advance God's mission in the world through cultural transformation.[35]

And this cultural transformation is then the basis for social, political, economic and ecological transformation.

Humans, as made in the image of God, occupy a place on the boundary between the natural and the super natural.[36] As "priest of creation," humanity has the function and privilege to assist the creation to realize and evidence its rational order and beauty and thus to express God's beauty and being back to God. According to Torrance, "through human cultivation and development nature should bring forth forms of order and beauty of

35. Flett, *Persons, Powers, and Pluralities*, 222. I am indebted to Flett for many of the ideas worked out in this paper.

36. Thomas F. Torrance, *The Christian Frame of Mind*, 41, 62; and "The Goodness and Dignity of Man in the Christian Tradition," 311.

which it would not be capable otherwise."[37] It is thus necessary to creation that humanity realize its vocation as priests, in order to bring forth the requisite praise that God requires. This is why humanity becomes "an essential member of the creation."[38] Men and women are the stewards or keepers of the Garden/creation, and by representing and respecting the earth they are meant to bring praise to the Creator. True priestly functions of humanity include caring for the environment, acting wisely and justly with all of creation, and both caring for and enjoying nature.

Conclusion

"God does not abandon his creation when he has saved man, for all creation, together with man, will be renewed when Christ comes again."[39] What will this redemption applied to nature look like? One can only speculate at this point based upon the limited biblical references. What we do know is that this present cosmos will be renewed and the earth, and all that is on it, will flourish. It is not hard to reflect further and envisage the perfection of the beauty, artistry, and fecundity of the creation itself. John of Patmos could speak metaphorically of golden streets, foundations of precious stones, and walls of costly jewels (Rev 21:19). The natural scientist could perhaps speak of eco-systems in equilibrium, the extinction of extinction itself, and the ordered-yet-free, harmonious-yet-new, ordering of the natural order. In Torrance's words:

> God made the creation for such a communion that it might sing His praises and reflect in gladness and joy His loving kindness and glory. Hence the restoration of creation involves the restoration of creation to communion and fellowship with Him in which the peace of God reigns over all, the joy and gladness in God the Father fills the whole of creation. Thus in reconciliation of atonement it is not only with obedience and justice that we have to do, but with the worship and adoration of creation, in which it faithfully reflects the Father's glory and love.[40]

Failure to understand and appreciate humanity's relationship with both God and creation has resulted in the environmental crisis we now

37. Torrance, *Divine and Contingent Order*, 130.

38. Torrance, *Reality and Evangelical Theology*, 25–26.

39. Torrance, *The Christian Doctrine of God*, 226.

40. Torrance, "The Atoning Obedience of Christ," 66. See also Torrance, *The Mediation of Christ*, 71–72.

face. Creation is now inseparable from humanity and journeys with us towards salvation when "all things" are brought under the dominion of Christ. The church has a special responsibility of gathering of world and creation together. With the Orthodox we can agree, "Participating simultaneously in the material and the spiritual world, man is able to form and give shape to matter in such a way that it retains the original orientation and purpose of its creation. Thus we have a "churching" of material creation and its participation in the glory of God . . . "[41] Both humans and creation are destined for deification, to participate in the divine nature by means of indwelling Christ. When the church, the earthly body of Christ, learns anew to live in the reality of the resurrected Christ *Pantocrator*, then creation will cease to be viewed instrumentally as a means to some greater end, and instead will be appreciated for the worth it has to God as a vehicle to display and declare divine glory.

Bibliography

Basil of Caesarea. *On the Holy Spirit*. Popular Patristics 42. Translated by Stephen Hildebrand. Crestwood, NY: St. Vladimir's Seminary Press, 2011.

Bell, Rob. *Everything Is Spiritual*. Grand Rapids: Zondervan, 2007.

Berry, Thomas. *The Dream of the Earth*. San Francisco: Sierra Club, 1988.

Bouma-Prediger, Steven. *For the Beauty of the Earth: A Christian Vision for Creation Care*. Grand Rapids: Baker, 2001.

Fesko, John V. *Last Things First: Unlocking Genesis 1–3 with the Christ of Eschatology*. Fern: Mentor, 2007.

Flett, Eric G. *Persons, Powers, and Pluralities*, Eugene, OR: Wipf and Stock. 2015.

Finger, Thomas N. *Self, Earth and Society: Alienation and Trinitarian Transformation*. Downers Grove, IL: InterVarsity, 1997.

Flett, Eric G. *Persons, Powers, and Pluralities: Toward a Trinitarian Theology of Culture*. Eugene, OR: Pickwick, 2011.

Gunton, Colin. *The Triune Creator: A Historic and Systematic Study*. Grand Rapids: Eerdmans, 1998.

Innes, Keith. *Caring for the Earth: The Environment, Christians and the Church*. Grove Ethical Studies 66. Nottingham: Grove, 1987.

Irenaeus. *Against Heresies*. In *ANF*, edited by A. Roberts and J. Donaldson, 1:309–567. 1887. Repr., Grand Rapids: Eerdmans, 1987.

Keselopoulos, Anestis G. *Man and the Environment: A Study of St Symeon the New Theologian*. Crestwood, NY: St. Vladimir's Seminary Press, 2001.

Linzey, Andrew. *Animal Theology*. Chicago: University of Illinois Press, 1995.

McFague, Sallie. *Models of God: Theology for an Ecological, Nuclear Age*. Minneapolis: Fortress, 1987.

Nash, James A. *Loving Nature: Ecological Integrity and Christian Responsibility*. Nashville: Abingdon, 1991.

41. Keselopoulos, *Man and the Environment*, 152.

Northcott, Michael S. "Ecology and Christian Ethics," in *Cambridge Companion to Christian Ethics,* edited by Robin Gill, 209–27. Cambridge: Cambridge University Press, 2001.

———. *The Environment and Christian Ethics.* Cambridge: Cambridge University Press, 1996.

O'Riordan, Timothy. *Environmentalism.* London: Pion, 1976.

McFague, Sally. *Models of God.* Philadelphia: Fortress, 1987.

The Pew Forum. "The Global Religious Landscape." Pew Forum, 18 December 2012. http://www.pewforum.org/2012/12/18/global-religious-landscape-exec/.

Phillips, Martin, and Tim Mighall. *Society and Exploitation through Nature.* Harlow: Prentice-Hall, 2000.

Sheldon, Joseph K. "Twenty-One Years after the Historical Roots of Our Ecological Crisis: How Has the Church Responded?" *Perspectives on Science and Christian Faith,* 41 no. 3 (1989) 152–58.

Schmemann, Alexander. *For the Life of the World: Sacraments and Orthodoxy.* 2nd edition. Crestwood, NY: St Vladimir's Seminary Press, 1973.

Staniloae, Dumitru. *The Experience of God: Orthodox Dogmatic Theology.* Vol. 2, *The World: Creation and Deification.* Translated and edited by I. Ionita and R. Barringer. Brookline, MA: Holy Cross Orthodox Press, 2000.

———. "The World as Gift and Sacrament of God's Love." *Sobornost* 9 (1969) 662–73.

Torrance, Thomas F. "The Atoning Obedience of Christ." *Moravian Theological Seminary Bulletin* (1959) 65–81.

———. *Calvin's Doctrine of Man.* London: Lutterworth, 1949.

———. *The Christian Doctrine of God: One Being Three Persons.* Edinburgh: T. & T. Clark, 1996.

———. *The Christian Frame of Mind: Order and Openness in Theology and Natural Science.* Edinburgh: Handsel, 1985.

———. *Divine and Contingent Order.* New York: Oxford University Press, 1981.

———. "The Goodness and Dignity of Man in the Christian Tradition." *Modern Theology* 4 no. 4 (1988) 309–22.

———. *The Ground and Grammar of Theology.* Charlottesville: University of Virginia Press, 1980.

———. *The Mediation of Christ.* 2nd ed. Edinburgh: T. & T. Clark, 1992.

———. *Reality and Evangelical Theology.* Philadelphia: Westminster, 1982.

Webster, John. "Trinity and Creation." *International Journal of Systematic Theology* 12, no. 1 (2010) 4–19.

White, Lynn. "Continuing the Conversation." In *Western Man and Environmental Ethics,* edited by Ian G. Barbour, 55–64. Reading: Addison-Wesley, 1973.

———. "The Historical Roots of Our Ecological Crisis." *Science* 155 (1967) 1203–7.

Wolters, Al M. *Creation Regained: Biblical Basics for a Reformational Worldview.* Grand Rapids: Eerdmans, 1985.

Wright, N. T. *Justification: God's Plan and Paul's Vision.* London: SPCK, 2009.

Conclusion

13

In Praise of Creatures

Pope Francis's Message of Hope for a Fragile Earth[1]

Celia Deane-Drummond,
Department of Theology,
University of Notre Dame

Introduction

In this chapter I will draw out the theological threads weaving through *Laudato si'* in order to show the deepest roots of its call for ecological conversion. The message is a universal one, given the common plight of those that are poor and the environmental problems facing humanity, including climate change. While this encyclical is open to insights from the sciences, social sciences, and philosophy, I will argue that the key motivation for this encyclical is theological, drawing its primary inspiration from the Franciscan tradition. The outcome is practical, ethical and brimming with hope, a renewed integral ecology and a common good that is inclusive of our common home, the earth, rather than exclusive.

1. This contribution was made possible in part by support (in the form of an International Travel Award) from the Institute for Scholarship in the Liberal Arts, College of Arts and Letters, University of Notre Dame. This chapter develops themes that have been published elsewhere (Deane-Drummond, 2012; 2016a, 2016b), as well as on various blog sites. I am grateful to Nicola Hoggard Creegan and A Rocha Aotearoa New Zealand for the invitation to deliver a public lecture as part of the *Ecology and Hope* Conference hosted by Carey Baptist College, Auckland on January 8th 2016 on which this chapter is based.

Pope Francis intends *Laudato si'* to be read widely and discussed by those who are not necessarily Roman Catholic or even Christian. He is likely to succeed since his appeal is one that begins where people are at; an observation of the world around him, what he terms, "our common home."[2] He is also likely to succeed because of his particular style of ministry; a pope who refuses to be shielded by batteries of bodyguards, who takes homeless people off the street to share a meal with him on his birthday, who refuses the grandeur of his office and who opts to live in shared accommodation. When he speaks, therefore, about the need for a simpler lifestyle this sounds authentic as it comes out of his own lived practice.

The theme of ecological conversion is one that builds, nonetheless, on the work of his predecessors, especially Pope John Paul II. In a pastoral letter addressed to the Bishops and leaders of the Church, Pope John Paul II claims:

> There is a need for *ecological conversion*, to which Bishops themselves can contribute by their teaching about the correct relationship of human beings with nature. Seen in the light of the doctrine of God the Father, the maker of heaven and earth, this relationship is one of "stewardship:" human beings are set at the centre of creation as stewards of the Creator.[3]

Pope John Paul II was also influenced by the Ecumenical Patriarch, Bartholomew I, and their joint letter published in June 2002 was one of the most significant statements on ecological conversion. What they pressed for was a change of heart:

> A solution at the economic and technological level can be found only if we undergo, in the most radical way, an *inner change of heart*, which can lead to a change in lifestyle and of unsustainable patterns of consumption and production. A genuine conversion in Christ will enable us to change the way we think and act.[4]

The difference with respect to the current encyclical is that this intent to ecological conversion is explicitly and more deliberately addressed to all of humanity, as well as rather more focus on the scientific aspects of the discussion that his predecessors only touched on tangentially and somewhat superficially. The conversation and warm relationship with Bartholomew I has continued in the episcopate of Pope Francis, with an additional initiative

2. Pope Francis, *Laudato si'*, §17.

3. Pope John Paul II, *Pastores Gregis*, §70.

4. Pope John Paul II and Bartholomew I, *Common Declaration on Environmental Ethics*.

towards the Russian as well as the Greek branches of the Orthodox Church.[5] Pope Francis's desire to heal broken relationships inside and outside of the Catholic Church is part of his wider intent to engage in peace making. While the details of the science could have been even more nuanced in places, the basic message is clear; he wants *all people* to be receptive to his message by drawing in the first instance on scientific accounts of environmental change, however controversial that might sound to some.

The first part of the encyclical lays out the ecological devastation now wrought on earth that eco-theologians and environmentalists have been pointing out for nearly half a century, and for which evidence is steadily accumulating. There is urgency, verve to his writing so that he does not mince his words, or try to wrap it up in a way that will make his message more palatable. He is aware, then, that the media "at times . . . shield us from direct contact with the pain, the fears and the joys of others and the complexity of their personal experiences."[6] So, he takes us to the root of the problems identified, both physical, such as turning the earth into a "pile of filth," and moral, such as a common indifference to the needs of the poorest and most oppressed peoples in the global community.

And behind that indifference there is another kind of attachment that he believes bedevils humanity in a way that is becoming much more widespread in the global economy and that is an attachment to technologies, social media and other forms of interaction that allow us to avoid human contact, and so become distanced from the needs of others. Although he does not use the language of idolatry, this is implied.

Pope Francis's approach to the earth and its creatures represents a shift in favor of giving those creatures a higher status and intrinsic value, though the notion that the earth has some sort of agency is also buried in some of the earlier encyclicals.[7] He is certainly rather bolder in his resistance to unwarranted anthropocentrism as we move deeper into this encyclical compared with his predecessors.[8]

As well as using flowery and perhaps figurative statements on mother earth at the beginning of *Laudato si'*, he also uses more instrumental scientific language of "ecosystemic services" to describe the contribution of other creatures to our common home.[9] Overall, his treatment of the scientific literature is balanced, coming down firmly on the side of those who support

5. Luhn, "Finally!"

6. Pope Francis, *Laudato si'*, §47.

7. See further discussion in Deane-Drummond, "Joining the Dance," 193–212.

8. Pope Francis, *Laudato si'*, §115.

9. Ibid., §25.

climate change, with adherence to the consensual view of the vast majority of scientists that human influence is primarily responsible for the sharp rise in greenhouse gases since the industrial revolution.

It is conservationists and ecologists, though, who will find most power in what he has to say here, calling on them to do more research, find better ways of using energy, and protect life in all its diversity. His overall message that we and all other creatures are caught up in the common problem of our own making will strike chords with those who have been working in this area ever since Rachel Carson published her *Silent Spring* in the early 1960s. But will this be a watershed document in the same way that *Silent Spring* was for that generation? Will it really wake up those who are slumbering in their own worlds, too caught up with an obsession with consumerism to notice what is happening around them?

The difference, of course, compared with environmentalists like Carson is that for Pope Francis an underlying faith in Christ and hope in the divine providence of God as Creator gives a special reason for his firm belief that another world is possible. And it is, I suggest, timely. In the last half-century the world has tried and repeatedly failed to find any way to move out of the trajectory of "progress" that for so many generations has locked in industrialist, capitalist societies bent on exploitative forms of profit. No wonder environmental philosophers such as Dale Jamieson resort to either a gloomy pessimism of locally negotiated agreements in *Reason in a Dark Time*, or attempts at story making in his subsequent work (written with Bonnie Nadzam), *Love in the Anthropocene.* [10]

And lurking in the background of this encyclical is a critique not simply of particular rival political parties, in the US context parsed as Republican and Democrat, or in the UK Labor and Conservative, but a wider critique of how the acceptance of destructive cultural values undermines the very possibility of democracy as such. So, Pope Francis claims:

> It is time to acknowledge that light-hearted superficiality has done us no good. When the foundations of social life are corroded, what ensues are battles over conflicting interests, new forms of violence and brutality, and obstacles to the growth of a genuine culture of care for the environment.[11]

10. Jamieson, *Reason in a Dark Time;* Jamieson and Nadzam, *Love in the Anthropocene.*

11. Pope Francis, *Laudato si'*, §229.

He points out earlier in the encyclical that a lack of sensitivity to the struggles of others "points to the loss of that sense of responsibility for our fellow men and women upon which all civil society is founded."[12]

It is worth pausing to consider for a moment as to why he has put so much stress on *cultural transformation.* One reason may be the kind of liberation theology that he enlists; a liberation theology "of the people" influenced heavily by his Argentinian background. This type of liberation theology stressed not just social-cultural change, but was also open to the insights of the social sciences and philosophy.[13] My own view is that the socio-economic transformation of the more dominant liberation theology stream is still present in the encyclical, but precisely how the economic transformation might take place is left underdeveloped. Liberation theologian Leonardo Boff's engagement with ecology is also a significant influence, but Pope Francis does not go as far as the kind of biocentrism that eventually characterizes Boff's writing.

Pope Francis, in keeping with the patron saint of ecology, Francis of Assisi, is not content just to be a prophet of doom, but provides concrete suggestions about how to act, along with a specific theological vision of an alternative. I am not going to dwell on the concrete details of his suggestions in this chapter; conservationists and ecologists have been discussing this for some time; except to say that he refuses, correctly in my view, to split apart care for the natural world from care for the most deprived and marginalized members of the global human community.

This is a theology informed by liberation motifs, even though he is comfortable using the language of "development," a word resisted by the majority of liberation theologians on the basis that it presupposes a particular model of growth. It is clear that when Francis uses words such as "development" he does not mean the standard model that apes a Western model of progress, but something very different, and much more akin to liberation theology.

Is he Marxist? Certainly not in that Marxist analysis resists careful consideration of the question of the transcendent. He puts at the heart of his liberation theology method a stress on *cultural change*, rather than structural societal change that has been the most dominant paradigm for liberation theology. Pope Francis's view emerges from the Christian option for the poorest members of the community, and is inspired by the example

12. *Ibid.*, §26.

13. Scannone, "Papa Francesco," 571–90. I am very grateful to Fr Gerard Whelan for a fascinating as yet unpublished article on this topic that deals with these issues.

of Christ who came to serve the poor, even if some social science is included in his treatment of economic or other social and political issues.

Media portrayal that sees the encyclical as further evidence of the Pope dabbling inappropriately in politics ignores over a hundred years of Catholic social thought, perhaps beginning with *Rerum Novarum* penned by Pope Leo XIII in May 1891. It also ignores the fact that there is a debate between liberation theologies; they are not uniform, and the Argentinian variety presses most of all for a cultural transformation rather than simply a societal transformation, and so it is easier to envisage.

Like all great encyclicals this one draws on magisterial teaching of both of his predecessors, but now includes Catholic social thought emerging especially from a Latin American context, and then parses out this rich tapestry through his own particular charism—one inspired by the life and teaching of Saint Francis of Assisi.[14] What I intend to do now is to look behind the tapestry to see the theological threads that inform this document.

Theological Threads Behind the Encyclical

The first thread is one taken directly from the title itself—*Praise*. Thanks and praise to the Creator of all life, including the life of humanity. This celebration of life finds common ground with ecologists investigating human impacts on natural ecologies through environmental science, including, but not exclusively, climate change. The difference between scientists' interpretation of the earth and this papal statement is that Pope Francis is prepared to give the earth, our common home, a sense of *agency*. The first words of the encyclical are ones of praise: "LAUDATO SI', mi' Signore"—"Praise be to you, my Lord." In the words of this beautiful canticle, Saint Francis of Assisi reminds us that our common home is like a sister with whom we share our life and a beautiful mother who opens her arms to embrace us."[15] Following biblical teaching in the New Testament letter to the Romans (8:22), the whole earth *groans* in travail: "This sister now cries out to us because of the harm we have inflicted on her by our irresponsible use and abuse of the goods with which God has endowed her."[16] In effect, the praise has now been silenced and replaced instead by groaning in travail.

Francis creates, then, a narrative of human interaction with the earth, where humans, instead of acting responsibly, now exist in a relationship of violence with it, with each other and with God. In theological language this

14. See Deane-Drummond, "Theological Tapestry."

15. Pope Francis, *Laudato si'*, §1.

16. Ibid., §2.

amounts to sin.[17] The language of war replaces that of peace, but now it is war against the earth that underpins breakdown in human relationships, environmental migration, and perpetuates all kinds of injustices.

So, the second thread is that of *Gift,* and humanity's abuse of the Gift of the earth, and the Gift of Life. So, "Nature is usually seen as a system which can be studied, understood and controlled, whereas creation can only be understood as a gift from the outstretched hand of the Father of all, and as a reality illuminated by the love which calls us together into universal communion."[18]

So how do we move back to a celebration of that Gift and a sense of the preciousness of all life, including human life? For that Francis relies on the idea of *ecological conversion* that comes at both the beginning and the end of the encyclical letter and that he picks up from Pope John Paul II, but uses in a new way.[19] The beginning is about conversion to a richer sense of human interrelationships with each other and the creatures in our common home. But at the very end of the encyclical we find an infusion of Christology; so at depth Gift is only recognized fully through Christ, the Savior and Redeemer of the whole world. Ecological conversion is also implied in the way he structures his argument according to the liberation theology tradition that asks us to *see* from an ecological perspective (chapter 1) and theological perspective (chapter 2); invites us to *judge* (chapter 3 and 4) and encourages us to *act* (chapters 5 and 6). Given his namesake of the patron saint of ecology, Francis of Assisi, the threads of another spirituality, namely, a Franciscan approach weave through this encyclical. A further Ignatian emphasis on detachment from material things is also present given his own Jesuit training, making this a richly diverse spiritual basis which inspires readers from many different Christian traditions.

The third thread in this document is that of *Love,* love towards each other and towards other creatures that flows from the love of God as Creator of the world. God creates not so much through power but through love. "Just as happens when we fall in love with someone, whenever he would gaze at the sun, the moon or the smallest of animals, he burst into song, drawing all other creatures into his praise."[20]

Such love will provide a basis for a check on human freedom that assumes it is limitless, and it is love that inspires awe and wonder at the beauty of the natural world. Love is "at the heart of what it is to be human," but it

17. Ibid., §66.

18. Ibid., §76.

19. Ibid., §216.

20. Ibid., §11.

is an inclusive love that refuses to exploit other creatures, and works for their protection.[21] Love also provides a basis for resisting what Francis calls "irrational confidence in progress."[22]

Hope, that another world is possible is the fourth thread of this encyclical. Such hope-filled messages may be met with cynicism or even skepticism in a world wedded to the technologies of their own making. However, hope is not the same as optimism, as optimism assumes that things will just get better. Hope puts its trust in the Creator and Savior of the world. Above all "Hope would have us recognize that there is always a way out, that we can always redirect our steps, that we can always do something to solve our problems."[23]

The common good is the goal that Francis wishes to instill on all people; whether Catholic or not, understood as the good for all and the good for each, including other creatures. So, significantly, "Because all creatures are connected, each must be cherished with love and respect, for all of us as living creatures are dependent on one another."[24]

Hope, too, extends to the poorest nations of the world in light of the global inequities that prevail and the lack of authentic relationships. This means that richer nations have a specific and differential responsibility to act so that poorer nations are able to build ecologically responsible governance. Population growth is barely mentioned; the stress is on overconsumption by the few at the expense of the poor.[25] The timing of the encyclical was strategically linked to the critical summit held in Paris in December 2015 and Pope Francis is clear in his hope for robust, rather than weak international agreements.[26] Above all, the hope is for flourishing communion between humans and other creatures in a common home, rather than one at the expense of the other: death is there, but limited rather than in excess and for excess.

The fifth thread, although rather less obvious, is that of *Glory*; premised first on the idea of interdependence, "a relationship of mutual responsibility between human beings and nature."[27] Living things are valuable to God and express God's glory: "Together with our obligation to use the earth's goods responsibly, we are called to recognize that other living beings have a value

21. Ibid.
22. Ibid., §19.
23. Ibid., §61.
24. Ibid., §42.
25. Ibid., §50.
26. Ibid., §54.
27. Ibid., §67.

of their own in God's eyes: "by their mere existence they bless him and give him glory."[28] And bubbling beneath the surface is a "faith" that "allows us to interpret the meaning and the mysterious beauty of what is unfolding."[29] Behind hope of glory is the presence of the Holy Spirit, present even in the midst of the present difficulties so that "something new can always emerge."[30] And, in this context, human beings have a special vocation "to lead all creatures back to their Creator."[31]

The sixth thread is that of *Joy*, which pervades all creatures, bringing forth a natural revelation.[32] But joy also comes in human living that takes its serenity from moderation rather than a grasping for more: "Christian spirituality proposes a growth marked by moderation and a capacity to be happy with little."[33] This is a liberating faith, but one that is a core aspect of Francis's approach.

The seventh thread is *Humility*, so "Once we lose our humility, and become enthralled with the possibility of limitless mastery over everything, we inevitably end up harming society and the environment."[34]

Integral Theology

And what joins up these seven threads of praise, gift, love, hope, glory, joy and humility? Namely, *peace*, expressed in an *integral ecology*, echoing the ideal of the Sabbath drawn from the Bible, the Sabbath being the crown of creation. Integral ecology is not a completely new concept; indeed, it was used by the International Theological Commission in their 2009 document on natural law. The passage in which it was introduced is worth citing in full since until Cardinal Turkson used the term when he gave a preview of what *Laudato si'* was all about, the possibility of something like an integral ecology being informative for Catholic social teaching was not really on the agenda. Pope Benedict XVI spoke of integral development and Pope John Paul II spoke of human ecology, so integral ecology might just be a combination of these ideas. But the ITC statement implies another root to this concept that is likely to be behind both the ideas of integral development

28. Ibid., §69.
29. Ibid., §79.
30. Ibid., §80.
31. Ibid., §83.
32. Ibid., §85.
33. Ibid., §222.
34. Ibid., §224.

and human ecology, and that is the natural law tradition. So, the ITC document claims the following:

> An integral ecology must promote what is specifically human, all the while valuing the world of nature in its physical and biological integrity. In fact, even if man, as a moral being who searches for the ultimate truth and the ultimate good, transcends his own immediate environment, he does so by accepting the special mission of keeping watch over the natural world, living in harmony with it, and defending vital values without which neither human life nor the biosphere of this planet can be maintained. This integral ecology summons every human being and every community to a new responsibility. It is inseparable from a global political orientation respectful of the requirements of the natural law.[35]

Pope John Paul II preferred the term "human ecology," as adopted by Pope Benedict XVI, but it is my contention that undergirding the shift to an expanded notion of "integral ecology" are theological threads that provide the deepest motivation for ecological conversion.[36] Further, joining integral to ecology is important, since it flags up the broader shift in his thought away from anthropocentrism. Christians have no choice if they want to claim authenticity: "what they all need is an 'ecological conversion,' whereby the effects of their encounter with Jesus Christ become evident in their relationship with the world around them. Living our vocation to be protectors of God's handiwork is essential to a life of virtue; it is not an optional or a secondary aspect of our Christian experience."[37]

Although Pope Francis avoids the term natural law, his basic theological orientation in *Laudato si'* and elsewhere in his writing is consistent with it, in so far as the common good is a prominent theme and in that he consistently gives primacy to the human person, even while insisting that human responsibility to the natural world is part of what it means to be human and a Christian.

Policies that will flow from such an approach are those that take on board an integrated and holistic view of the human person, entangled with others and richly embedded in the natural world. Even if Christian believers prefer to use the language of glory rather than beauty, and sin rather

35. International Theological Commission, "Universal Ethic," §82.

36. Integral mission *misión integral* or holistic mission has been used by evangelical Liberation theologians to describe the integration of evangelical and social justice teachings. I think it is unlikely that "integral" stems from this reference but it is not impossible given the openness of Pope Francis to other Christian traditions.

37. Pope Francis, *Laudato si'*, §217.

than violence, the Pope's message is intended to be a universal one, namely towards a common good, so it is one that should be recognizable by all. He therefore gives *lines* of approach and action (Chapter 5) rather than spelling out the details. He is prepared to be tough on some issues. For example, "technology based on the use of highly polluting fuels—especially coal, but also oil, and to a lesser degree gas—needs to be progressively replaced without delay."[38] He does, however, admit to the possibility of having to choose "the lesser of two evils" in order to find short-term solutions.

What this might mean in practice is harder to discern, but he urges a much greater sense of urgency in addressing the issues. But he wants to start small, to start with the relationships that make up our daily lives and build from there. So, drawing inspiration from Saint Therese of Lisieux, he claims:

> An integral ecology is also made up of simple daily gestures which break with the logic of violence, exploitation and selfishness. In the end, a world of exacerbated consumption is at the same time a world which mistreats life in all its forms.[39]

He is also prepared to speak of harmful forms of inequity even in the midst of poor nations, and so of the "scandalous level of consumption in some privileged sectors of their populations."[40] It is therefore hardly surprising that he concludes that one way forward is not just through local agreements but through putting greater weight on "enforceable international agreements."[41] The gross disparity within as well as between nations shows sensitivity to the ambiguity of laying the blame on one community or nation over against another. Sins of injustice are pervasive.

Rather than political revolution, then, Francis speaks of *covenantal* relationships which are bonds that need to be nurtured through educational programs of justice and peace.[42] So, "environmental education should facilitate making the leap towards the transcendent, which gives ecological ethics its deepest meaning."[43] This calls for a special kind of compassion and solidarity. Moving towards such a practice is more like a cultural revolution that turns away from an over dependence on technology and a narrowing towards concern for human interests alone.[44]

38. Ibid., §165.
39. Ibid., §230.
40. Ibid., § 172.
41. Ibid., § 173.
42. Ibid., §209.
43. Ibid., §210.
44. Ibid., §114–15.

Integral ecology is premised on a stress on relationships that come up throughout the encyclical, an openness to other religious traditions, and the need to engage in dialogue; the breakdown of misunderstandings between the sciences, and the mutual benefit of theology and science working together rather than in isolation. He affirms the need for dialogue between religions "for the sake of protecting nature, defending the poor, and building networks of respect and fraternity."[45] He also stresses that sciences need to be open to insights from other scientific fields, since specialization means that "each can tend to be enclosed in its own language," and, citing *Evangelii Gaudium*, he insists that faith is beneficial to science in reminding it of its own limits. In all this, he emphasizes that effective dialogue demands "patience, self-discipline and generosity."[46]

The message of the encyclical ends with an ecclesial tone, bringing in a richly Eucharistic and cosmic understanding of the sacraments in a way that echoes the thought of Pierre Teilhard de Chardin.[47] Citing Pope Benedict XVI, Francis explains, "creation is projected towards divinization, towards the holy wedding feast, towards unification with the Creator himself.[48] In the Eucharist, fullness is already achieved; it is the living center of the universe, the overflowing core of love and of inexhaustible life.[49]

And the basis for right relationships between creatures, including human beings, is not so much political as Trinitarian, grounded in the pattern of mutual love of the three persons. And, in keeping with his predecessors, he gives Mary, the mother of God the special place of caring not just for broken humanity but the wounded world. So, "Just as her pierced heart mourned the death of Jesus, so now she grieves for the sufferings of the crucified poor and for the creatures of this world laid waste by human power."[50] This is not the end, for she remains, along with Christ, an icon of hope, so "transfigured, she now lives with Jesus, and all creatures sing of her fairness."[51]

Above all, Francis puts forward a theological vision of the whole that is consistent with traditional Catholic teaching, reinforcing strong and traditional Catholic concepts such as the dignity of the human being, faith in God as Creator, hope in Christ who renews all things. He ends the

45. Ibid., §201.

46. Ibid., §201

47. Teilhard de Chardin, "The Mass," 159–66.

48. Pope Francis, *Laudato si'*, §236.

49. Ibid.

50. Ibid., §241.

51. Ibid.

encyclical with a reminder of the value of the family and the hope that, though mortal, humanity, along with all creatures, will one day share in the Sabbath of celebratory inclusiveness. Eternal life, then, the hope for which the human heart longs, is one of transfiguration, liberation from the bonds of sin and death.[52] And it is joy that will accompany the struggle in this life, not the superficial joy of consumerist pleasures, but the deep joy of knowing that we will one day dwell in the presence of the eternal God, who is Lord of all life.[53]

Are such theological threads sufficient to convince his readers and undertake the kind of cultural revolution and ecological conversion that he believes are the next step? Certainly, for the Catholic church my hope is that this will be a wake-up call to act, a new way of understanding that ecology is not separate from Christian discipleship or an extra responsibility, but central to its mission. The stakes are high, since the poorest regions of the world are waiting in expectation as to how the world might act. While Pope Francis may not have the philosophical sophistication of his predecessor, his intelligence is expressed in paying attention to the heart as well as the mind; a deliberate strategy of praxis, so following our ability to see what is the case, make judgments about what to do, and then act accordingly. It seems to me at least, that the buried theological threads reaching out to communion with others and the natural world are effective and full of promise. So, in common with Denis Edwards, I agree that a summation of the theological vision of the encyclical is one of *sublime communion* between God, humanity and all creatures.[54]

> The created things of this world are not free of ownership: "For they are yours, O Lord, who love the living" (*Wis* 11:26). This is the basis of our conviction that, as part of the universe, called into being by one Father, all of us are linked by unseen bonds and together form a kind of universal family, a sublime communion which fills us with a sacred, affectionate and humble respect.[55]

This occasion for recognition of the glory of God should not detract from an earthy realism and greater attention to human beings that I believe is also present. Rather, such recognition allows us to face such difficulties with courage, and see hints at the possibility of such communion now, even if its fullest expression can only be realized in the future. For Francis, even in the context of the awareness of sublimity of all things and their expression

52. Ibid., §243.

53. Ibid., §245.

54. Edwards, "Sublime Communion."

55. Pope Francis, *Laudato si'*, §89.

in terms of the Trinity—he draws here from Aquinas—is down to earth in his insistence that ethical priority must go to the poorest and most deprived peoples of the world:

> Certainly, we should be concerned lest other living beings be treated irresponsibly. But we should be particularly indignant at the enormous inequalities in our midst, whereby we continue to tolerate some considering themselves more worthy than others.[56]

His reference to "mother earth" should not, therefore, be thought of as any kind of leaning towards divinization, but in as much as he stays tuned to the theology of the people, he recognizes that the spirituality and insights of other religious traditions and indigenous cultures in particular have something to contribute to the discussion.

To sum up, this bold encyclical shows lines of continuity and discontinuity with previous papal statements. It represents a significant shift of what have been somewhat peripheral concerns about the natural world to the center. At the same time in as much as Pope Francis is still firmly grounded in priority of the poorest members of the human community it is in keeping with traditional Roman Catholic social thought. He cites Latin American Bishops to a much greater extent than his predecessor, and his push towards socio-cultural transformation is significant. He also takes into account ecological and social scientific research in a way that is refreshingly open to insights outside the immediate ecclesial community. This is a multidisciplinary liberation theology that is targeted at the liberation of the materially rich caught up in habits of consumption and fascination with new technologies. However, above all Francis wants his listeners to be inspired to change their hearts and minds, to see and recognize what is at stake, and to appreciate that a new way of living and being is possible. Praise, hope, humility, joy, love, respect; all these virtues are necessary in order to glimpse the glory of God in the sublime communion of creation. They are also virtues that will help humanity work towards the kind of cultural revolution and ecological conversion that is so desperately needed in the face of such enormous social and political challenges. His message may be upbeat, but that positive emphasis is based upon his hope and an awareness that only such hope can encourage deeper and more lasting change.

If we rip out the theological threads from this encyclical we are left with a worn carpet that lacks the vibrancy that flows from a lifetime of prayer and contemplation. Thus, it is appropriate that the afterword to this encyclical is itself a prayer, and a dedication to pray for the earth so that we

56. Ibid., §90.

come to recognize more fully how human lives are intricately linked with that of other creatures and each other. This prayer of praise to the Father, Son and Spirit undoubtedly came from his own pen, rather than that of his advisors. It is reminiscent, too, of the prayer of Saint Francis of Assisi, in speaking of the need for all humanity to become channels of love and peace in the world. "Let us sing as we go. May our struggles and our concern for this planet never take away the joy of our hope."[57]

It is fitting, then, to end this chapter with the final words of this encyclical—a prayer, which reads as a cry from the heart: "O Lord, seize us with your power and your light, help us to protect all life, to prepare for a better future, for the coming of your kingdom of justice, peace, love and beauty: Praise be to you! Amen."[58]

Bibliography

Carson, Rachel. *Silent Spring*. Boston: Houghton Mifflin, 1962.

Deane-Drummond, Celia. "Catholic Social Teaching and Ecology: Its Promise and Limits." In *Fragile World: Ecology and the Church*, edited by William Cavanaugh. Eugene, OR: Cascade/Wipf and Stock, 2017 (in press).

———. "Joining in the Dance: Ecology in Roman Catholic Social Teaching." *New Blackfriars* 93 no. 1044 (2012) 193–212.

———. "*Laudato si'* and the Natural Sciences: An Assessment of Possibilities and Limits." *Theological Studies* 2017 (in press).

———. "The Theological Tapestry of *Laudato si'*." http://www.abc.net.au/religion/articles/2015/06/19/4258547.htm

Edwards, Denis. "Sublime Communion: *Laudato si'* and a Theology of Nature." Public lecture presented at the University of Notre Dame, November 2nd, 2015.

International Theological Commission. "In Search of a Universal Ethic: A New Look at Natural Law." http://www.vatican.va/roman_curia/congregations/cfaith/cti_documents/rc_con_cfaith_doc_20090520_legge-naturale_en.html.

Jamieson, Dale and Bonnie Nadzam. *Love in the Anthropocene*. New York: OR Books, 2015.

Jamieson, Dale. *Reason in a Dark Time*. Oxford: Oxford University Press, 2014.

Luhn, Alec, "Finally! Pope and Russian Patriarch Meet for the First Time in 1,000 Years." *The Guardian* (February 13th, 2016). , http://www.theguardian.com/world/2016/feb/12/pope-francis-russian-orthodox-patriarch-kirill-make-history-cuba-first-meeting-in-1000-years. Accessed April 21, 2016.

Pope Francis, *Laudato si': On Care for Our Common Home*. Huntington: Our Sunday Visitor, 2015.

Pope John Paul II and Ecumenical Patriarch Bartholomew I. *Common Declaration on Environmental Ethics*. http://www.vatican.va/holy_father/john_paul_ii/

57. Ibid., §244.

58. Ibid. From *A Christian Prayer in Union with Creation* following *Laudato si'*.

speeches/2002/june/documents/hf_jp-ii_spe_20020610_venice-declaration_en.html.

———. *Venice Declaration., June 10, 2002.* http://www.vatican.va/holy_father/john_paul_ii/speeches/2002/june/documents/hf_jp-ii_spe_20020610_venice-declaration_en.html. Accessed June 15th, 2007.

Pope John Paul II, *Pastores Gregis.* London: Catholic Truth Society, 2003.

Scannone, Juan Carlos "Papa Francesco e La Teologia del Popolo," *La Civiltà Cattolica* 3930, no. 165 (2014) 571–90.

Stevens, Scott. "'Care for Our Common Home': Taking Up the Moral Challenge of Pope Francis" *ABC Religion and Ethics,* June 19, 2015. http://www.abc.net.au/religion/articles/2015/06/19/4258547.htm.

Teilhard de Chardin, Pierre. "The Mass on the World." In *Thomas King, Teilhard's Mass,* edited by Thomas King, 159–66. New York: Paulist, 2005.

14

Conclusion

Nicola Hoggard Creegan,
A Rocha Aotearoa New Zealand

THIS IS AN AUSPICIOUS few years (2015–2018). In 2015 *Laudato si'* was published and has been much acclaimed and much discussed. Pope Francis is the fitting end of 50 years of dispute about the role of nature in Christian faith, and a fitting beginning of the new era ahead. For 2017 is also the 50th anniversary of Lynn White Jr.'s expounding of the material that was to form the article in *Science*, excoriating Christians as one of the major causes of the ecological crisis. In the 1960s this said crisis was new in awareness, if not in reality. Five years before Rachel Carson had broken the ground of the ecological age, with *Silent Spring.*[1] DDT was one of the agents she identified as the cause of widespread loss of wildlife. Only in 1972 was DDT banned in the United States, and the billowing clouds of pesticide eliminated from the streets of suburbia. Green New Zealand would not ban the substance until 1989.

In those toxic decades, Christian fundamentalism was strong and growing stronger; premillennialism was still in the ascendancy, with its particularly devastating disregard for the earth and for human actions regarding creation. Nevertheless, winds of change were evident. Vatican II began its radical outward-turning deliberations, and the 1960s were also the decade in which the works of French theologian and palaeontologist, Teilhard de Chardin would be published posthumously. Teilhard de Chardin was one of the first theologians to grasp the phenomenon of nature and its vital indwelling by the Spirit, its direction and its purpose in complexity

1. Carson, *Silent Spring.*

and consciousness.[2] He was the first to have a vision which combined evolution's grand narrative and sacred history. For Teilhard de Chardin matter was sacred, was sacrament. God was working inside of history toward an omega point, the cosmic Christ, inside of nature and not only from afar.

In many ways, we might assume that Aotearoa/New Zealand, in its extreme geographical isolation, is very far away from all this drama. This would be a false assumption. In some ways the flora and fauna of New Zealand were more vulnerable than in many other places, being acclimatised and adapted to a low-predator environment. The waves of migration silenced our wildlife and birds long before this happened in other places. The massive Moa bird was largely gone before Pākehā arrived here.[3] We are a country of water, but water is scarce, and often falls in all the "wrong" places for our human needs. Our intensive farming has polluted rivers and waterways as Kath Rushton has emphasized in this volume.

New Zealand's Pākehā pragmatism has been deeply influenced by an almost vitalistic Māori deep knowledge of nature from which Sue Burns has "borrowed" for her paper in this collection. Although Māori spirituality has truly not penetrated very far into our common psyche, it is protected in law and has influenced our intellectual and artistic landscapes. Māori language and custom in its deepest sense are important strands in our spirituality, strands that speak to the vibrancy and spirit of nature long after this was forgotten in many parts of the West. The acute sense of nature is evident in post-war artists and writers. The New Zealand poet, James K. Baxter, sought some sort of spiritual redemption in nature, as well as being a Christian convert, and his poetry was imbued with religious longing and a Spirit-filled sense of the New Zealand landscape.[4] Similarly, with the work of the prominent artist Colin McCahon whose scripts painted over brooding landscapes also typify the artistic response to place and creation in Aotearoa. Finally, the poet and novelist Janet Frame, wrapped words into linguistic lyrical prose that reflected the inwardness of both mind and nature.[5] Thus, the Teilhardian dream is not absent here, at least implicitly. For these or for other reasons New Zealand has a strong green presence a strong and active Green Party, and conservation movements, and increasing numbers of young Christians eager to put the world back into balance.

2. Teilhard de Chardin, *The Divine Milieu*; Teilhard de Chardin, *The Phenomenon of Man*.

3. Scholarly consensus makes the Moa extinct since the fourteenth century, but reliable witnesses suggest the extinction took place fully only in the nineteenth century. See Anderson, "On Evidence for the Survival of Moa in European Fiordland."

4. Baxter, *Selected Poems*.

5. Janet Frame, *To the Is-Land*.

We have our own experience, as our somewhat melancholy artists reveal. To live in New Zealand/Aotearoa is to experience the rivers, the water, the dense bush (or southern notafagus), along with sandflies and fickle weather. We experience pristine beaches (and sometimes the raising of these beaches) the ground shaking, the steam and volcanic ash; and the sparse but still present sound of the ubiquitous birds which have filled every biological niche in this country. Many of the writers in this compendium have noted this experience, and its deep resonance with both Māori spirituality and the biblical narrative. The phenomenon of the bush and its wildlife is an important underlying basis of our ecological awareness, and our willingness to work for change. Hence A Rocha's decades long commitment to bringing back birds (and especially *oi*) to the slopes of Mount Karioi on the coast outside Raglan. *Oi* are a voice of God, one that we had silenced; a voice that only we can return.

Thus, predominant themes of this volume have centered around entanglement, a newly discovered invigorating niche dependent interdependence of all species in a place. The interdependence is spiritual, biological, earthy, social, historical, conscious and unconscious. Although we refer most often to the wildness of nature, an important aspect of human evolution is our co-evolution with other species, cats and dogs, farm animals and so on, as Yael Klangwisan has eloquently expounded in her reflections on the relatedness of cats. We learn about ourselves and our depths as we encounter these animals. "Humans and animals share much of the experience of vitality: pleasure, bodily sensation if not the Heideggerian fullness of Being," she says. They are our companions and our mirrors, and they carry hints of otherness and praise.

Lest we be accused of abandoning the plain sense of Scripture we have other papers here which speak directly to the text. Stephen Pattemore insists that against the widespread belief of many evangelical Christians, that salvation is for all the earth. Philip Church insists that dominion *is* the God-ordained role of humans (against those who would always put nature first), but this dominion should be a role of care and attention to all other life. Myk Habets explores the journey towards perfection that involves the whole creation.

The authors in this volume do not speak with one voice. While all would agree that we must work for justice as a part of any ecological hope, few critique capitalism as strongly as Scott Kirkland. Kirkland ties his critique to a thoroughgoing affirmation of life and hope as possible only by the gift of God and not because hope is "immanent" within nature itself. Hope exists in spite of signs to the contrary. This is of course a replay of similar conversations throughout church history relating to the balance of human effort and God's initiative. While we would all agree with gift and with the revealed hope of the world, we would disagree on the place of nature in securing and supporting that hope. Selwyn Yeoman's paper resonates here with Kirkland in his insistence that Sabbath rest is the end of creation, the divine end, and that Sabbath relativizes all human endeavor. The celebration of Sabbath reinforces our absolute dependence and hence our hope in God's final restoration of all things.

For those of us who have for whatever reason indwelt the evolutionary process or nature itself some part of the basis for hope involves either an encounter with nature, or at the very least the inclusion of nature and our entangled habitat in sacred story. Celia and I have both pointed to the ways in which superficial understandings of evolution as mechanical and random—and based mostly at the chemical level—have undermined our hope and our spirituality and also our health, because they deprived us of vital contact with the life of nature. The new evolutionary synthesis, which affirms the slow long ascendancy of language, community, compassion, tools, cunning, and self-consciousness over an underlay of animal sentience in a community context prevents us from making objective, transactional understandings of our engagement with God. For God was in and of the creation long before humans arrived. Whatever the basis of hope we would argue it must have been implicit in and for creation and evident in creation as a whole long before humans arrived.

Nevertheless, God is a God of surprises and of the constantly new. Whatever we might see in creation it can give us only hints of transcendence, hope and "messianicity"; the particular character of our hope will always involve a handing over of power and autonomy to the God who will make all things new, even as we work to do what we can to restore species and habitats in the present time. These incomplete fragments of understanding accompany our reflection in this volume, and our hope that although we have every reason to despair, God is still working out God's purposes for the flora and fauna, and even humans on this planet.

Bibliography

Anderson, Atholl. "On Evidence for the Survival of Moa in European Fiordland." *New Zealand Journal of Ecology* 12 (1989) 39–44.

Baxter, James K. *Selected Poems of James K. Baxter*. Edited by Paul Miller. Auckland: Auckland University Press, 2013.

Carson, Rachel. *Silent Spring*. New York: Houghton/Mifflin, 1962.

de Chardin, Pierre Teilhard. *The Divine Milieu*. New York: Harper & Row, 1960.

———. *The Phenomenon of Man*. New York; Harper & Row, 1961.

Frame, Janet. *To the Is-land: An Autobiography*. New York: Braziller, 1982.

Author Biographies

Sue Burns emigrated from England to Aotearoa with her kiwi husband three decades ago. They farm in the Waikato. Sue is ordained and was Dean of Anglican Studies at St. John's College Auckland for nine years where she also taught pastoral theology and ministry practice. She is now working as a ministry enabler for the Anglican Diocese of Auckland. From her interest in biblical hermeneutics and narrative theology she is researching a framework for pastoral theology and practice that emerges from the language and landscapes of Aotearoa. This will be a doctoral project from 2017. Sue's family is involved in ethical environmental management and conservation research.

Philip Church taught biblical studies at Laidlaw College from 2002 to 2016. Prior to that he had a thirty-year career in accountancy. His PhD from the University of Otago was a study of Temple Symbolism in the Book of Hebrews, now published by E. J. Brill in the Supplements to Novum Testamentum series as *Hebrews and the Temple: Attitudes to the Temple in Second Temple Judaism and in Hebrews* (2017). He was editor of *Stimulus: The NZ Journal of Christian Thought and Practice* from 2012–2014. He is a trustee and the treasurer of A Rocha Aotearoa New Zealand and is also on the Board of New Zealand Christians in Science. He is married to Dorothy and they have three grown children and three grandchildren.

Celia Deane-Drummond is Professor in Theology at the University of Notre Dame and Director of the Center for Theology, Science and Human Flourishing. She was editor of the journal *Ecotheology* for six years and has served as Chair of the *European Forum for the Study of Religion and Environment* from 2011 to present. A selection of her recent books include *Ecotheology* (2008), *Christ and Evolution* (2009), *Creaturely Theology*, ed. with David Clough (2009), *Religion and Ecology in the Public Sphere*, ed.

with Heinrich Bedford-Strohm (2011), *Animals as Religious Subjects*, ed. with Rebecca Artinian Kaiser and David Clough (Bloomsbury, 2013), *The Wisdom of the Liminal: Evolution and Other Animals in Human Becoming* (2014), *Re-Imaging the Divine Image: Humans and Other Animals* (2014), *Technofutures, Nature and the Sacred*, ed. with Sigurd Bergmann and Bronislaw Szerszynski (2015), *Religion in the Anthropocene*, ed. with Sigurd Bergmann and Markus Vogt (2017).

Myk Habets is Dean of Faculty and Director of Research at Carey Baptist College and Head of Carey Graduate School, where he teaches systematic theology and ethics. He is the author or editor of many books, including *Theology in Transposition* (Fortress) and *Third Article Theology* (Fortress, 2013), and has written numerous journal essays. He lives with his family by the beach in Auckland and enjoys God's creation.

Nicola Hoggard Creegan is a theologian based in Auckland. She is the author of *Animal Suffering and the Problem of* Evil (Oxford University Press, 2013). She and Andrew Shepherd also edited *Taking Rational Trouble Over the Mysteries* (Wipf and Stock, 2013). Nicola was co-editor of *Colloquium* for six years, and wrote a column in science and theology for *Stimulus* for over a decade. She was Chair of TANSA (Theology and the Natural Sciences in Aotearoa) for seven years and part of the *Human Nature Project* at CTI in Princeton, 2012–2013, and the *Human Distinctiveness Project* at Notre Dame, 2015–2016. She is currently working on a book on free will in dialogue with the sciences. Nicola has taught theology in the US and NZ. She is an Anglican, is on the Board of A Rocha NZ, works for NZCIS (New Zealand Christians in Science), and enjoys hiking with her husband Charlie, in New Zealand and other countries.

Scott A. Kirkland is the Project Officer for Australian Catholic University's "Atheism and Christianity: Beyond Polemic" project in the Institute for Religion and Critical Inquiry, Melbourne. He is also an Honorary Postdoctoral Associate at Trinity College, University of Divinity. He is the author of *Intro the Far Country: Karl Barth and the Modern Subject* (Fortress, 2016). He is also the co-editor of *Correlating Sobornost: Karl Barth and the Russian Orthodox Tradition* (Fortress, 2015), *Kenotic Ecclesiology: Select Writings of Donald M. MacKinnon* (Fortress, 2016), and the forthcoming monograph series *Dispatches: Turning Points in Theology and Ethics* (Fortress, from 2016). He has appeared in journals such as *Heythop Journal, New Blackfriars,* and *Irish Theological Quarterly.*

Yael Klangwisan is a senior lecturer in the School of Social Practice, Laidlaw College, and the Laidlaw Graduate School, in Auckland. She writes books and articles about French literary readings of the Bible, such as, *Jouissance: A Cixousian Encounter with the Song of Songs* (Sheffield, 2015). She lives in a cottage beside the Huruhuru Stream, West Auckland with her partner, children, cocker spaniel, cat, four chickens, two goldfish, and a rooster named Napoleon.

Stephen Pattemore is Translations Director for Bible Society New Zealand. He works with Bible translation projects in New Zealand, Papua New Guinea and Thailand, and is Executive Editor of the journal *The Bible Translator*. He has postgraduate qualifications in Physics, Linguistics, and Biblical Studies, and his research interests include the book of Revelation, translation theory, issues of science and faith, and ecological hermeneutics. Stephen and his wife Raewyn live in Auckland where they help with restoring a local reserve as part of their involvement with the Auckland Branch of A Rocha Aotearoa NZ.

Kathleen Rushton of Nga Whaea Atawhai o Aotearoa/Sisters of Mercy New Zealand works as an independent scholar and is contracted to teach Scripture courses for The Catholic Institute of Aotearoa New Zealand at the Christchurch Catholic Education Office. Her doctorate on birth imagery in the Gospel according to John has been published along with several articles. Her current research interests in using the cosmological framework of prologue to interpret John's Gospel and its implications for spirituality and ecology began when she was the 2011 Cardinal Hume Scholar at Margaret Beaufort Institute, Cambridge, U.K. Kathleen writes a monthly gospel reflection in *Tui Motu InterIslands*. As a 2017 Residential Scholar at Vaughan Park Anglican Retreat Centre, Auckland, her project is to work on an accessible book that explores the ethical implications of the cosmology of John for whakawhanaungatanga/making right relationships between Atua/God, whenua/land, and tangata/people. She delights in her vegetable garden.

Andrew Shepherd is the National Co-Director for the Christian conservation organization, A Rocha Aotearoa New Zealand. His working life has been spent on the interface between theological, outdoor education, and conservation, and he particularly enjoys facilitating learning experiences that blend place-based environmental education, practical conservation, and biblical/theological reflection. Alongside his work with A Rocha he also teaches theology and ethics for a range of US and NZ tertiary institutions, and is a Research Affiliate with the Department of Theology and Religion, University of Otago. He researches and writes widely in the area of ecotheology and theological ethics. Recent publications include: *The Gift of the Other: Levinas, Derrida, and a Theology of Hospitality* (Wipf and Stock, 2014), and *Taking Rational Trouble over the Mysteries: Reactions to Atheism* (Wipf and Stock, 2013), also co-edited with Nicola Hoggard Creegan. He seeks to "ground" his life with his family in the Makarora valley, on the doorstep of Mount Aspiring National Park in Otago, New Zealand.

Selwyn Yeoman is an ordained minister of Christ in the Presbyterian Church of Aotearoa New Zealand, currently serving a congregation of the Christian Churches in New Zealand, in Dunedin, New Zealand. Twenty-seven years of the past thirty-eight have been in rural or semi-rural parishes where issues of land use and relationship with the land have been central concerns in most people's lives. The remainder have been in urban contexts where the issues are as pressing but the consciousness of connection much attenuated. He has degrees in Geography and Divinity and a University of Otago Doctorate addressing the nature of Human Dominion over Creation. His chapter arises partly out of reflection upon growing up in a family that kept a strict Sunday. This was sometimes embarrassing but did issue in the discovery that he did not have a bad conscience about not working on Sunday, which remains exceptionally liberating!

www.ingramcontent.com/pod-product-compliance
Lightning Source LLC
LaVergne TN
LVHW010935100826
845153LV00001B/53

* 9 7 8 1 5 3 2 6 0 9 7 5 6 *